THE UK DEFENCE INDUSTRIAL BASE

Development and Future Policy Options

THE UK DEFENCE INDUSTRIAL BASE

Development and Future Policy Options

by

TREVOR TAYLOR

and

KEITH HAYWARD

BRASSEY'S DEFENCE PUBLISHERS

(A member of the Maxwell Pergamon Publishing Corporation plc)

LONDON · OXFORD · WASHINGTON · NEW YORK · BEIJING
FRANKFURT · SÃO PAULO · SYDNEY · TOKYO · TORONTO

UK (Editorial)	Brassey's Defence Publishers Ltd., 24 Gray's Inn Road, London WC1X 8HR, England
(Orders)	Brassey's Defence Publishers Ltd., Headington Hill Hall, Oxford OX3 0BW, England
U.S.A. (Editorial)	Pergamon-Brassey's International Defense Publishers, Inc., 8000 Westpark Drive, Fourth Floor, McLean, Virginia 22102, U.S.A.
(Orders)	Pergamon Press, Inc., Maxwell House, Fairview Park, Elmsford, New York 10523, U.S.A.
PEOPLE'S REPUBLIC OF CHINA	Pergamon Press, Room 4037, Qianmen Hotel, Beijing, People's Republic of China
FEDERAL REPUBLIC OF GERMANY	Pergamon Press GmbH, Hammerweg 6, D-6242 Kronberg, Federal Republic of Germany
BRAZIL	Pergamon Editora Ltda, Rua Eça de Queiros, 346, CEP 04011, Paraiso, São Paulo, Brazil
AUSTRALIA	Pergamon-Brassey's Defence Publishers Pty Ltd., PO Box 544, Potts Point, N.S.W. 2011, Australia
JAPAN	Pergamon Press, 5th Floor, Matsuoka Central Building 1-7-1 Nishishinjuku, Shinjuku-ku, Tokyo 160, Japan
CANADA	Pergamon Press Canada Ltd., Suite No. 271, 253 College Street, Toronto, Ontario, Canada M5T 1R5

Copyright © 1989 Royal United Services Institute

First edition 1989

Library of Congress Cataloging in Publication Data
Taylor, Trevor.
The U.K. defence industrial base/Trevor Taylor and Keith Hayward. — 1st ed.
p. cm.
1. Munitions — Great Britain. I. Hayward, Keith. II. Title.
UF535.G7T39 1989 355.2'6'0941 — dc19 88-39448

British Library Cataloguing in Publication Data
Taylor, Trevor
The UK defence industrial base
1. Great Britain. Military equipment industries
I. Title II. Hayward, Keith
338.4'7623'0941

ISBN 0-08-036713-5

Printed by A. Wheaton & Co. Ltd., Exeter.

Contents

v

List of Tables

List of Figures

Abbreviations

ACARD	Advisory Council for Applied Research and Development
ACDA	Arms Control and Disarmament Agency
ACOST	Advisory Council on Science and Technology
AFVG	Anglo-French variable geometry (aircraft programme)
AMRAAM	advanced medium range air-to-air missile
AOR	Auxiliary Oiler Replenishment (vessel)
ASRAAM	advanced short-range air-to-air missile
AWACS	airborne warning and control system
BAe	British Aerospace
BAOR	British Army of the Rhine
BMARC	British Manufacture and Research Company
BMY	Bowen Mclaughlin York
CAD/CAM	Computer-aided design and manufacture
CEST	Centre for the Exploitation of Science and Technology
C^3I	Communication, Command, Control and Identification
CNAD	Conference of National Armaments Directors
DARPA	Defence Advanced Research Projects Agency
DIB	Defence Industrial Base
DoD	Department of Defense
DTE	Defence Technology Enterprises
DTI	Department of Trade and Industry
EAP	European Aircraft Programme
EC	European Community
EDC	European Defence Committee
EEA	Electronic Engineering Association
EFA	European Fighter Aircraft
ELINT	electronic intelligence
GATT	general agreement on trade and tariffs (UN)
GDP	gross domestic product
GEC	General Electric Company

GKN	Guest, Keen and Nettlefold
GRP	glass reinforced plastic
HCDC	House of Commons Defence Committee
IEPG	Independent European Programme Group
IT	information technology
LSL	landing ship logistic
MLRS	multi-launch rocket system
MMC	Monopolies and Mergers Commission
MoD	Ministry of Defence
MRCA	multi-role combat aircraft
NAD	National Armaments Director
NFR–90	NATO frigate requirement
OECD	Organisation for Economic Cooperation and Development
PAC	Public Accounts Committee
QSEs	qualified scientists and engineers
R&D	research and development
RAFG	Royal Air Force Germany
RDE	research and development establishment
ROF	Royal Ordnance Factories
RPE	relative price effect
RSRE	Royal Signals and Radar Establishment (Malvern)
SDE	Statement on the Defence Estimates
SLM	Singer Link Miles
V/STOL	vertical/short takeoff and landing
VHSICS	very high speed integrated circuits
VLSICS	very large scale integrated circuits
WEU	Western European Union

Preface

The RUSI Technology and Defence Procurement Programme

Within the broad scope of its work, the RUSI focuses upon particular areas of study. These study programmes include one on Technology and Defence Procurement. The programme is concerned with the technological, industrial, political and military criteria which determine defence procurement policies. The correlation between new technologies, defence budgets and possible force structures is of notable relevance. The programme also reflects the RUSI's strong links with industry. The specific aim of the programme is to produce realistic policy options at a time when resources for defence are increasingly constrained.

This book on the UK's Defence Industrial Base is the outcome of considerable research, commitment and rigorous analysis both of Trevor Taylor, Keith Hayward, as well as the Study Programme. It forms the basis for and examination of competition and collaboration within Europe and in international consortia, particularly those in which American companies are involved.

Defence research and development of the relationship between price and performance and the costs of conventional defence procurement are areas of further work and interest. The Programme seeks to maintain a continuing commitment to the assessment of future technologies as they apply to current and prospective military and industrial thinking.

The RUSI is privileged to be able to call upon the assistance of those within its membership with direct responsibility, considerable experience, and a depth of knowledge, to guide its work. This is evidenced by the Advisory Group for the Technology and Defence Procurement Programme to whom the Institute is especially indebted:

Dr James Barnes
Vice Admiral Sir Jeremy Black, KCB, DSO, MBE
Dr William Fraser
Air Marshal Sir Donald Hall, KCB, CBE, AFC
Professor Sir Ronald Mason, KCB, FRS
Professor Ronald Smith

David Bolton
Director, RUSI

Executive Summary

Since 1979, the British Government has placed great emphasis on value-for-money in procurement, both to minimise waste and to head off a major review of defence commitments. However, has this, some might say over-zealous, quest for greater efficiency led to a neglect of other critical defence industrial issues?

It is clear that the United Kingdom cannot afford a comprehensive range of domestically produced weapons systems to provide all of the capabilities required to meet current commitments. Nevertheless, the UK defence industries represent a key element of the British economy; but, despite their importance, there appears to be no explicit Government policy for the nation's Defence Industrial Base (DIB).

These issues have been addressed by Professor Trevor Taylor and Keith Hayward in a RUSI study which examines fundamental questions concerning the structure and operation of the UK DIB. It reviews the effects of recent procurement policies and identifies future policy options.

The Study specifically considers:

- [ ] The consequences, stemming from successive British defence policies, for the UK defence industries.
- [ ] Those fields in which the UK is industrially and technologically strong.
- [ ] Whether there are specific industrial capabilities which, for military or economic reasons, should be retained.
- [ ] The impact of competition policy on defence contractors.
- [ ] The choices open to Government concerning the future of the British DIB.

and, [ ] How closely should UK defence industries be linked to European and other foreign companies.

The study finds that, in some respects, the UK DIB has not been driven by a proper regard for efficiency and effectiveness. Equally, Government procurement policy has sometimes contributed to inefficiency and cost escalation. However, there are a number of companies with outstanding records of technical and commercial success extending beyond a possibly unhealthy dependence upon the British defence market. To endanger these firms by a seemingly heedless regard for a narrowly defined concept of 'value-for-money' would be a waste of human and material capital invested in the defence industrial sector. It is argued that there is a need for a more structured approach to procurement if a dynamic UK DIB is to be maintained.

There are no easy policy options. It is proper for the Government to be concerned about the rising cost of domestic development and production. Competition is also to be welcomed as a spur to increased efficiency and it has already had a positive effect on British firms. However, the Government has made no explicit attempt to define the outer limits of competition, especially the extent to which it would accept the permanent loss of certain elements of the UK DIB. Many decisions appear to have been taken on an *ad hoc* basis. There would seem to be a clear need for a more coherent policy.

In examining a range of choices, the study strongly argues for:

- ☐ A distinct, but not an exclusive, commitment to a European defence industrial strategy.
- ☐ A DIB which optimises the return to the British economy from investment in defence R & D.
- ☐ An approach to the DIB which, while stressing the importance of efficiency, is aware of the dangers of unrestricted competition.

Above all, the study advocates the view that, whatever the specific components of the defence industrial base may be, the UK should have a clearly stated DIB policy. This should extend beyond *ad hoc* solutions and recognise the broader national and international implications of the Government's role as the single most important customer for advanced technology.

The most promising area for development would appear to be greater cooperation within Europe. This would offer increased opportunities for:

- ☐ Promoting efficiency through competition.
- ☐ Reducing costs.
- ☐ Maintaining a degree of European autonomy in key defence technologies.
- ☐ Creating a structure capable of cooperating on equal terms with the United States.

and, ☐ Making the best use of scarce alliance resources.

Introduction

In the spring of 1987, the House of Commons Defence Committee (HCDC) made the following observations:

> There are various considerations and some fine judgements involved in deciding how far the Government should go to maintain the defence-related elements of the industrial base. . . .
> . . . To try to stay at the forefront of weapons technology may make the cost of independence unacceptably high, but there is little point in seeking to remain independent if it means relying on outdated equipment which will not be effective in countering the threat posed by an increasingly sophisticated enemy.[1]

Thus, as it had already done in 1986, the HCDC drew specific attention to the question of the future of Britain's defence industrial base (DIB), recognising that Britain's traditional policy of being broadly self-sufficient in armaments development and production was no longer appropriate because of the costs involved. Yet it acknowledged that there were disadvantages associated with alternative policies which meant reliance on other nations. In brief the HCDC indicated that the DIB was a difficult area for Government yet one which needed further attention. This study reviews relevant government policies both on procurement and on the DIB itself, with one of its starting points being that the Government has in fact been reluctant to address issues relating to the optimum shape of the British DIB, in the main either because it felt there was no need or because it has had other priorities. To explain why this has been so, it is necessary to consider the evolution of British defence policy as a whole.

British defence policy since the Second World War has clearly been marked by an inevitable focusing of effort. By 1979, when Mrs Thatcher came to office, its basic shape was normally identified in terms of the four established tasks to which British forces were devoted.[2] These tasks, in no order of priority, were

- [ ] to defend the United Kingdom territorial base itself;
- [ ] to contribute to forward defence in Western Europe, most importantly through the British Army of the Rhine (BAOR) and RAF Germany (RAFG);
- [ ] to contribute to the defence of the North Atlantic; and
- [ ] to operate an independent strategic nuclear deterrent.

In addition, the Government deliberately maintained some capability for a fifth task: military actions outside the NATO area. After Mrs Thatcher became Prime Minister, debate about defence policy intensified, not least because of the 1980 decision to procure Trident C4 (which was amended in 1982 to the selection of Trident D5) and the British role in the 1979 NATO decision on American cruise missile deployment in Europe. A series of points emanated from the major political parties, the Press and independent analysts which suggested that Britain either could not or should not continue to meet all these five tasks. One frequently cited ground was that of cost. Defence equipment costs had tended to rise for many years at rates well above the general rate of inflation and Britain, with an all-volunteer force, had also to keep up pay levels in its armed forces in order to recruit new personnel and to retain valuable trained people.

In 1981 the Government accepted that some modifications of policy had to be made despite the 1978 NATO commitment to increasing defence spending in real terms by 3 per cent a year which it inherited from the Labour Government. The consequence was a review introduced by the then Defence Minister, John Nott.[3] This, among other measures, scheduled a substantial reduction in the surface fleet. The Falklands Conflict produced a significant modification to this plan although by 1986 a substantial reduction in the number of destroyers and frigates had been achieved. Yet developments in the 1980s in the Iran-Iraq War led the British Government once more to deploy ships to the Gulf on a long-term basis.

In addition, by the mid-1980s, the Government came round to the view that defence spending should not be allowed to increase in real terms. This was after several years of increased spending had brought greater capabilities. Moreover, Britain already spent a higher proportion of its Gross Domestic Product (GDP) on defence than any other member of the Western European Union (WEU) (although not as much as the United States). Even slight cuts in real spending were introduced towards the end of the decade.[4] In the light of these budget restraints, analysts such as defence economists David Greenwood and Malcolm Chalmers reiterated that Britain could not continue to afford to maintain all five tasks.[5] Yet despite the views of such 'pessimists', as they are described in Chapter Five below, there was said to be no need for a further defence review. By the 1987 election, the Government was emphatic that defence resources and commitments were matched and were consistent with United Kingdom needs and policies.

A specific further focus for debate was the view that, for a number of reasons not necessarily related to cost, Britain should not continue to be a nuclear weapon power. The Labour Party went into both the 1983 and 1987 elections with a commitment to the cancellation of the Trident contract and unilateral nuclear disarmament. The Liberal-Social Democrat position was more ambivalent and essentially involved specific opposition to Trident, however, the Conservative victory in the 1987 election meant that this issue area lost much of its political salience.

A central economic issue in the United Kingdom was that Britain's relative industrial position had continued to decline since the Second World War (although there were signs of improvement particularly during the second Thatcher Administration). The argument that, over decades, Britain has devoted too much of its national capability in terms of skills and material resources to defence research and development (R&D), and that civilian industry has therefore suffered, explicitly links defence production to economic problems.[6] The Government is the only United Kingdom customer for defence equipment and historically it has funded R&D for the equipment which it has defined as needed. Statistically, Britain has devoted a higher proportion of government R&D spending to defence than its allies. Also defence has accounted for a high proportion of the total (public and private) British R&D effort.[7] Although counter arguments assert that defence R&D expenditures are not central to the British economy and that a major problem is the general reluctance of British industry and financial institutions to invest in R&D, the Conservative Government has accepted that Britain should reduce, to a degree, the share of government R&D spending going to defence. This conclusion was announced publicly in the 1987 Statement on the Defence Estimates and in the 1987 White Paper on United Kingdom Research and Development.[8] The latter set up the Government's Advisory Committee on Science and Technology (ACOST) whose tasks included providing the Government with advice on R&D priorities.

Overall, however, the Government argued that Britain's (effectively five) defence roles could be maintained within planned funding levels. The Government claimed that it could adopt a policy of holding down spending whilst simultaneously maintaining its defence capabilities. This, in large part, was because it expected to make substantial savings in procurement derived from more rigorous and competitive practices and from much greater use of collaboration, particularly with European partners. Better value for money was to be obtained from defence equipment spending and Mr Peter Levene was brought into the Ministry of Defence (MoD) as Chief of Defence Procurement specifically to introduce these more effective practices. He felt that savings of at least 10 per cent in procurement costs could be made within his five year contract period. Although he acknowledged that no one would ever be able to prove or disprove overall savings, the MoD on occasions in its Statements on the Defence Estimates (SDEs) has sought to demonstrate specified savings from the use of greater competition in individual projects.[9] The 10 per cent target has not been clearly defined and it has emerged as a mix of securing 10 per cent more equipment for the same budget and obtaining the same amount of equipment using reduced funding.

The emphasis on procurement savings as a means of maintaining Britain's immediate military capabilities raised questions about an implicit but nevertheless central element in British defence policy since the Second World War. This was the British practice of buying the great majority of its defence equipment from British suppliers. An alternative possibility was that Britain might be able to secure optimum defence 'value for money' from its procurement budget only by buying more equipment from overseas suppliers. Thus Government procurement policy had major implications for the British DIB and consequently this issue is one of the central concerns of this study, a work which seeks to identify the main elements affecting DIB policy and to identify some policy options for government and industry.

Traditionally, countries have often sought to rely on their own defence producers for a number of reasons, including guaranteed security of supply and a sense of political autonomy. In the world as a whole, more countries, especially in the developing world, are seeking to build up their arms industries. In the United Kingdom, it cannot be expected that debate on the national DIB would be confined to concerns about the immediate needs of the armed forces. Most obviously, employment and the balance of payments would be considerations, as would arguments about how best Britain could act to meet the wider technological and industrial challenges of the 1990s. The Ministry of Defence is a major customer for high technology. Overall it is by far British industry's biggest single customer and so DIB policy has clearly direct repercussions for national industrial policy in general. Yet responsibility for industry in the United Kingdom lies with the Department of Trade & Industry (DTI) and, as the 1986 Westland crisis and the discussions on the proposed 1986 GEC-Plessey merger showed, the MoD and the DTI do not always cooperate easily. On industrial issues, the thrust of the Thatcher Administrations, with some qualifications, was rather to rely on market forces of competition to generate effective UK industrial performance, although defence products have certain characteristics which make it hard for the government to disassociate itself completely from their manufacture.[10]

But also of relevance to discussion of those characteristics desirable for the UK DIB is the likely wider world in which British defence policy will have to be implemented. Will it be one in which Britain will have reliable sources of defence equipment for any conflict in which it may become involved? If so, which suppliers are to be regarded as reliable? Is it a reasonable assumption, even in support of a strategy of deterrence, that any conventional war in Europe would be short and thus fought largely with weapons in stock? Does Britain need to be prepared for protracted conflict anywhere outside Europe? Clearly these are weighty, even uncomfortable questions, to which it is hard to give responses with confidence, especially in the light of some of the current international political trends. Such trends include the apparent American preference to scale down the role of nuclear weapons in European defence and the periodic differences of view between Western Europe and the United States, on such matters as burden-sharing, arms control, technology transfer and out-of-area issues. These issues persistently contribute to the pressures for greater European defence cooperation.

Taking these factors into account, the specific aims of this study are to provide an outline of the shape, trends and capabilities of the British DIB, to identify and analyse critically government policy in terms of words and deeds towards procurement and the DIB, and to identify options for future policy action.

The study is outlined as follows. It considers first the concept of a DIB. The next section analyses the actual structure of the United Kingdom DIB in terms of technologies, products and companies. There is a separate section devoted to the all-pervasive electronics sector because of its growing importance, its implications for civil industry and its complexity. The study then moves to analyse the range of procurement choices in principle for specific systems. Next, attention is turned to existing government policy on procurement and the stances it has adopted towards the DIB. Clearly these two areas are inter-related and overlap to a considerable degree. Yet particularly, because it is possible to procure equipment without considering the DIB, it is valuable to treat them separately for purposes of analysis. The chapters are concerned mainly with explicit manifestations of policy in terms of written or spoken general commitments but they also take into account implicit policy, which is revealed mainly in decisions on individual systems. The final sections articulate the range of DIB policy options open to the British Government, with their implications for industry, in the light of technological and market trends and the anticipated nature of British security challenges.

1

The Defence Industrial Base: A Conceptual Analysis

The expression defence industrial base (DIB) is not self-evident in its meaning either in terms of its definition or its implications and it is therefore appropriate to begin by considering briefly some of the dimensions of the DIB. This section introduces some variations on the general notion of the DIB and raises issues for further discussion.

The concept of the DIB is clear at first glance. The DIB can be thought of simply as that section of a country's industry which supplies equipment for the state's armed forces. The British Secretary of State for Defence, George Younger, told the House of Commons Defence Committee that ' "the defence industrial base" is the term we adopt for convenience to describe the wide range of firms which supply the Ministry of Defence with the equipment and services it requires.' However, this definition gives rise to difficulties when it is necessary to identify specific elements in the DIB and to raise fundamental policy questions.[1] The House of Commons Defence Committee took a much wider view, noting that 'in general the defence industrial base consists of those industrial assets which provide key elements of military power and national security. These assets thus demand special attention by government'.[2]

Military Equipment, Militarised Civil Equipment and Civil Equipment

An initial question is whether all equipment supplied to a state's armed forces should be considered to have a military value and thus be DIB-related. It may be helpful to distinguish three groups of products which, although not falling into clear-cut categories, have different foci. At one extreme of the spectrum, and clearly emerging from the DIB, are products with the clear aim of killing or disabling people and the destruction of property. Also in this category are the specialist vehicles (tanks, warships, combat aircraft) on which are mounted the missiles, guns, bombs and projectiles whose purpose is destruction. Although such equipment is designed to destroy, it is often procured to threaten and to deter.

1

In the middle there is a broad category of equipment which in itself is non-lethal yet it is concerned directly with specific military activities. Included here are such items as air defence radars, communications networks, bridge-laying equipment and so on. A piece of equipment may have a close civilian equivalent but the military version will probably have been given special features to meet the needs of armed forces. Normally it will have been made more rugged and tough. Military trucks, transport aircraft and most heli-copters fall into this category.

In times of operational need, equipment in this grouping which began life in the civil sector is often recruited to serve the military. To take a recent example, Britain lacked sufficient specialist troop transport ships in the Falklands Campaign, and therefore adapted civilian ferries and liners. Civil trucks can be used instead of military trucks or even transport helicopters. There is a long history of such utilisation in many countries and a policy preparing for requisitioning can provide capabilities at modest cost. The United States Government will pay for modifications to civilian passenger aircraft so that they can be adapted easily for military use and thus form part of the American emergency airlift capabilities. In the context of the NATO debate about the Alliance's merchant fleet stocks, there has been some discussion in the West of the fact that containerised merchant ships which are in common use today are hard to convert to the carriage of military cargoes.

Industries producing goods in this middle category, where the civil-military distinction is blurred, should most easily be able to argue that advances made under military R&D programmes produce a 'spin-off' that is useful in the civil sector. On the other hand, such firms may be tempted to concentrate on the military side of their business if they feel that the competition there is less fierce.

At the other extreme are products used by the military but which are produced en masse for the civilian population as well. Such goods include word processors, staff cars, food, diesel oil and medicines or, in the words of the Ministry of Defence, 'everything from boots to breakfast cereal'.[3] In general, the military market for these items is much smaller than the civil one. A state which, in conflict, is deprived of such items will eventually see its fighting capabilities substantially diminished and thus they are as central to its war efforts as ammunition. Historically, it has been much harder to supply armies with food than ammunition. But, on the other hand, in times of shortage the government is well placed to ensure that the military receive priority.

Governments tend to recognise these three groups of products in policy terms by referring to items exported from the first and second categories as defence exports and by subjecting them to additional regulations. Items in the third category are not normally thought of as being generated by the DIB and in Britain other ministries or government bodies often handle their procurement on behalf of the Ministry of Defence. The Department of

Health & Social Security, for example, supplies drugs and medicines to the MoD.

The groupings present several DIB policy questions. Is it logical for a government to seek self-sufficiency in items from one category to give it greater freedom of action to decide if, how and when it will use force, although it may not be self-sufficient in less direct but nonetheless vital areas such as fuel? To what extent is defence manufacturing within a state dependent upon foreign components, sub-systems, machine tools and/or licences? Can supplies of lethal items be expected to be more difficult to acquire from external sources in times of crisis than non-lethal items, such as wheeled vehicles? To what extent can the effects of reliance on foreign suppliers be offset by the holding of considerable stocks or by making sure that several suppliers are available? In Britain in the 1950s the government sought to offset the loss of autonomy which reliance on imported oil might have brought by increasing oil stocks and by developing refining facilities in the UK.

Defence dependence for firms and the residual DIB

It is debatable whether all firms supplying the armed forces should be considered part of the DIB and whether some firms which do not currently supply the armed forces should be included. Stances on these issues depend very much on the angle from which the DIB is being examined.

For Secretary of State George Younger, only those companies which depend on the MoD for a significant proportion of their business should be included in the DIB. 'I would not like to put a firm percentage on it, but a significant proportion'[4]. The Minister's definition would yield a very small DIB and his views may not have been carefully considered. Many firms are important suppliers and competitors for MoD contracts and yet defence accounts for considerably less than 15 per cent of their turnover. GKN, Vickers, Pilkington and British Petroleum are among such companies. Many large firms have specialist but comparatively small defence divisions. Firms which deal only on a minor scale with defence ministries can supply items, such as semi-conductors, microchips, and some materials which are of enormous military importance but perhaps of small cost. Moreover a given volume of business is much less important for a big firm than a small one. Defence does not have a major share of Siemens business but Siemens is nonetheless an important element in the German DIB. Moreover, some firms not currently producing defence equipment could change to so doing if required.

From a wider political point of view, a state's defence potential, as opposed to its present capability, is much affected by the overall capacity of its industry. Japan's DIB, in the sense of which industries serve the defence ministry, is still relatively modest, although the Japanese defence budget is larger than that of the United Kingdom or France and Japanese equipment needs are met predominantly by Japanese industry. It is apparent and significant that Japan's industry could change direction and has the potential, perhaps within a decade, to equip much more extensive Japanese forces. Japan, then, has a substantial residual DIB and a smaller, growing extant DIB.

Strategic and operational autonomy from a DIB

One feature of a comprehensive DIB is that it should give a government more freedom in its decisions concerning the application of military force or the sending of arms supplies. Clearly, states dependent on external arms supplies can wage war, even when their main suppliers do not cooperate. But their efforts, like those of the Iranians against Iraq, can be severely hampered by reliance on black market or covert deals and by the absence of reliable supplies. However, the time-scale of decision-making is also of considerable significance, as is illustrated by the concepts of strategic and operational autonomy. Operational autonomy or freedom from constraint focuses on situations where a decision is imminent on the use of armed force. In such cases, the possible consequences of dependence on outsiders for military supplies can be minimised in several ways. Thus a state could in principle:

avoid signing legal agreements limiting the use of weapons it buys;

build up stocks so that military activities can be undertaken with minimal need of further supplies from overseas sources;

build up a partial domestic DIB which can produce the main consumables of war, such as ammunition and frequently-failing components; and

develop a range of suppliers to minimise the consequences should one supplier disappear.

Each of these has real disadvantages. The first may be difficult to achieve, particularly with regard to purchases from the United States. The second would definitely be costly, the third would provide only limited self-sufficiency, as the Israelis know well, and the fourth assumes that a range of suppliers of suitable equipment is available. It also hinders the development of equipment interoperability within a state's armed forces.

On the other hand, operational freedom can be restricted even for a state which produces its own defence equipment if:

the production base is unable to step up output quickly enough (this is often referred to as 'surge capacity,') to meet the extra demands which the use of force or related arms sales might make;

the government does not have control over other elements essential to the smooth prosecution of operations. The American pressure which led to Britain and France halting their invasion of Egypt in 1956 was directed not at the fighting potential of British and French forces but on sterling and the British economy;

the country does not have the necessary access to imports, such as minerals or machine tool spare parts, which are necessary for local defence production.

The elements of 'operational autonomy' vary. Thus Britian would claim to have operational autonomy regarding the use of its strategic nuclear forces because it can threaten their use and could use those forces if it so chose, even though they are largely supplied by the United States. Operational autonomy is achieved by having a national capability to target the missiles and by having a national command and control system. For conventional force operations, however, which can involve more protracted conflict and heavy consumption of spares and ammunition, operational autonomy is much harder to achieve.

'Strategic autonomy', on the other hand, is relevant to the long term and to future decisions on the use of force. Here the central concern is with a state's actual defence producers and its residual capabilities which together could turn it into a much more self-sufficient defence equipment manufacturer should the need arise.

The determinants of a country's strategic autonomy include the breadth of capabilities across its industries as a whole. West Germany, if it built upon the expertise of its civil nuclear industry, could build its own nuclear forces if it chose, although such an action would involve basic changes to the German constitution and would cause enormous political disruption. The potential of Japan to develop and produce defence equipment has already been noted.

Another direct determinant is the extent of research effort. By spending on research across a range of technological areas, but by not incurring the expense of developing and producing specific systems incorporating that technology, a state can maintain considerable potential. It can build a platform from which to launch industrial and technological projects if need be. In the West German debates on a new fighter aircraft in 1980, Messerschmitt Boelkow Blohm calculated that they could remain potential developers and builders of modern combat aircraft, even if the West German Government chose the F-18, so long as they spent some hundreds of millions of dollars on research to carry them to the next German programme.[5]

Until the mid-1950s, British policy was to spend very broadly on research and, although there was a relative and steady diminution of the research effort from 1956, one consequence was to give Britain considerable strategic autonomy today, ie a capacity to develop, if necessary, a broadly comprehensive range of military equipment.

Other techniques by which states can increase their strategic autonomy include engaging in licensed production of equipment developed elsewhere and undertaking projects on a collaborative basis. Often of most value with licensed production are the manufacturing techniques involved. In general, licensed production means that the licensee starts from a position of inferiority to that of the licensor but knowledge gained from licensed manufacture can be built on over the years. Licensed production does not, however, provide the capability totally to design and develop a system, although obviously it can lead to relevant insights being gained.

By engaging in collaborative development projects, a state can develop and produce part of a wider system, while getting access to information and technology which would permit it to develop and produce a full system for itself should the need arise. Britain and France have both tended to view collaboration as a means of maintaining the comprehensive capabilities of their DIBs. However, using collaboration in this way, which can include duplicated test facilities, multiple production lines and duplicated research, does push up costs.

The concept of strategic autonomy, then, concentrates on a state's potential, and thus on the R&D aspect of the procurement process, whereas operational autonomy is concerned with current capabilities. The latter is much more oriented towards the production and support in the procurement process.

Here a few words are appropriate to review what it is that gives a government and its officials a sense of 'political autonomy', a psychological condition of not feeling unacceptably tied to the preferences of outside governments. A sense of political autonomy is clearly something which the leaders of sovereign states would prefer to possess and for which they will pay a price. What gives a government such a sense seems to vary from state to state and is a function of the culture and history of the society in question. West Germany's recent assertiveness in European technological issues would seem to reflect a growing preference to put aside the experience of the Second World War and to have confidence in Germany's industrial achievements and the strength of the Deutsch Mark. France's national self-esteem is apparently much strengthened by the success of high technology projects such as Ariane. Traditionally, a sense of political autonomy in Britain has, perhaps, been tied to the existence of a wide-ranging British DIB but a DIB where the emphasis was on strategic rather than operational autonomy, on high technology achievements and R&D rather than on immediate fighting capabilities. Ascribing importance to psychological elements in policy is always dubious because unambiguous supporting evidence is particularly scarce. Nevertheless, the distinction is clearly noteworthy between operational and strategic autonomy, which are measurable in principle, and political autonomy, which may be related to the other forms of autonomy but which exists to a degree in the mind of the statesman.

2

The UK Defence Industrial Base

Selling in the defence market

Companies selling defence equipment to the British Ministry of Defence have an unusual variant of a free-market commercial relationship. Within the United Kingdom there is only one eventual customer for military equipment, the MoD. Normally the Ministry states its requirement, made up of the key characteristics which it wants a piece of equipment to possess, before equipment is bought and often before it has been developed. Clearly the MoD delegates much purchasing of subsystems in equipment to prime contractors, although the MoD oversees subcontracting activities. Regarding the equipment produced, compared with most goods in the civilian economy, military items have to be rugged because they may have to be used in hostile environments and to survive rough handling. Also, because people's lives and the nation's security are associated with defence equipment, reliability has always loomed large as a consideration. On the other hand, because the West perceives that it cannot match Soviet numerical strength, it has felt the need for its equipment to be technologically advanced. Technological sophistication may not always be easily reconciled with reliability, or with available budgets.

A major characteristic of the external defence market, where governments are again the only significant customers, is that it is highly politicised. For many regimes, buying a major piece of equipment from a foreign source sends important political messages. Governments, for instance those of Saudi Arabia and Jordan, sometimes want to buy American equipment in part because they want the American support which they feel a sale signifies. On the other hand, many states deliberately diversify the sources of their arms suppliers in order to avoid too close association with any one nation. Arms exports can also raise security questions, sometimes about technology transfer. In security terms, no government wants to sell arms which are likely to be used against it in the future.

To a large degree, the domestic customer, the home defence ministry, must be won over to the virtues of a product before a foreign sale can be made, as Northrop found to its cost with the F-20. If a company's home defence ministry does not endorse a product by buying it, other states may also be

7

reluctant to purchase it. In part this is because many pieces of military equipment are extremely complex and it is difficult for a potential customer to evaluate them, even with the aid of demonstrations, trials and so on. The purchase of equipment by the manufacturer's home government is a straight-forward sign that the equipment does in fact work broadly as specified. These then are some of the characteristics of the defence market and clearly it is very different from most civil markets.

British firms and their products: a brief survey

In the 19th century, the British capacity to produce equipment for its military forces depended essentially on the country's capacity to build ships and its expertise in the characteristics and fabrication of metals. Specialist munitions companies such as Vickers appeared and chemical industries became import-ant as manufacturers of explosives. Today, however, specialist munitions companies are comparatively few (two cases in the United Kingdom are the Royal Ordnance Factories (ROF), now a British Aerospace (BAe) subsidiary, and the British Manufacture & Research Company (BMARC), which is a subsidiary of Oerlikon. The contemporary DIB in many ways simply per-meates manufacturing industry. The goods required by the military for transport, for information collection and transmission, for protection and for destruction, are today so varied and dependent on expertise in so many technologies that there is more or less no industrial sector which does not or could not contribute to the DIB. This is illustrated by Table 2.1.

The diversity of technology involved (and the rapid rate of advance in many of them) is posing problems for firms when these technologies have to be integrated within a single system such as an aircraft. Today's aircraft manufacturer must be expert not just in aerodynamics, but also in the performance characteristics and processing techniques of advanced metals and other materials (particularly composites), and in most aspects of electro-nics. In addition, the company needs access to modern engine technology. Finally, the company must have the managerial and technical capacity to integrate all these elements to produce an effective, capable aircraft. The need to accommodate new technologies is, however, affecting smaller enterprises as well, as is shown, for example, by the growing involvement in electronics of Normalair Garrett, a Westland subsidiary traditionally strong in mechanical engineering.[1] Many UK 'defence' companies in the late 1980s were seeking to market their wider technology skills in wider civil and military sectors.

This range of technologies relevant to military endeavour helps to explain the pyramid shape of the British DIB. At the top are those very large companies which often serve as prime contractors for major projects and whose names are closely associated with defence. British Aerospace (BAe), Rolls-Royce and GEC are in this category. Next there are a range of

TABLE 2.1
*Defence Expenditure in the United Kingdom: estimated breakdown by
commodity*

	SIC(80) Group[1]	£ million		% change		% change
		1981–2	1985–6	change	1986–7	change
Solid Fuels [3]	111.20	8	10	25	12	20
Petroleum Products [3]	140	512	601	17	385	– 36
Gas. electr., water supply [3]	161–70	160	213	33	231	8
Ordnance, small arms, ammun.	329	437	675	54	683	1
Other mechan. and marine eng.	320–328	278	415	49	427	3
Data processing equip.	330	90	121	34	130	7
Other electrical engineering	341–348 nes	131	135	3	145	7
Electronics	344, 345	1219	1557	28	1599	3
Motor vehicles and parts	351–3	162	288	78	253	– 12
Shipbldg. and repairing	361	544	660	21	700	6
Aerospace equip.	364	2007	2531	26	2418	– 4
Instrument engineering	371–4	173	118	– 32	114	– 3
Food[3]	411–429	103	132	28	127	– 4
Textiles, leather goods, clothing	431–456	73	124	70	133	7
Other prod. industries	111–495 nes	158	271	72	290	7
Other industries and services	nes	124	253	104	272	8
TOTAL [2]		6180	8128	32	7919	3

1. Groups in Standard Industrial Classification (1980 revision)

2. Gross expenditure at current prices excluding VAT, pay and allowances, general administrative expenses (£704 million in 1985-6), Property Services Agency expenditure on behalf of MoD and other expenditure on land, buildings and works services.

3. Includes payment for goods and services purchased overseas.

Source: Statement on the Defence Estimates 1987, Vol. II, p. 11, Cmnd. 101-II.

companies, some with annual turnovers in the hundreds of millions of pounds, which also work regularly for the MoD directly and whose internal procedures for quality assurance and other elements have been approved under the MoD qualification system. They have become formally 'defence qualified', a difficult and sometimes expensive status to attain.[2] Some of these firms are well known for their defence work while others are not. Hunting Engineering, Racal, Vickers Shipbuilding & Engineering Ltd (VSEL) and Plessey are notable cases in this area but this whole top part of the pyramid consists largely of those firms which the annual Statement on the Defence Estimates (SDE) lists as having had work worth more than £5 million in a year from the MoD. Table 2.2 lists all the companies which have appeared in this list since 1981. In the 1987 SDE the Government revealed which companies had contracts in excess of £250 million.

TABLE 2.2

United Kingdom-based MoD Contractors Paid £5 million or more by MoD

Companies	Tax Year									
	1976	1977	1978	1979	1980	1981	1982	1983	1984	1985
Acrow plc								+10	+5	
Airtech Ltd				+5		+5				
Angle Nordic Holdings plc										+5
Ameeco (Hydrospace) Ltd								+5		
J. C. Bamford Excavators Ltd										+5
Bell & Howell Ltd							+5			
BICC plc				+5				+5	+5	
British Aerospace (BAe) plc (Aircraft Group)	+100	+100	+100	+100	+100	+100	+100	+100	+100	+250
British Aerospace (BAe) plc (Dynamics Group)	+100	+100	+100	+100	+100	+100	+100	+100	+100	+250
British Airways plc									+25	+25
British & Commonwealth Shipping Co Ltd			+5						+10	+10
British Electric Traction (BET) plc		+5	+10	+10	+10	+10	+10	+10	+10	+25
British Leyland (BL) plc (Austin Rover Group)	+25	+25	+50	+50	+50	+25	+50	+50	+50	+50
British Petroleum Co. plc									+100	+100
British Railways									+50	+5
British Shipbuilders	+100	+100	+100	+100	+100	+100	+100	+100	+100	+250
British Telecommunications plc									+25	+5
Bodycote International plc										+5
B Thompson Ltd								+5		
BTR plc				+5	+10	+10	+10	+10	+25	+10
Cable & Wireless plc				+5	+10	+25	+10	+10	+10	+5
Caltex (UK) Ltd								+10		
Cambridge Electronics Industries plc							+10	+10	+10	+10
Cap Group Ltd										+5
Chloride Group Ltd			+5	+5	+5		+5		+10	+5
Clarke Chapman Ltd			+5							
Computing Devices Ltd								+5		
Conoco (UK) Ltd								+5	+10	
Control Data Ltd										+10
Cossor Electronics Ltd					+10	+10	+10	+10	+25	+25
Courtaulds Ltd			+5	+5	+5				+5	+5
Cranfield Institute of Technology									+5	+10
Cray Electronic Holdings plc										+10
CT Group Ltd									+5	
David Brown (Holdings)Ltd	+25	+25		+5	+10	+5	+5		+5	+5
Decca Ltd	+5	+5	+5	+10						
Dickenson Robinson Group (DRG) plc					+5	+10	+10	+10	+10	+10
Digital Equipment Co (DEC) Ltd						+5				+25
Dowty Group plc	+10	+25	+25	+25	+25	+25	+25	+50	+50	+50
Dunlop Holdings plc	+5	+5	+5	+5	+10	+10	+10	+10		+10
Englehard Industries Ltd								+5		
Esso UK plc									+100	+100
Ferguson Industrial Holdings plc						+5		+5	+10	+10
Ferranti plc	+25	+25	+50	+50	+100	+100	+100	+100	+100	+100

Fisher Controls Ltd									+5	
Flight Refuelling (Holdings) plc					+5	+5	+5	+10	+10	+25
Fodens Ltd	+5	+5	+5							
Ford Motor Co Ltd				+5	+5					
Frazer Nash Group Ltd										+5
The General Electric Co (GEC) plc	+100	+100	+100	+100	+100	+100	+100	+100	+100	+250
General Motors Ltd (Vauxhall)	+10	+10	+5	+10	+25	+50	+50	+25	+50	+50
George Blair										+5
Goodyear Tyre and Rubber Co					+5		+5	+5	+5	+5
Gresham Lion plc		+5	+5	+10	+10	+5	+5	+5		
Grindleys Holdings Ltd				+5						
Guest, Keen & Nettlefolds (GKN) plc			+5	+5	+10	+10	+25	+10	+25	+25
Harland & Wolff Ltd								+10	+5	
Hawker Siddeley Group plc		+10	+5	+10	+10	+10	+10	+10	+10	+10
Hewlett Packard						+5	+5		+5	+10
Hillsdown Holdings Ltd									+5	+5
Honeywell Ltd										+10
Humber Shiprepairers Ltd										+5
Hunting Associated Industries plc	+25	+25	+25	+50	+50	+50	+50	+50	+50	+100
IBM United Kingdom Holdings Ltd										+5
ICI plc		+5	+5			+5	+5			
ICL plc							+5	+10		
Imperial Continental Gas Association									+5	+5
Inchcape plc									+5	+5
The Inqram Maritime Co Ltd						+5			+5	
International Thompson Organisation plc									+5	
ITM Offshore								+10	+5	
ITT (United Kingdom) Ltd							+10			
John Brown plc										+5
Loqica Ltd										+5
Louis Newmark plc						+5		+5	+5	
Lucas Industries plc	+25	+25	+25	+25	+25	+25	+25	+25	+50	+50
MacTaggart Scott (Holdings) Ltd						+5	+5		+5	
Marlborough Communications Ltd								+5	+5	
Marshall of Cambridge (Engineering) Ltd	+5	+10	+10	+10	+25	+25	+25	+25	+50	+50
Martin Baker Aircraft Co Ltd									+5	+5
Massey Ferguson Holdings Ltd									+5	
Matheson & Co Ltd							+10			
ML Holdings Ltd					+5					+5
Mobile Holdings Ltd									+10	+10
Monsanto plc									+5	+5
Mullard Ltd	+5	+5	+5							
Negretti and Zambra Ltd						+5				
Northern Engineering Industries plc (NEI plc)								+10	+10	+10
Oerlikon Buerle Holdings Ltd (BMARC Ltd)							+25	+10	+10	+10
Other British Government Departments									+25	+25
Paccar UK Ltd									+5	+10

Company										
Petrofina (UK) Ltd									+25	+25
Philcom plc										+5
Philips Electronic & Associated Industries plc	+10	+10	+10	+5	+50	+50	+25	+50	+25	+25
Pilkington Bros plc (Barr & Stroud)	+5	+10	+10	+10	+10	+10	+25	+25	+50	+50
The Plessey Co plc	+50	+50	+50	+100	+100	+100	+100	+100	+100	+250
Portsmouth Aviation				+5	+5		+5	+5		
Racal Electronics plc	+10	+10	+25	+25	+50	+50	+50	+100	+100	+100
Rank Organisation plc	+5	+5	+5	+5	+5			+5	+5	+5
RCA Ltd				+5	+5	+5	+5	+10	+10	
Raytheon Co						+5				
Remploy Ltd				+5	+5	+5	+10	+10	+10	
RFD Ltd							+5	+5	+5	
Richard Dunstan (Hessle) Ltd				+5						
Rockwell-Collins (UK) Ltd										+5
Rolls-Royce Ltd	+100	+100	+100	+100	+100	+100	+100	+100	+100	+250
Ropner Holdings Ltd				+5	+5	+10			+5	+5
Royal Ordnance Factories (ROF)	+100	+100	+100	+100	+100	+100	+100	+100	+100	+250
Saft (UK) Ltd							+5	+5	+5	+5
Sandbach Engineering Co						+5				
Schlumberger Measurement & Control Ltd						+5	+5	+5	+10	+5
The Shell Transport & Trading Co plc									+100	+50
Short Bros Ltd	+10	+10	+10	+25	+25	+25	+25	+25	+25	+25
Siemens Ltd					+5	+5	+5	+5	+5	
Singer Co (UK) Ltd		+5	+5	+10	+10	+10	+10	+10	+10	+10
Smiths Industries plc	+10	+10	+10	+10	+10	+25	+10	+25	+25	+25
S Pearson & Son plc						+5	+5	+5		
Sperry Rand Ltd	+10	+10	+25		+25	+50				
STC plc	+5	+5	+5	+10	+10	+10		+10	+25	+50
Stone Platt Industries Ltd				+5	+5	+5				
Systems Designers International plc								+5	+5	+10
Taddale Investment plc									+5	
Tate & Lyle plc									+10	+10
Texaco Ltd										+5
Thorn EMI plc	+25	+25	+25	+50	+50	+50	+50	+100	+100	+100
The Throgmorton Trust plc							+5	+5	+10	+10
Thomas Tilling plc								+5		
Total Oil (GB) Ltd									+10	+5
Trafalgar House plc									+10	+5
Tube Investments plc				+5						
Tyne Ship Repair Group Ltd				+5						
United Kingdom Atomic Energy Authority (UKAEA)	+5	+10	+10	+10	+5	+10	+25	+10		
United Scientific Holdings plc (inc. Alvis)						+25	+25	+25	+10	+10
UK Universities										+5
Vantona Viyella plc			+5	+5			+5	+5	+10	+10
Vickers plc	+50	+100	+10	+10	+10	+10	+25	+25	+10	+25
Volvo BM UK Ltd									+5	+10
Watercraft Ltd										+5
Waverley Electronics Ltd										+5
The Weir Group Ltd	+5	+5	+5	+5	+10	+10	+10	+10	+10	+10

	1	2	3	4	5	6	7	8	9	10
Western Scientific Instruments Ltd							+5	+5	+5	
Westland plc	+50	+50	+50	+100	+100	+100	+100	+100	+100	+100
Wilkinson Sword Group Ltd							+5	+5	+5	+5
Yarrow plc	+25	+25		+5	+5	+5	+5	+5	+5	+10

Source: Statement of Defence Estimates, Part 1., various years.
Note: Before 1984 suppliers of defence equipment only were listed. From 1984 the list was broadened to include the suppliers of food, fuels, and services.

Obviously the overall composition of this MoD group is fairly stable since many MoD contracts take some years to fulfill and many of the companies are involved with a range of products. However, it is possible to see some newcomers and some whose position has not strengthened. Additionally, however, there are defence companies which, because they do not often have direct contracts with MoD, do not often appear on the SDE lists. One notable case is Martin Baker, the famous manufacturer of ejector seats.

One clear trend is the rising importance of electronics companies in defence procurement. The rise of companies such as Plessey and Racal is quite apparent. Not yet making much showing but likely to do so in future are the major software houses of which Logica and the CAP Group are perhaps the best known independent companies. The electronics involvement in the DIB is specifically discussed in the next chapter.

Perhaps the clearest guide to the pyramid structure of the DIB is given by the fact that each year the MoD lists about 100 firms as its major contractors. A few of these hold financial prominence. On the other hand, the Defence Manufacturers Association of Great Britain has a membership of about 300. Other relevant trade associations — the British Naval Equipment Association, the Computing Services Association, the Electronic Components Industry Federation, the Electronic Engineering Association and the Society of British Aerospace Companies — also have company memberships in the low hundreds. Overall, defence equipment catalogues and other publications indicate that there are about 800 firms in the United Kingdom which make equipment designed specifically for military use. The MoD itself asserts that about 10,000 firms a year in Britain benefit from its contracts, though many of these are involved in supplying food, undertaking civil enginering and providing other civilian goods and services. About 8,000 firms are qualified on the MoD Defence Contractors list.

While the DIB might have some collective characteristics, in the main it is the sum total of the individual companies concerned. At the centre of the UK DIB are a few companies of which the most important in defence financial terms is British Aerospace (BAe). The SDE lists BAe Aircraft and Dynamics sections as separate companies, although they are under central control, and each had work worth more than £250 million from the MoD in 1986. In all, BAe's contracts for the MoD are probably worth between 33 per cent and 40 per cent of its total turnover, currently a sum of £1-1.2 billion.

BAe's turnover in military aircraft and support together with guided weapons and electronics was £1,868 million in 1985.[3] It has some defence-oriented space work, in particular the Skynet satellite system. With its acquisition of the Royal Ordnance Factories (ROF) in 1987, BAe became even more central in the British DIB, being a major supplier to all three services and often acting as a prime contractor. Should its 1988 bid for the Austin Rover group succeed, BAe would become a diversified engineering group which included a range of softskin military vehicles among its products.

Before and after privatisation, BAe adopted a positive corporate strategy for future success. It committed itself to two new national civil projects — the 146 short range airliner in the 100-seat class and the Advanced Turboprop airliner (ATP) in the 60-seat class. The 146, in particular, represents a substantial gamble with a four-engined product in a highly competitive market and its immediate future success depends on the evolution of the dollar-pound exchange rate and how well the substantial commitment of the air freight TNT organisation to the aircraft proceeds.[4] BAe has built on the earlier commitment of Hawker Siddeley (now an element in BAe) to Airbus Industrie and in general is seeking to play a more active lead role in that organisation. In short, BAe has shown a preference to reduce the relative weight of defence in its corporate activities and to develop its civil activities. This was dramatically signalled by its bid for the Austin Rover group. In 1988, excluding the ROF, the civil side of BAe generated about 30 per cent of turnover and the company's aim is to increase it to 50 per cent by the early 1990s.[5]

In the defence field itself, BAe has sought to build up its capabilities across the range of relevant technologies. It has developed capabilities in composite material manufacture and it has become increasingly involved in electronics systems and components. For instance, its Naval & Electronics Systems Division developed a declarative language machine claimed to be the fastest artificial intelligence machine in the world.[6] It bought Sperry UK and in 1987 it applied to buy the West German military optics firm Steinheil Lear Siegler, for which it needed the approval of the West German Government. It also acquired a major interest in Systems Designers, a leading British software house (see Chapter 3). As noted, in 1987 it took over the ROF, seeking to improve its overall cash flow position and to couple the ROF capability in explosives, shells and other ground weaponry with its expertise in guidance systems, aerodynamics and so on. Clearly the company aimed to be well placed in the whole smart weapons field but BAe became so large in the United Kingdom that any further domestic growth tended to provoke concern about its central position in the British defence industrial structure.

In the 1980s, several of BAe's military aircraft and some missiles were highly successful commercially. Two generations of the Harrier were sold to the United States Marine Corps and the Hawk trainer to the United States

Navy among other customers. The collaborative aircraft Tornado was sold to Saudi Arabia, Jordan and Oman and had chances of further sales. The Rapier anti-aircraft missile in particular sold well in outside markets. Moreover, BAe products acquired a reputation for being ready on time, at something approaching the agreed cost and meeting the set requirement. When projects with BAe involvement went wrong, as did AEW Nimrod and the ALARM anti-radiation missile, it was clear that the responsibility lay elsewhere.

BAe was also sensitive to the utility of collaboration. For more than two decades the company, and the firms from which it was established, have actively endorsed collaboration and have been involved with a range of collaborative projects (involving over 20 other countries) including Tornado. Of particular note were the collaborative arrangements it made with McDonnell Douglas in the United States for joint manufacture and further development of the Harrier and the Hawk. It also established a partnership with Rockwell-Collins to promote its Terprom navigation system in America. But perhaps most significant was its approach to finding collaborative partners for a follow-on project to Tornado. The discussions around such a project date back at least to the start of the 1980s and BAe adopted a dual posture. On the one hand it appreciated that a successor project would almost certainly have to be collaborative and it therefore made sure that its links with MBB and Aeritalia were consolidated. On the other hand, it also made sure it would have an authoritative voice in any future project by undertaking national work on a fly-by-wire version of the Jaguar and on the Experimental Aircraft Programme. BAe felt that collaborating with Dassault of France would provoke some problems and was less keen on that possibility. The consequence was that, when the governments in the European Fighter Aircraft discussions reached deadlock in 1985, there was effective industrial and other pressure on Germany, which held the key, to go for a solution with its Tornado partners. In the summer of 1985 West Germany decided to go ahead with the EFA project without France.

BAe still has problems. Its turnover per employee remains lower than that of other major aerospace companies although it has made substantial improvements. BAe leaders often stress the need for productivity increases. Technologically it faces the challenging task of staying abreast of US companies in such areas as fabrication using composite materials. Its civil side is still unprofitable, due in part to the depreciation of the dollar and to the volume of investment made in that area which has not yet had time to bring returns. Sales of the 146 and the ATP must build up and A320 sales turned into production and revenue. As an amalgam of many other former aircraft companies spread all over the UK, BAe developed centralised arrangements which left it perhaps rather bureaucratic and ponderous in responding to business opportunities. On the other hand, there is also still a considerable amount of intra-company rivalry between, for instance, War-

TABLE 2.3
Rolls-Royce turnover in 1986 (£ million) Business

	Overseas	UK	Total
Civil Aero	627	130	757
Military Aero	522	220	740
Industrial and Marine	95	58	153
Other	33	119	152
TOTAL	1275	517	1802
	(71%)	(29%)	(100%)

Source: Company Prospectus, 1987.

ton (the home of the Tornado) and Kingston (the home of the Harrier). Separate design teams are maintained at each site and the company overall would appear to have surplus capacity in the design area. The future of the Warton site is very much dependent on continued Tornado production and on progress in the development of the EFA.

Yet the company also has a growing order book which stood at well over double annual turnover. Although its shares slumped in the 1987 crash, they had risen strongly in value since 1981 and certainly the company performed effectively after full privatisation in 1985. It is in a much stronger financial position than MBB, its German equivalent, which the German Government is pressing on to Daimler Benz.[7] BAe has adopted a positive approach towards dealing with problems of new technology and developing the civil side of its business. It cannot easily be accused of resting on reliable defence orders from the UK MoD and overall it is Britain's second largest exporter of manufactures (after ICI), selling over 60 per cent of its output overseas. Its real exports increased by 72 per cent between 1979 and 1985, a better performance than any other major British manufacturing company.[8]

Rolls-Royce, Britain's other main aerospace company, is often BAe's rival for government political and financial backing. Defence accounts for probably just under half of Rolls' work and Rolls exports something over 70 per cent of its ouput (see Table 2.3).

Rolls is a specialist gas turbine/aero-engine company whose products have been adapted for power generation, for instance on oil and gas platforms, and for ship propulsion. In general Britain's frigates, destroyers and aircraft carriers are powered by Rolls-Royce 'aircraft' engines, mainly Tyne and Olympus. Building on expertise originally obtained from the United States, Rolls has also become a developer and manufacturer of nuclear submarine propulsion systems. Whereas BAe has in particular had to meet the broad challenge of the ever more diverse range of technologies relevant to aircraft, Rolls has had to deal with the new materials and the development and manufacturing techniques needed to increase engine performance. Although it is an over-simplification, the development of military jet engines is mainly about making very precise machines work at very high temperatures. Yet the costs of engine manufacture and development have meant that Rolls is in a league which includes only two other companies, both American conglomerates. They are Pratt & Whitney (which is part of United Technologies) and General Electric (GE). Snecma of France is pushing very hard to join this club. It has invested heavily in manufacturing technology and has derived great benefit from its cooperation with GE in the successful CFM-56 project. In terms of the differences between military and civil engines, quietness and fuel economy are clearly greater considerations for the latter group, while power is central in the military section, but all the jet engine companies have a mix of civil and military business.

It has become conventional wisdom in the aircraft industry that, because engines take longer to develop than airframes, a new airframe should therefore use an established engine. Engine development time tends to be extended because much of the process still involves building an engine by hand, testing it at great length and sometimes having to rebuild. On the other hand, computers have contributed more to engine design in recent years and manufacturers have developed a modular approach to engines so that families of engines can be developed (and maintenance problems eased). Rolls-Royce was driven into bankruptcy in 1971 by its contract terms with Lockheed for the development of the RB-211 but since then many variants on that engine have been produced and sold in large numbers. Rolls invested extensively in productivity improvements involving modern techniques of design and manufacture and was able to reduce its workforce by over 20 per cent to 42,000 between 1982 and 1986.[9]

Rolls' performance on the military side has had many positive elements. It has developed and continuously improved the Pegasus engine which powers the Harrier and it has maintained its position in vectored thrust technology. Rolls-Royce has intra-firm and cooperative arrangements with Pratt & Whitney (P&W) for studies to lead to the development of an engine for a supersonic V/STOL aircraft. Rolls and P&W appear to have a secure position in the fast jet V/STOL field since the main alternative V/STOL concept, the tilt rotor, threatens the helicopter rather than the Harrier. The gains which Rolls can make in this field eventually depend on how many countries decide to follow Britain, Spain, India and probably Italy in using Harriers on 'cut-price' aircraft carriers, and on the perceived vulnerability of long runways for land-based aircraft. Rolls' product range also includes the Adour engine whose reliability contributed much to the acceptance by the United States Navy of the Hawk trainer as a single-engined aircraft. In 1987, Rolls had 'over 110 military customers in 87 countries operating over 7,700 aircraft with over 11,600 engines across the spectrum of military aircraft types' and across the Atlantic 'approximately nine per cent of the combat aircraft in service are powered by engines supplied or designed by Rolls-Royce'.[10]

In the civil area Rolls-Royce has had a corporate product strategy based mainly on the RB-211 and a commercial strategy aimed mainly at the United States. Rolls took a long time to become associated with Airbus and is so today only through its participation in the collaborative V-2500 project, a candidate engine for the Airbus. In general, Rolls has not been enthusiastic about collaboration on the civil side, having had a failed relationship with GE on very large engines and never having got on easily with Snecma. In the military sector, however, it recognised the need to collaborate with Europe, initially on the RB-199 engine. Rolls was the effective leader of this project, which was not an easy one. The project meant passing some technology to German and Italian companies but the development work that these companies could undertake undoubtedly eased the overall burden for Rolls. The RB-199 has been further developed to be a contender for the initial EFA engine contract and for other aircraft.

Rolls adopted a similar approach to BAe in preparing for the successor to Tornado. It undertook its own work on experimental engines, designated the XG-20 and XG-40, but also prepared the ground for a collaborative project.[11] To produce the eventual EFA engine (the EJ-200) the Eurojet consortium was formed without difficulty with Rolls again having a central place. Rolls is also involved with Turbomeca of France in an ambitious collaborative helicopter engine package centred on the RTM-322 and with Turbomeca and MTU of Germany on an engine for the planned Franco-German battlefield helicopter.

BAe civil aircraft are not powered by Rolls engines and clearly Rolls engines are used in many non-British aircraft. While this on occasion promotes tension between the two British companies, the trend for more states to develop their own aircraft of limited sophistication but substantial capability provides Rolls with further sales opportunities. These are being pursued, for instance, in Italy and Yugoslavia. Overall, Rolls expects that sales of its military engines into foreign build aircraft will rise shortly from its current level of 38 per cent of total military aero sales to more than 50 per cent.[12]

Like BAe, Rolls was privatised by the Conservative Government. Although its turnover growth in the 1980s was modest, some doubts were raised about its long term prospects, particularly in terms of its capacity to develop a successor to the RB-211 family using prop-fan or related technology. The problems of the civil US-Europe-Japanese V-2500 project were also apparent. Yet the company received a major endorsement from the British public in a share issue that was heavily oversubscribed. Like BAe, Rolls has sought vigorously to compete successfully in the world as a whole. In the future it looks to move more into missile engines and its technology was one of the driving forces behind the BAe Hotol spaceplane proposal.

At the centre of political controversy in 1985 was Westland, whose helicopters serve all three services of Britain's armed forces. Westland almost went bankrupt in that year since it lacked orders to keep its production facilities employed, although its long-term involvement in a range of collaborative development projects made its long-term prospects look reasonable.

The management team brought in, headed by Sir John Cuckney, adopted a strategy of securing capital support from the American firm United Technologies which includes Sikorsky helicopters. Westland had successfully built Sikorsky helicopters under licence for many years. The then UK Defence Minister, Michael Heseltine, pressed an alternative rescue package from a group of European companies on the company. In the resulting political furore, Mr Heseltine resigned, as did Trade & Industry Minister Leon Brittan. United Technology participation in Westland eventually went ahead in 1986.[13]

By 1987 Westland's position had clarified further. Financially, it had become profitable once again but, its hopes that the United Kingdom would buy a version of the Sikorsky Black Hawk to be built by Westland had not materialised. Also, its prospects of exporting Black Hawks manufactured under licence in Britain appeared limited in a depressed world market for helicopters, although the company's hopes remained. As Sir John Cuckney recognised, Westland clearly have to survive the next few years with limited British helicopter orders for Lynx and with such exports, in particular from India and perhaps for Lynx from Brazil, as it can find. Work from Sikorsky began to flow in 1987 but, with Sikorsky's target being only two million man hours over five years, it seemed unlikely to be on a scale which would change the company's fortunes markedly in the long term.[14] Westland could well seek to expand its more general high technology sectors and it had some success in winning contracts for civil aircraft parts.[15] However, the 1,100 job losses which it announced in 1987, and which meant major cuts at its Weston Super Mare plant, were unlikely to be its final word.

On the other hand, there were bright spots. The excellence of its advanced rotor technology was widely acknowledged and the commitment of the British Army as well as the British and Italian navies to the EH 101 enhanced the prospects of that aircraft. A major order for the EH 101 also seemed likely to be forthcoming from Canada.

Also in the aerospace sector, the state-owned Short Brothers is Northern Ireland's biggest industrial employer and makes the Blowpipe and Javelin anti-aircraft missiles. It is building, under licence from Brazil, the Tucano trainer for the RAF, although not without meeting some problems, and delays and has a £225 million MoD contract to develop the supersonic Starstreak anti-aircraft missile. It has won contacts to supply its Sherpa small transport aircraft to the United States Air Force and it builds civil aircraft sections for Boeing. It clearly has limited capacity to compete against BAe for major systems but it has benefited from its military-civil small transport aircraft programmes and to its credit has won contracts for aircraft and components from the United States.[16] However, it faces problems in establishing follow-on projects for its existing light transports, a field where global competition is fierce. Its image has also suffered from the militant Protestantism of much of its work force.

TABLE 2.4
British Shipbuilding Capacity

Yard	Berths and Docks	Maximum Length (m)	Maximum Beam (m)	Maximum Capacity (dwt)
Appledore Shipbuilders	3	110	, ,	, ,
Brooke Marine	6	128	, ,	, ,
Cammell Laird	7	290	, ,	140,000
Richard Dunston (Hessle)	8	100	, ,	, ,
Richard Dunston (Doncaster)	8	100	, ,	, ,
Ferguson-Ailsa	4	100	, ,	6,000
Goole Shipbuilders	6	106	15	, ,
Govan Shipbuilders	3	275	, ,	70,000
Russell Hall	5	120	21	, 8,000
Harland & Wolff	8	335	50	1,000,000
N. Holman & Sons	6	107	, ,	1,600
Lithgows Ltd	3	, ,	, ,	500,000
Scott's Shipbuilding Co.	10	304	44	, ,
Smith's Dock Ltd	3	185	, ,	, ,
Sunderland Shipbuilders	, ,	, ,	, ,	80,000
Swan Hunter Shipbuilders	10	310	, ,	, ,
Vickers Shipbuilding	7	304	, ,	, ,
Vosper Thorneycroft (Camber)	2	60	, ,	, ,
Vosper Thorneycroft (Portchester)	6	60	, ,	, ,
Vosper Thorneycroft (Woolston)	5	137	, ,	, ,
Yarrow Shipbuilders	9	207	, ,	9,000

Source: *Lloyd's Ship Manager Marine Equipment Guide 1986* (Lloyd's of London Press Ltd, Colchester, 1986) pp. 311–360.

Rolls and BAe are two leading national champion companies which were built up by mergers with other companies, by and large under government guidance, from the late 1950s. In shipbuilding, the recent trend has been different with the former central company, British Shipbuilders, having been largely broken up and its defence constituent parts having been privatised. However, the number of warship/building yards has been concentrated. Between 1955 and 1964 a total of 18 British shipyards built major warships and between 1965 and 1974 the corresponding figure was 15. Between 1975 and 1984 the figure was eight.[17]

Table 2.4 provides an assessment of British shipbuilding capacity and Table 2.5 shows the military product range of the companies concerned. However, this must be contrasted with the number of major warships and auxiliaries actually launched by the various yards in the 1960-88 period and with the decline in the average total launches per year from eight to three (see Table 2.6).

Under the Conservative Government many elements of the former British Shipbuilders have been sold off, the last being Swan Hunter in 1986. The remaining British Shipbuilders company is essentially concerned with civilian vessels only. British defence orders went mainly to the Vickers (VSEL) yard

TABLE 2.5
British Shipyards Product Range

Yard	Submarines	Major Warships	Minor Warships	All Types of Merchantmen — Sea	Coastal	Utility	Oil Rigs
Appledore Shipbuilders					×	×	
Brooke Marine			×				
Cammell Laird	×	×		×			×
Richard Dunston (Hessle)					×	×	
Richard Dunston (Doncaster)					×	×	
Ferguson-Ailsa					×	×	
Goole Shipbuilders					×	×	
Govan Shipbuilders				×			
Russell Hall			×	×		×	
Harland & Wolff				×			×
N. Holman & Sons						×	
Lithgows Ltd				×			
Scott's Shipbuilding Co.				×			
Smith's Dock Ltd.					×	×	
Sunderland Shipbuilders				×			
Swan Hunter Shipbuilders		×		×			
Vickers Shipbuilding	×	×					
Vosper Thorneycroft (Camber)			×				
Vosper Thorneycroft (Portchester)			×				
Vosper Thorneycroft (Woolston)			×				
Yarrow Shipbuilders		×				×	

Notes: Major Warships = Carriers, Destroyers, Frigates.
Minor Warships = Patrol Vessels, Mine Warfare, Fast Attack Craft.
Sea Merchantmen = Tankers, Bulk Carriers, Ro-Ro Ferries, Container Ships, Naval Auxiliaries, etc.
Coastal Merchantmen = Smaller versions of "Sea Merchantmen".
Utility = Trawlers, Oil Rig Service Vessels, Tugs, Dredgers.
Oil Rigs = Semi-submersibles, Jack-ups.

Source: *Lloyd's Ship Manager Marine Equipment Guide 1986* (Lloyd's of London Press Ltd, Colchester, 1986) pp. 311–360.

at Barrow, which is Britain's submarine constructor, Cammell Laird on Merseyside (which is owned by VSEL and is now building conventional Type 2400 submarines), the Glasgow firm Yarrow, which was bought by GEC in 1985 for £35 million, and Swan Hunter, which is privately-owned and has a much reduced workforce of 3,600 on Tyneside. However, the state-owned Northern Irish concern Harland & Wolff came back into naval construction with a 1984 £50 million contract to convert a container ship into an aviation training ship and a £120 million order for a Royal Navy advanced oiler replenishment (AOR) vessel in 1986. The Government had been ready to provide orders from some smaller vessels to Scott Lithgow but that company failed to come up with prices acceptable to the MoD.[18] Late in 1987, Scott Lithgow's owners, Trafalgar House, scheduled the yard for closure.

TABLE 2.6
Royal Navy Major Warship and Auxiliaries Launched 1960–88

Yard/Year	60	1	2	3	4	5	6	7	8	9	0	1	2	3	4	5	6	7	8	9	0	1	2	3	4	5	6	7	8	T
	1960s										1970s										1980s									
John Brown				1	1																									2
J. Samuel White		1	1																											2
Alex Stephen	1			1	1		1	2																						6
Fairfield	1			1			1																							3
Harland & Wolff			2				1	1	1																					5
Vickers (Newcastle)		1			2	1																								4
Hawthorn Leslie		1	1			3	1	1																						7
Scott Lithgow	1	1	1	1		1	1												1											7
Vosper Thorneycroft									1	1	1	1	2			1	1	1			1									8
Yarrow	1	1	1			1	1	1	1	1	1	1	1	1	2	1	1	1			1	1	1	1	1	1				23
Vickers (Barrow)	1		2	1	1	1	1	1	1	2	1	1	1	2	1	1	1	1			1	1	1	1	1	2	1	1		27
Cammell Laird	1		1	1	1	1	1	1			1	1	1	1	1		2				1	1	1	1						16
Swan Hunter	1	1	1			1	1		2	3			2	1	2	2		2	1			1	1			2	1		1	20
HMDY Chatham	1												c		c	c		c		c		c	c							2
HMDY Devonport	1			1		1			c		c		c	c	C	C						C	C	C	c					4
HMDY Portsmouth	1					1		1						c																3
Totals	7	8	8	8	x	3	8	x	7	5	2	4	4	4	5	5	5	2	5	2	4	4	4	3	2	5	3	3	1	
	1960s (74)										1970s (36)										1980s (29)									
5 Year Moving Average	8	7	7	8	8	6	6	6	4	3	3	4	3	4	4	4	4	4	3	3	4	3	4	3	3	3				

Notes: x = 10, c = One Conversion, C = Two Conversions.

In shipbuilding, the capacity to build warships is more a function of construction facilities than of high technology knowledge, although computer-aided design and manufacture (CAD/CAM) is increasingly used in ship manufacture. Also, despite some innovatory suggestions such as that of the 'short, fat frigate', the SWATH hull and the hydrofoil, ship designs have remained relatively conservative. In consequence, many countries have retained or acquired a capacity to build naval ships, while buying in the high technology systems for propulsion, radar and so on which they cannot make for themselves. Thus the question has been raised as to whether hull constructors should always be the prime contractor. In 1987 BAe, with a ship design partner, was competing for an aviation support ship contract.

Perhaps not surprisingly, in contrast to the aerospace sector, British major warship exports were virtually non-existent for much of the 1980s. Progress was made in the spring of 1987 when Pakistan chose to buy three Type 23 frigates, two of which would be built at Yarrow at a total cost of £557 million.[19] However, financing arrangements and command and control equipment issues remained to be finalised. There were also possibilities that VSEL might sell nuclear submarines to Canada and up to 10 diesel submarines to Saudi Arabia. The limitations of the British shipbuilding industry, including the presence of restrictive work practices, had not helped British industry, especially as the global competition among warship builders was considerable. Also few countries wanted to procure ships with the 'blue water' capabilities required by the Royal Navy. Partly in consequence the Type 23 was designed to be a simpler and more exportable ship than previous Royal Navy frigates. In the autumn of 1987, VSEL announced a private venture small submarine which, with the aid of computers, could be produced in a range of versions.[20]

In shipbuilding, where there is excess capacity, it might be expected that competition policy would generate good deals for the government. In practice the government has tended to use competition to secure a good price and then to spread orders for a single type among different yards, with all broadly having to meet the best quotation received in competition. By and large, shipyards are located in areas of high structural unemployment and this has, perhaps, operated to the disadvantage of Vosper Thorneycroft, located in the South of England, where unemployment problems are not so serious. Vosper Ship Repairers collapsed in February 1987. Vosper Thorneycroft announced a further 400 jobs would be lost in the same month, reducing its workforce to 1,900 and the firm has not won any recent frigate orders. However, after a management buy-out, its fortunes have been turned around to a considerable degree. The company has been successful with smaller warships (minesweepers and fast patrol boats) with hulls made of glass-reinforced plastic (GRP). Such smaller warships have been built for the Royal Navy and export customers and the company has also built up its non-shipbuilding work. Thus, at the beginning of 1988, it had orders worth over

£200 million and it looked set for a successful Stock Exchange flotation.[21]

Which are the stronger major warship yards has not finally emerged, but the Vickers/Cammell Laird group (whose parent company is VSEL) with its Trident and other submarines contracts, and with the possibility of exports, is clearly in the best position. VSEL is already using its facilities for modular ship construction and has invested heavily in CAD but Cammell Laird has not won a frigate contract since it got a vital Type 22 order in January 1985.[22] Its previous naval order to that was in 1983. Swan Hunter has had a difficult time with contracts won rarely matching its hopes. It received an order for one Type 23 frigate in 1986 and work on HMS *Marlborough* began in 1987[23]. Its fortunes in the three to five year future could be boosted by an order for the two replacement assault ships needed by the Navy, for which they were awarded a feasibility study contract in 1986. In December 1987, the yard won a £100 million-plus order for the second Auxiliary Oiler Replenishment vessel (AOR) for which they were the only company initially invited to bid.[24] They had done the original AOR feasibility study but the contract for the first vessel (including its detailed design) had gone to Harland & Wolff. In September 1986 a major productivity deal was concluded with the work force and labour relations and efficiency are reported to have improved substantially.[25] Swan Hunter, which launched the Type 22 frigate HMS *Coventry* in April 1986 and the landing ship logistic (LSL) *Sir Galahad* in December 1987, won a £25 million civil contract from Cable & Wireless in August 1987. It also won a £10 million order to refit coastal patrol vessels from an African state.[26] The company's approach to survival is to concentrate shipbuilding on one yard and to look for work with smaller ships. It is also seeking to sell its technical and design skills to foreign shipbuilders. Nevertheless it will probably need to lay off more workers unless additional Royal Navy orders (it has bid for frigate contracts) can be won.

Yarrow, which got the order for the first Type 23 frigate, received orders for two more in 1986, and in early 1982 it had a Royal Navy Type 22 frigate near completion. It is probably regarded by the Navy as the lead yard for frigates and, alongside Vosper and VSEL, is a member of the Supermarine consortium which represents British industrial interests in the NFR-90 (Nato frigate) project.[27] In 1988 the MoD planned to order up to four Type 23 frigates, perhaps from a single yard. An obvious compromise would be to spread the orders between Yarrow and Swan Hunter. In addition to shipyards are the naval dockyards for the repair and refitting of naval vessels. As the Falklands conflict showed, the dockyards are central to any effort to prepare ships at short notice for war. In terms of workloads, although the number of 'normal' refits held up since the beginning of the decade, the number of major refits taking place fell from six in 1979-80 and eight in 1980-81 to three in 1984-85 and 1985-86.[28] The government decided that there was insufficient work to justify the continued existence of Chatham Dockyard. Naval work going to the dockyard at Gibraltar was largely stopped and the

TABLE 2.7
New naval vessels

	No. brought into service			No. ordered		
	85–6	86–7	87–8	85–6	86–7	87–8
Trident subs.	–	–	–	–	1	1
Nuclear Fleet sub	1	1	–	1	–	–
ASW Carrier	1	–	–	–	–	–
Destroyer Type 42	2	–	–	–	–	–
Frigate Type 22	1	1	2	–	–	–
Frigate Type 23	–	–	–	–	3	–
MCMVs Hunt	2	1	1	2	–	–
MCMVs River	6	2	–	–	–	–
Single Role Mine Hunter	–	–	–	1	–	4
Auxiliary Oiler	–	–	–	–	1	1
Coastal Training Craft	2	–	–	–	–	–
Coastal Survey	–	1	–	–	–	–
Landing Ship Logistic	–	–	1	–	–	–

Source: SDEs 1986 and 1987, Vol. 1., Tables 2 and 4.

scale of operations at Portsmouth was also reduced. Work was concentrated on Rosyth in Scotland and Devonport whose management was handed over to private companies. Extensive job cuts have taken place at both and the number of Royal Dockyard employees fell from 34,049 in 1979-80 to 19,264 in 1985-86. The management at Devonport announced in the middle of 1987 that a further 3,400 jobs would disappear there.[29] Part of corporate strategy at Devonport is to diversify into wider engineering fields.

British naval shipbuilding is undoubtedly becoming more and more efficient but exports will continue to be very difficult to bring about and the government's extant nominal defence policy of maintaining a fleet of 'about 50' major surface warships will not produce work for all the facilities available, especially if a minimum of three ships a year is not ordered and if the fleet strength is upheld by keeping hulls in service for longer.[30] Table 2.7 shows the numbers of various classes of naval vessel brought into service and ordered in recent years.

Overall it appears that not enough work will be forthcoming even for all the larger yards. As the *Financial Times* noted, 'Britain's warship yards are in a precarious position . . . there are too many yards chasing too few orders'.[31] A Kleinwort Grieveson survey in 1986 concluded that within a decade there might be only one shipyard building surface ships and one building submarines. A slightly less pessimistic view could be that VSEL would build submarines, Yarrow frigates, Swan Hunter larger mainly non-combatant ships, and Vosper smaller ships including minesweeper/hunters. This approach would raise questions about Cammell Laird's role, about the size of Swan Hunter and about the scope for competition.

As already noted, Rolls-Royce and BAe are national champions in aero-space while in shipbuilding the Government has promoted a diversity of competing suppliers. When attention is turned to traditional land equipment such as guns and ammunition, the former national champion, the Royal Ordnance Factories (ROF), was felt to be too weak by the mid-1980s.

Historically the ROF had developed as the British Army's supplier of equipment, being owned and controlled by the government. For many years it did not operate at all as a commercial enterprise but from 1974 it was given some autonomy and financed from a trading fund. The Conservative Government, however, wanted to privatise the organisation and this took place in two stages. First, the Leeds tank plant was sold to Vickers (today a separate company from VSEL), who also received a substantial contract for Challenger tanks. Then it was decided to sell the remainder of the ROF to a single private buyer. The limited commercial prospects of the ROF as an independent entity would have made it difficult to dispose of the company through a public share subscription. BAe won the 1987 competition in which its chief rivals were GKN and, for a while Ferranti. BAe paid £190 million for the ROF (which included a poor factory on very valuable land assets at Enfield).

As the main British manufacturer of light arms, ammunition, guns and explosives, the ROF occupies a central place in the operational DIB of the United Kingdom. It produces lethal equipment rather than platforms or communications systems. However, many countries can produce much of what the ROF makes and it has a hard time in being internationally competitive, although it continues to export around 15 per cent of its output. It had and continues to have some very successful lines including its 105 mm gun made at Nottingham and 81 mm mortars. On the other hand, its future tank gun business was hit by the commitment of Germany, the United States and France to 120 mm smooth bore guns while the British Army (and hence the ROF) persisted with the rifled barrel. Overall, however, the ROF has a range of products made in a series of plants of various ages around the country. Its tank plant in particular was old and unsuitable for the introduction of modern manufacturing techniques; UK orders were insufficient to keep it running at anywhere near full capacity. Vickers, which bought it, was about to open its own much more modern tank facility in Newcastle on Tyne. In any case, question marks over the performance of the Challenger tank have raised doubts as to whether the Government would again want to sponsor a solely British-developed tank. The Enfield small arms plant was also outdated and BAe decided to close it soon after taking over the ROF, moving SA-80 production to a modern plant in Nottingham. For both the SA-80 and many ammunition contracts, the ROF needs the assurance of large although fixed price, government contracts to justify the investment needed in automated, modern production facilities.

Given its limitations and the highly competitive international environment in which it must operate, the ROF needed a high technology partner to lead into successful subcontracts on such projects as the multiple-launch rocket system (MLRS). ROF products are clearly central to any notion of British operational autonomy and traditionally the British Government has, at least implicitly, allowed the ROF to keep some surplus capacity to allow expanded production in time of emergency. BAe will have little commercial incentive to maintain any such surplus capacity. Soon after taking over, BAe reorganised the ROF corporate structure and introduced a more vigorous commercial culture to the company.

These companies are among the more prominent names in British industries and, with the exceptions of the ROF, they are very much concerned with producing means of transport and weapons platforms. One tendency in defence equipment, however, is for electronics to play a more important role in determining both the operational effectiveness of a system and its cost. Electronics can account for even 40 per cent of the cost of a combat aircraft and 30 per cent of a ship. Predictably then, Britain's main electronics company GEC, is heavily involved with defence and has been specifically associated with three recent problem products (AEW Nimrod, the Air Defence Variant Tornado radar (Foxhunter) and the Stingray torpedo) as well as with many successes. Because of the growing significance of electronics, it is discussed separately in the next section but here it is worth noting that many conventional 'engineering' defence contractors such as Rolls-Royce, Hunting Engineering and BAe have felt it worthwhile to develop their own substantial electronics expertise (see Chapter 3).

While the companies noted above comprise the most publicised sectors of the British DIB, it must also be accepted that they are both supported and competed against by many other firms which are associated with defence to a greater or lesser degree. Smiths Industries and Dowty are, among other activities, major manufacturers of aircraft mechanical and electrical systems. Dowty also makes mining machinery but its aerospace turnover now exceeds £500 million, much of it for overseas civil contracts. Even after buying two American companies in hydraulics and polymer engineering, its chairman described it as 'hungry' to add to its high technology capabilities by further acquisitions.[32] As traditional manufacturers of car components, Lucas reduced emphasis on that part of its business as the British car industry declined, and has bought in the United States in order to get access to sensor and test equipment technology. It is also developing its medical equipment section with some success.[33]. Hunting Engineering, which is involved with a range of technologies, has moved to being a prime contractor for the JP233 anti-runway weapon system and the British element in the MLRS system which is being procured under licence from America.

These are companies which are publicly associated with defence but there are hundreds of others which are not. Vickers is a diversified engineering group whose results impressed the City in early 1988.[34] Despite its role as a tank producer, defence is a small element of its business. The major Northern Engineering Group has a range of machining and other capabilities which make it an important subcontractor on many projects and its capabilities run into the nuclear field. The glass firm Pilkington owns Barr & Stroud which, among other things, makes submarine periscopes. Pilkingtons have moved into electro-optics as an important element in growing more involved with high technology. Guest, Keen and Nettlefold (GKN) opened a new plant in Telford in 1987 to produce the Warrior infantry fighting vehicle. The earth-moving equipment manufacturer J.C. Bamford is seeking to have its products bought for defence civil engineering purposes and it became a qualified MoD contractor in 1987. United Scientific Holdings is an unusual multi-national defence company, beneficially owned in Britain, which concentrates on niche markets in the civil and military fields. Among its British companies it owns Avimo, which is involved with thermal imaging equipment, and Alvis, the armoured vehicle manufacturer. Chloride, a company whose fortunes fell and revived during the 1980s, had defence as a small and fairly static part of its business but its batteries are important in many British military systems, including the lightweight Stingray torpedo. Inco, benefi-cially owned by a Canadian multinational, is a metal fabrication firm making, for instance, parts for ships and aircraft using titanium, nickel and aluminium.

This list is merely illustrative and could be expanded almost indefinitely to the point where almost all British manufacturing industry is represented. As noted at the beginning of this section, the activities of at least 800 companies would be relevant. Solely by way of illustration, using information from the industrial associations, Table 2.8 brings together British manufacturers from a sample of defence-related product areas.

TABLE 2.8
A Sample of British DIB Manufacturers

Airframes
    AVR Aviation
    Aviation Eng. & Maintenance
    Bramah Eng.
    British Aerospace
    J. S. Chinn Holdings
    Dowty Group
    GEC Avionics
    Hindustan Aeronautics
    Hunting Engineering
    The Norman Aeroplane Co.
    Optica Industries
    Pilatus Britten-Norman
    Short Brothers
    C. F. Taylor
    W. Vinten
    Westland
    Westland Helicopter Div.

Anti-Missile Systems
    British Aerospace

Filters, Air
    Aircraft Porous Media
    AP Precision Hydraulics
    Ador Engineering
    B.I. Engineering
    Bristol Pneumatics
    BTR Industries
    C.M.T. Wells Kelo
    Fairey Microfiltrex
    Gallay
    Hymatic Engineering
    Leyland & Birmingham Rubber
    Marston Palmer
    RFI Shielding
    Siebe Gorman
    Vokes

Guided Weapon Control Equipment
    Barr & Stroud
    British Aerospace
    Computing Devices Co.

EASAMS
GEC Avionics
MEL
The Marconi Co.
Racal Electronics
Royal Ordnance
Smith Associates

Armoured Personnel Carriers
Alvis
Aviation Jersey
GKN Defence
Land Rover
Mountain Range
Sleeman Engineering
Stonefield Military Vehicles
United Scientific
Vickers, Def. Systems

Bayonets
HPC Engineering
Wilkinson Sword

Carbon Fibre Materials
Bristol Composite Materials Eng.
British Aerospace
CIBA-GEIGY
Dunlop Aviation Division
Hysol Grafil

Carbon Fibre Reinforced Materials
Air-Log
BAJ
Fothergill & Harvey
Freeman Chemicals
Halmatic
Hysol Grafil
Imperial Chemical Ind.
National Plastics
Northern Eng. Ind.
Permali
Plastechnol
Primco
Royal Ordnance Summerfield
H. R. Smith (Tech. Dev.)
St. Bernard Plastics
W & J Tod
Triton Oliver
Mark Tyzak

Casting Non-Ferrous
Aurora
British Steel
Butler Foundries
Ceramicast (Prec. Inves. Castings)
Deloro Stellite
Deritend Stamping
Finecast

Dowty Boulton Paul
Dowty Electrics
Dowty Group
Fairey Hydraulics
GEC Avionics
The Hymatic Engineering Co.
Louis Aerospace
Louis Industries Australia
MEL
The Marconi Co.
Louis Newmark
Normalair-Garrett
The Plessey Co.
Smith Associates
Thorn EMI Electronics

Guided Weapons, Missiles and Rockets
BAJ
British Aerospace
Dowty Group
Ferranti
Graseby Dynamics
Hunting Engineering
The Marconi Co.
Portsmouth Aviation
Royal Ordnance
Short Brothers
Smith Associates
Thorn EMI

Machine Guns
Dince Hill
Manroy
Engineering
Pylon Industries
Royal Ordnance

Niobium and Niobium Alloy Materials
Aircraft Materials
Cabot UK
IMI Titanium
Spencer Clark Metal Ind.
Titanium International

Optical Fibres
BICC
Barr & Stroud
British Aerospace
ITT Cannon Electric (GB)
MBM Technology
Sperry

Radomes
Adame Aviation Supply Co.
Bristol Composite Materials Eng.
British Aerospace
Chelton (Electrostatics)
Flight Spares

GKN Defence
Grant Castings
Inco Eng. Products
Maycast Prec. Products
Northern Eng. Ind.
P.I. Castings
Vickers Shipbuilding & Eng.

FR Hitco
The Marconi Co.
H. R. Smith (Tech. Development)
Westland
Westland Helicopter Div.

Chaff/Chaff Dispensers
British Alcan Alum.
Cristie Defence Systems
Hunting Engineering
MEL(M)
Pains-Wessex/Schermuly
Plessey Aerospace
Pylon Industries
Radamec Defence Systems
Richard Unwin
Vickers Shipbuilding & Eng.

Components, Kevlar
Advanced Composite Comp.
BAJ
Fothergill & Harvey
Freeman Chemicals
Hunting Engineering
National Plastics
Plastechnol
Southbourne Sheet Metal
W. & J. Tod
Woodville Polymer Eng.

Electromagnet-Pulse Protected Materials
Air-Log
Hellerman Deutsch
Icore International
Imhof-Bedco
Raychem
Romag Holdings
Vactite

Surveillance Systems Equipment, Submarine Underwater
Andromica (T.V.)
Barr & Stroud
Calne Electronics
Compact Energy
DBE Technology
Graseby Dynamics
Hymatic Engineering
Insten Computer Systems
MEL
Nicolet Instruments
Osprey Electronics
Radamec Defence Systems
Rediffusion Radio Systems
Thorn EMI Electronics
UDI
Ulvertech
Vosper Thorneycroft

Titanium and Titanium Alloy Materials
Aerospace Metals
Avco Eng.
B.A.S. (aircraft components)
Cabot U.K.
Fine Tubes
H.D.A. Forgings
IMI Titanium Inco Eng. Products
Middleton Sheet Metal Co.
Raychem
Short Brothers
Smith-Clayton Forge
Spencer Clark Metal Ind.
Titanium International
Titanium Metal & Alloys

Source: SBAC and DMA Publications.

Further elements in the DIB are the institutions where research work is carried out. Outside industry itself, this means the universities which attract a very small amount of MoD work, and the Government's own research and development establishments (RDEs). There are now just seven of these dealing with aerospace, airplane and armaments testing, armaments and land systems, sea systems, chemical weapons defence, signals and radar, and nuclear weapons. After the Second World War, the UK undertook a very wide defence research effort. It still spends money across a broad spectrum but the scale of the RDE operations has been reduced. Some RDEs have been closed and their number of employees fell from 34,000 in 1971 to 23,000 in 1985.[35] Although the RDEs enjoy a very favourable technical reputation in their fields (British RDEs invented composite materials and Chobham armour, for example), their range of expertise has thinned to the point where they cannot always serve one of their past roles — to assess defence proposals from British and foreign industry. Thus to act as an expert customer, the Government has also turned to consultants from the commercial system/ software houses which have little experience of actually developing equipment.

The RDEs work closely with British industry and scientists from industry are seconded there to work, although it is unusual for the reverse movement to take place. The RDE's have been marked by a double trend since the early 1980s. Their development work has declined in relative importance as the government has sought to push this more to industry and they have undertaken a growing proportion of research work. Nonetheless they still receive over a quarter of the development budget, much of it presumably for nuclear weapons, and they receive about 60 per cent of the research budget.

The United Kingdom DIB generates almost all the equipment needed by the British Armed Forces. According to official figures, about 5 per cent of British equipment is imported, around 15 per cent (mainly in aerospace projects) is supplied through international collaborative arrangements in which the principal of *juste retour* means that the British exports work to the value of work imported, and the remainder is accounted for by national projects. However, imports of raw materials, components and subsystems constitute an element in national projects. Among other things, aircraft include substantial amounts of aluminium and titanium, some of which is processed in Britain by such firms as the multinational Alcan Corporation. Even in products of relatively limited technological complexity, imports have a role. For instance, Heckler & Koch of West Germany produces parts for the ROF which go into the SA-80 small arms family of weapons.[36] There are American Texas Instruments avionics in Tornado and the British Spearfish torpedo will have an American motor. An MoD official has stated that 'as regards the UK, imported components and supplies comprise about 25 per cent of the cost to the MoD of defence equipment produced in the UK'.[37] The presence of foreign components sometimes reflects a specific governmental choice but more often the decision of the prime contractor interested in holding down costs. In the case of the Spearfish motor and of the German motor which it is now intended to use in the Alarm missile, after a ROF development effort had gone wrong, it is because an equivalent British product was not available. It would appear that most imported defence equipment comes from America although clearly some is bought from Europe.[38]

Table 2.9 lists major British defence imports in the 1980s. Table 2.10 gives identifiable British defence imports according to the MoD. MoD categories

TABLE 2.9
Major Identified United Kingdom Arms Imports (July 1980–June 1985)

Supplier	Date of Agreement	System	Quantity	Cost ($m)
Brazil	3/85	Tucano training a/c	130	140
France	2/85	Falcon fleet spot. a/c	5–10	–
France	81	Exocet anti-ship missile	48	–
Netherlands	1/84	Goalkeeper Ship defensive gun system	6	56.3
USA	12/86	E.3A AWACs a/c	6	1370
USA	5/85	Harpoon anti-ship missile	31	33
USA	84	Harpoon anti-ship missile	300	–
USA	10/84	Tristar tanker a/c	4	68
USA	9/84–10/85	Phalanx ship defensive gun system	22	215
USA	7/82	Trident II SLBM	72	3000
USA	2/83	F.4J fighter a/c	15	51
USA	3/83	MLRS (rocket launcher)	10	–
USA	5/83	Chinook helics.	8	143
USA	12/81	Harrier GR.5 (collab)	60	1400
USA	5/82–6/82	Phalanx ship defensive gun system	4	29.4
USA	–	MLRS rocket launcher	10	–

Source: IISS, *The Military Balance*, 1981–2 to 1986–7 editions; SIPRI, World Armaments & Disarmament Yearbook, 1985; Various press sources.

TABLE 2.10
Imports of Defence Equipment

	£ million						
	1981	1982	1983	1984	1985	1986	1987
Identified Defence equipment	137	199	207	253	246	295	285
Guided weapons and missiles	57	108	85	102	119	175	145
Ammunition	16	18	17	16	35	58	41
Guns, small arms and parts	29	27	36	33	40	38	67
Armoured fighting vehicles and parts	4	14	21	10	10	5	4
Radio, radar and optical equipment	21	28	47	38	24	17	28
Military aircraft including helicopters	11	3	–	54	18	3	–
Origins of identified equipment							
NATO countries and other W Europe	128	184	178	239	220	268	266
Asia and Far East	3	5	3	5	16	11	5
Others	6	9	25	9	10	16	14

Source: SDE's 1987 and 1988

and the import list make clear that Britain has bought mainly components and specific sea-launched missiles ranging from Trident to Harpoon and Exocet. The MoD list, however, does not pick up all defence imports, especially of components.

What systems are currently beyond Britain's capabilities? Clearly she struggled recently in the area of advanced large-scale airborne early warning and United Kingdom limitations in some aspects of missile propulsion have been noted. But overall it is unusual for the British not to have the broad knowledge base to build any given type of equipment, even ballistic missiles or reconnaissance satellites. It is, however, the case that Britain finds it difficult to fund development programmes and that British technology perhaps lags behind the United States in some defence areas. Thus, while Britain has no equivalent to the long range air-to-air Phoenix missile, BAe has done further work on the medium-range Skyflash air-to-air missile, which it originally based on the US AIM-7 Sparrow, to give it some autonomous homing capacity. The company hopes this missile will be a cost-effective rival to AMRAAM. British industry has developed terminal guidance systems for the Sea Eagle anti-ship missile and is working on navigation/guidance equipment which could be used in cruise missiles.

Furthermore, considerable extended-range missile technology could flow to the UK from participation in transatlantic collaborative projects covering the AMRAAM-ASRAAM family of air weapons and the modular stand-off weapons. The latter programme was just getting established in 1988 but regarding the air-to-air missiles there were doubts whether the US would meet its commitment either to transfer AMRAAM-related technology to Europe, or to procure ASRAAM, if and when it was ready, from Europe.

Assessing British strengths across the range of technologies associated with defence is not easy, not least because technological capabilities are often classified and because there is variation in the extent to which they are integrated into effective defence systems.

Certainly some American officials feel that, because of the dimensions of United States R&D spending, particularly under the Reagan Administration, the United States has pulled far ahead of Europe in almost all fields. This would not be accepted in Britain, and British strengths would certainly be seen to include submarine propulsion, air defence for ships, armour, helicopter rotors and aircraft engines. This does not take account of the defence electronics sector covered in the next section.

British technology is broadly comparable with that of Western Europe as a whole and the research commissioned by the Independent European Programme Group (IEPG) Vredeling Commission found that:

> Looking at the European technology base, that is, the underlying science and technology status including innovative capability, concepts, research resources and experimental hardware up to the demonstration phase . . ., Europe appears to be better placed in many sectors of the defence field than exemplified, often, by its final competitive position in product sales.[39]

The report noted several areas where the United States had some real advantage, for instance in Stealth technology and torpedo and armoured vehicle propulsion systems. It also noted that, in several high technology fields, including aircraft subsystems and helicopters, the scale of its production gave it a real advantage in holding down costs. America was also found to have a lead in high temperature thermodynamic cycles and high temperature materials 'which could assume importance in future engine developments'.[40] Nevertheless, there were areas too of European strength such as armour and conventional munitions. British expertise in nuclear submarine propulsion was noted. Overall, the picture painted was of European current competence. However, effort and collaboration was stressed as needed for Europe to compete in the face of the American and Japanese challenges. An extract from the Report summarising its findings is published at Appendix A.

Overview

Precise statistics about the defence sector are elusive, not least because there is no clear border between defence and non-defence equipment. That said, there are some data available and they can be used to draw some conclusions.

In all, defence is said to provide jobs for some 515,000 people in Britain. The SDE 1986 said that MoD defence orders provide work for 225,000 directly and a further 170,000 indirectly. British defence exports supported a further 120,000. The corresponding employment figures given in SDE 1981 were 220,000 direct MoD defence jobs, about 220,000 indirect jobs and 142,000 arms sales jobs. A 1987 study forecast a fall in the near future by as much as 100,000, taking into account the reduction planned in equipment spending, reduced manpower at the dockyards and so on.[41]

In broad brush terms, using about three per cent of the United Kingdom population at work, a senior MoD official noted in 1985 that 'the UK defence industrial base produces just over three per cent of UK GDP, about one quarter of which is exported'.[42] However, the Labour Party Research Department presented the situation differently, assessing that the 10 per cent of the industrial workforce which is involved with defence produced over 13 per cent of industrial output.[43]

Both these figures are in their way correct but an initial problem is how to measure defence industrial output. Table 2.11 generates an estimate by taking the value of the United Kingdom defence procurement budget, adding British defence exports, and deleting the best available approximation of British arms imports. This latter consists of the value of American arms exports to Britain in the nearest United States Fiscal Year (which runs from October to September), converting from dollars at the end of year rate recorded by the International Monetary Fund (IMF), and adding 5 per cent as an allowance for imports from other states. The 5 per cent is included on the basis that the American Arms Control & Disarmament Agency (ACDA) data show that Britain imports all save about five per cent of its arms imports from America. The ACDA data, while understating the value of British arms imports, might nevertheless be thought to have the ratios between different suppliers about right. British MoD figures of 'identifiable' defence imports, which are published in the SDE and reproduced here in Table 2.10, also

TABLE 2.11
UK Defence Equipment Procurement Spending, Defence Exports and Defence Imports

Year	Procurement Spending (£ million)[a]	Defence Imports (Est.) (£ million)[b]	Defence Exports (£ million)[c]
1979	4017	138	1075
1980	5324	170	1537
1981	6121	271	1746
1982	6815	301	2064
1983	7504	505	2064
1984	8573	736	2135
1985	8979 (+ 123.6% on 1979)	368 (+ 167% on 1979)	2500 (+ 132.6% on 1979)
1986	9048	403	3000 +[d]

[a]Source SDEs 1984 and 1987, 1986 figure is an estimate, figures cover nearest UK FY.
[b]Estimate based on sources explained in text.
[c]Sources SDEs 1984 and 1987, 1985 figure is an estimate in SDE 85.
[d]*Financial Times* 15/12/87.

TABLE 2.12
Defence Output, Manufacturing Output and Employment

	Defence Equipment Production Estimate	1980 £	1985 £	% increase
A)	UK Defence procurement budget[a]	5,324m	8,979m	+ 68.6
B)	UK Defence equipment exports[b]	1,537m	2,500m	+ 62.6
C)	UK Defence equipment imports[c]	170m	368m	+116.4
D)	Total (A + B − C)	6,691	11,111	66.1
E)	Defence equipment for UK market[d]	440,000	395,000	− 10.2
F)	Defence equipment employees for export market	142,000	120,000	− 15.5
G)	Total employees (E + F)	582,000	515,000	− 11.5
H)	UK manufacturing, industry output[e]	53,833m	76,800m	+ 42.7
I)	UK product, industry output[e]	73,931m	111,135m	+ 50.3
J)	UK exports of goods	47.4b	78.1b	+ 64.7
K)	UK Manufacturing, industry employees	6,940,000	5,533,000	− 20.3
L)	Defence output per employee (D/G)	11,497	21,575	+ 87.6
M)	Manufacturing, output per employee (H/K)	7,757	13,880	+ 78.9
N)	Defence output per export, employee (B/F)	10,824	20,833	+ 92.5

[a]Source SDE, covering nearest UK FY.
[b]Source SDE and author's estimate.
[c]Source US DoD for US FYs.
[d]Source SDEs, 1981 and 1986.
[e]HMSO *National Income 'Blue Book' Statistics 1986*.

understate the position. The British Defence Minister said in 1987 that the United Kingdom spends 7 per cent of its defence equipment (ie over £600 million) in the United States alone.[44]

Table 2.12 gives a series of figures which show British defence manufacturing in comparison with manufacturing in general in the United Kingdom.

Using the data, defence employees appear more productive than employees in the manufacturing sector as a whole and their performance, both in terms of output and exports since 1980, has improved by a large percentage. The data clearly have their limits (they refer only to current money values) and not too much weight should be placed on them. Nevertheless they do not offer support for the view that British defence production is inefficient compared with manufacturing in the national economy as a whole or with defence manufacturing throughout the world. However, a characteristic of the defence sector compared with British manufacturing industry in general, is its lower share of total output being exported. The little over nine per cent of British manufacturing employees who work in the defence sector generated just 3 per cent of export goods in the mid 1980s. However, orders suggest that defence export deliveries will be increasing in future years, and these figures ignore the possibility that civil manufacturing may import more per United Kingdom employee and add less value before exporting.

It is difficult to gauge the impact of the British DIB on the balance of payments, even by simple arithmetic rather than in any dynamic sense. Interestingly, although it is often observed that British defence equipment spending has risen rapidly under the present Administration, it is noticeable that British defence exports have also performed strongly, even though demand in the global arms market has not been buoyant. Britain claimed 9 per cent of the world arms market in 1985 and 16 per cent in 1986 in terms of contracts concluded. British orders in 1986 reached £5.3 billion.[45]

In Table 2.11, taking the bare difference between British defence imports and exports overstates defence industries' contribution to the balance of payments since some of the related goods such industries use will have been imported but not classified as defence equipment. Taking the import content of British defence equipment at 25 per cent, as noted at the beginning of this section, would suggest that defence exports do little more than offset imports but this too would seem to be an exaggeration. In the broad field of aerospace, which clearly includes the extensive civil sector, the Society of British Aerospace Companies says that, in 1986 British aerospace turnover was £8 billion, exports totalled £4.6 million and the overall industry trade surplus came to £1.9 billion, taking account of goods bought by industry for further processing. The US was the industry's main market taking 28 per cent of United Kingdom exports.[46] What is quite clear is that the United Kingdom DIB undertakes high value-added activities and prevents defence from being a major drain on the balance of trade, which it would be if Britain maintained today's level of defence effort and imported most of the equipment concerned.

Although there have been problems, the British defence industry has not performed badly in recent years, as the growth of exports indicates. Aerospace has been an area of particular growth as a publication by the technicians' union TASS stressed.

TABLE 2.13
Aerospace Industry Final National Turnovers (in M, ECUs)

	1979	1984	% change
Britain	4029	9889	+ 145
France	4733	9962	+ 110
Germany	2590	4515	+ 74
Italy	773	2331	+ 201
USA	28059	84349	+ 201
Japan	934	2109[a]	+ 125[a]

[a]1983 Figure only available
Note: An estimated 65% of the UK aerospace industry is defence-related.

Source: Commission of the EC, The European Aerospace Industry Trading Position and Figures 15/7/86.

> Aerospace is a growth industry. Its annual turnover in Britain increased from below £2,000 million in 1975 to over £7,000 million in 1985. In the same period exports increased from £801 million to £4,200 million .... Britain's aerospace industry supplied 10 per cent of the aerospace goods in the non-socialist world. By the 1970s the figure had risen to 14 per cent and now, despite increasing competition from abroad, it has reached 17 per cent.[47]

In 1988, aerospace appeared as an industry where output, productivity and exports were rising, while employment was falling.[48] Even a report critical of the impact of defence equipment on the economy and of the efficiency of defence industries accepted that aerospace had considerably increased productivity and exports.[49] This is reflected in Table 2.13. Certainly companies with substantial defence interests were prominent in a list of successful British firms published in *The Sunday Times* in 1987 (see Table 2.14). Table 2.15 lists some British arms deals of recent years. George Younger, the British Defence Minister, told an American audience in 1987 that

> the United States has a fine defence industry. But the British industry too is as efficient as any in the world. It is no accident that last year we were the second largest exporter of defence equipment in the free world .... the British defence industry is quite capable of producing products which can match any of the world today and our arms are world leaders in many areas of technology.[50]

TABLE 2.14
We're Rolling Again: The Numbers Tell The Story

Company	Employees			Turnover £ per employee			Profit £ per employee			Capitalisation Figures in £m			Earnings per share Figures in pence		
	1980	Latest	Change	1980	Latest	%rise	1980	Latest	%rise	1980	Latest	%rise	1980	Latest	%rise
British Aerospace[1]	79,300	75,000	− 4,300	17,944	41,826	133	701	2,426	246	300	1,566	422	32.1	51.4	60
British Steel	166,400	54,200	− 112,200	18,659	68,911	269	− 10,721	701	NA	NA	NA	NA	NA	NA	NA
BTR	24,600	79,200	+ 54,600	20,723	50,744	145	2,857	6,376	123	583	5,556	853	4.4	21.2	381
Coats Viyella	21,785	72,000	+ 50,215	13,633	24,305	78	381	2,524	NA	17	1,622	9,441	NA	47.2	NA
Courtaulds	93,000	68,000	− 25,000	18,387	31,955	74	54	2,103	3,794	150	1,669	1,013	5.9	30.0	408
Dowty	17,072	15,673	− 1,399	18,479	33,114	79	2,226	3,037	36	261	566	117	17.1	14.4	− 15
Fisons	11,308	10,239	− 1,069	40,060	68,561	71	336	8,238	2,351	50	1,613	3,126	0	27.5	NA
GKN	93,000	41,200	− 51,800	20,674	49,975	142	13	3,203	NA	284	806	183	NA	28.5	NA
Glynwed	17,400	11,100	− 6,300	20,471	43,225	111	927	4,153	348	47	486	934	16.2	27.5	69
Hanson Trust	36,000	92,000	+ 57,000	19,000	46,869	147	1,083	4,989	361	224	8,057	3,496	2.5	14.3	472
ICI	143,200	121,800	− 21,400	39,909	83,218	108	2,318	8,341	260	1,987	8,677	336	22.1	92.0	316
ICL	33,087	20,000	− 13,087	21,640	59,450	174	1,396	4,510	223	92	NA	NA	NA	NA	NA
IMI	29,858	20,200	− 9,658	21,049	38,628	83	884	3,629	310	117	701	499	10.2	17.1	68
Jaguar	9,725	11,000	+ 1,275	17,110	75,490	320	− 4,863	10,981	NA	2 297	1,058	256	2 31.7	46.1	45
Lucas	82,700	64,100	− 18,600	14,340	25,257	76	258	1,485	NA	125	727	480	− 38.6	56.2	NA
Pilkington[3]	35,000	44,700	+ 9,700	17,971	49,217	173	2,611	5,592	114	319	1,726	441	52.0	72.0	27
Plessey	53,000	33,000	− 20,000	15,900	44,270	178	1,585	5,151	225	232	1,909	722	7.5	13.5	80
Rolls-Royce	62,000	42,000	− 20,000	20,290	42,857	111	387	2,857	NA	NA	NA	NA	NA	NA	NA
Smiths Industries	19,400	11,600	− 7,800	16,494	34,569	110	1,340	4,913	268	114	559	390	9.3	16.4	76
Vickers	31,590	15,871	− 15,719	18,882	43,588	131	905	3,402	276	109	490	349	22.5	40.7	81

Source: *The Sunday Times*, 29 March 1987.   [1] BAe for 1981–6.   [2] Jaguar fig. for '84.   [3] Pilkington est. for '86 based on profits forecast.

TABLE 2.15
Major Identified United Kingdom Arms Exports

Recipient	Date of Agreement	System	Quantity	Cost ($m)
Europe/Nato				
Austria	87	Gun. fire simulation equipment	68 + 33	10.0
Canada	81	Blowpipe div. defence missiles	–	–
West Germany	11/84	Sea Lynx helicopters	2	8.7
Netherlands	87	Spey naval turbines	–	24
Netherlands	87	Lynx engine modifications	70	16.0
NATO	1/87	Skynet satellites	2	150
Spain	1/85	Scorpion AFV	17	6.7
Sweden	10/86	Helicopter engines	35	22
Sweden	2/87	Surveillance radars	3	4.5
Sweden	7/81–4/82	Skyflash air–air missiles	–	46.9
Switzerland	80	Rapier SAM (Blindfire)	60	678.9
Turkey	9/83	Rapier SAM (Blindfire)	36	220
USA	10/87	M252 81mm mortar	800	168
USA	10/87	Naval Communications system development	–	430
USA	up to 7/87	Air data computers	–	135
USA	7/87	Personal radiation dose meters	–	15
USA	86	Holographic HUDs	450	72
USA	11/86	HUDs for C.17s	–	9
USA	86	81mm mortars + ammunitition	–	c.30
USA	12/85	Bloodhound SAM	–	300
USA	12/84–5/85	81mm mortar bombs	860	48.6
USA	3/84	Sherpa transporter a/c	18	54.6
USA	11/81	Hawk trg a/c	300 +	1000
USA	11/80	Auxiliary replenishment vessel	1	20.0
USA	1/81	81mm mortar	300	12.5
USA	2/81	Rapier SAM (Blindfire) launchers	32	290.0
		Rapier SAM (Blindfire) missiles	128	
Yugoslavia	86/87	Twin giro platforms		11
Middle East				
Algeria	4/82	LST	2	–
Algeria	4/82	Patrol craft	6	–
Bahrain	1/85	Wasp patrol vessel	1	2.7
Egypt	9/84	Stingray torpedoes	–	19.6
Egypt	83	HS.748 transport a/c	–	–
Kuwait	10/83	Hawk COIN/trg a/c	12	105
Kuwait	9/84	Landing craft	4	8.1
Kuwait	4/83	Navy support vessel	12	9.3
Iran	86	Air surveillance radars	6	380
Iran	84	Naval support ships	2	–
Jordan	87	LAW 80 anti-tank missiles		16
Jordan	87	Explos. repress systs.	c.560	19
Jordan	86	Engineering equipment		20
Jordan	86	Air def. radar modernisation		24
Jordan	11/80	Bulldog trg a/c	5	–
Oman	6/85	Marconi 3-D radar	2	27.2
Oman	3/83	Chieftain tanks	15	–
Oman	82	Blowpipe SAM	–	–
Oman	82	Support ship	1	–
Oman	11/81	Chieftain tanks	15	–
Oman	7/80	Jaguar a/c	12	–

Oman	7/80	Blindfire radar for rapier	28	–
Oman	2/81	Province Fast attack craft	2	19.2
Qatar	81	Commando ASW helicopters	8	–
Qatar	81	Rapier SAM	24	–
Saudi Arabia	2/86	Tornado IDR & ADV a/c	72 ⎫	
Saudi Arabia	2/86	Hawk trg a/c	30 ⎬	c.8000
Saudi Arabia	2/86	PC.9 trg a/c	30 ⎭	
Saudi Arabia	2/83	FH.70 howitzer (with Germany & Italy)	72	c.50
Saudi Arabia	82	BH.7 Hovercraft	8	–
Sudan	2/84	Strikemaster COIN/trg a/c	7	–
Unit. Arab Emir.	2/83	Hawk trg a/c	24	156
Unit. Arab Emir.	82	Coastal patrol craft	5	–
Sub-Saharan Africa				
Botswana	84	Islander light transport a/c	2	–
Kenya	9/84	Province patrol craft	2	–
Kenya	81	Towed guns	70	–
Kenya	10/80	56 metre fast attack craft	4	–
Nigeria	8/84	Vickers main battle tank	36	81.0
Nigeria	2/82	Tiger Hovercraft	5	–
Nigeria	11/83	Swingfire ATGW	–	235.0
Nigeria	7/81	Vickers main battle tank	36	125.0
Nigeria	10/81	Lynx ASW helicopters	3	23.0
Nigeria	81	Blowpipe SAM	–	–
Nigeria	7/81	Bulldog trg a/c	4	–
Nigeria	80	Bulldog trg a/c	5	–
South Africa	83	Islander light transport a/c	2	–
Upper Volta	4/81	HS.748 transport a/c	1	7.7
Zimbabwe	83	Hunter FGA a/c	5	–
Zimbabwe	1/82	Hawk trg. a/c	8	35.0
Zimbabwe	1/81	Hawk trg. a/c	8	–
Zimbabwe	1/81	Hunter FGA a/c	4	–
Zimbabwe	1/81	Hunter FGA/trg a/c	1	–
Zimbabwe	1/81	Canberra bomber/bombing trg a/c	2	–
Asia & Australasia				
Australia	87	Pericope sets	6	48
Australia	87	Tactical radios	6000	c.250
Australia	86	Land Rover vehicles	2900	A$110
Australia	85	Sea King	6	–
Australia	3/84	National communicators system		40.8
Australia	8/81	Sea King ASW helicopters	2	–
Australia	82	Invincible ASW carrier	1	324.0
Bangladesh	3/82	Type 41 frigate	1	–
India	87	Combat engineers tractors	14	–
India	86	Howitzer aiming system		40
India	86	WG.30 helicopters	30	–
India		Aircraft carrier	1	–
India	83	Sea Eagle anti-ship missiles	24	–
India	8/83	Sea King helicopters (Sea Eagle)	12	375.6
India	3/84	Sea Harrier attack a/c	11	–
Indonesia	87	Rapier air defence missile system		64
Indonesia	12/84	Rapier SAM (Blindfire)	–	120.0
Indonesia	8/83	Hawk trg a/c	3	–
Indonesia	4/84	Tribal frigates	3	29.1
Indonesia	1/83	Hawk trg a/c	5	–
Indonesia	5/81	Hawk trg a/c	4	8.0

Japan	7/84	FH.70 (with Germany & Italy)	100	–
Malaysia	2/82	Scorpion light tank	38 ⎤	
Malaysia	2/82	Stormer APC	20 ⎦	331.0
Malaysia	2/82	Scorpion SPAA gun	18	
Nepal	84	Skyvan light transport a/c	1	–
New Zealand	10/81	Leander frigate	2	83
New Zealand	8/80	Scorpion light tank	26	10.7
Pakistan	10/84	Amazon Type 21 frigate	3	1200
Pakistan	2/81	County destroyer	1	–
Singapore	6/81	Rapier SAM (Blindfire)	–	85.6
South Korea	86	Electro-optical sights	–	48
South Korea		Surface ship C^2 system		35.0
South Korea		Javelin SAM	–	30
South Korea		Combat patrol boats	–	–
Sri Lanka	2/85	Cougar patrol boats	10	–
Sri Lanka	2/85	Saladin armoured cars	–	–
Thailand	8/84	Stingray torpedoes	12	7.4
Thailand	9/84	Short's utility transporter	2	–
Thailand	12/81	Blowpipe SAM	–	–
Latin America				
Brazil	11/82	Tigerfish Mk.24 torpedo	c.60	39.0
Bahamas	1/85	Protector patrol boats	3	9.5
Chile	4/84	County DDG	1	–
Chile	81	County destroyer	1	–
Chile	81	Fleet tanker	1	–
Columbia	8/81	HS.748 transport a/c	1	–
Guyana	84	Skyvan light transporter a/c	1	–

3

The Defence Electronics Sector

Introduction: the significance of electronics in defence.

In 1975, Roger Facer wrote that 'the capacity of a country's industry to meet its own defence needs rests more on the capacity of its electronics industry than that of any other sectors.'[1] More recently, an IEPG report regarded electronics as 'an essential enabling technology which pervades all modern defence weapons and operational systems. Its prime manifestation is in the collection, transfer and processing of information. Advances in electronics technology and its closely related field of Information Technology (IT) have had the greatest impact of all technological advances on the nature of warfare in modern times.'[2] Similar sentiments were expressed by the United States Defence Science Board: 'electronics technology is the foundation upon which much of our defence strategy and capabilities are built and is one of the technologies that can be leveraged most highly.'[3]

Western defence has always relied on the force multiplier effect of having a qualitative superiority over the Warsaw Pact in terms of its weapons. This advantage has depended increasingly upon electronics. In some areas of electronics, particularly integrated circuitry and computing, the Soviet Union is still inferior to the West. In others, however, this may no longer be the case, or the West's lead is under considerable pressure. For example, the Soviet Union has a sound optical technology capability and consequently, is well placed to develop sophisticated opto-electronic systems. The Soviet Union also has the ability to focus on a narrow range of militarily significant technologies with a potential for leap-frogging current generations of electronics. Under such circumstances, Western investment in electronic based systems must be maintained.

The importance of electronics in military equipment and operations can vary from the minimal to almost total dependence, with a myriad of intermediate cases. At one end of the spectrum, is the infantry rifle; at the other would be a multi-tiered ballistic missile defence system. However, even a rifle may be improved by the addition of an opto-electronic sight, and the effective deployment of its user is considerably enhanced by electronically based communications systems. The impact of electronics has been most evident in military aerospace. Over the past 30 years, electronics and aerospace have become symbiotic, both in technological and commercial terms. Indeed, the point has been reached where many combat aircraft cannot fly without a flight control system based on electronic assistance.

If the strike aircraft represents the pinnacle of electronic sophistication, naval and land warfare, even if at a slower rate, has been affected by a similar technological dynamic. The torpedo, for example, first developed in the 19th century, was, for many decades, no more than a casing, explosive and motor, targeted by sight and crude computation. Using electronics, the humble torpedo has become a 'smart' weapon, with sophisticated homing and fusing devices. By the same token, electronics are vastly increasing the complexity of 'battle management' at strategic and tactical levels. Humans now have to cope with, and to use effectively, considerably more information and offensive and defensive capability. Paradoxically, only electronics and information technology can resolve this problem by easing the work load in cockpit and general headquarters alike. Logistics and training have also been revolutionised by computerised stock control and the use of increasingly sophisticated simulators. The significance of electronics is reflected in the increasing proportion of defence equipment funding attributed to electronic equipment and associated technologies. Lockheed, for example, estimates that avionics and systems generally will make up 42 per cent of the unit cost of future combat aircraft compared to a third a decade ago.[4]

What is 'defence electronics'?

'Defence electronics' is a complex of inter-related technologies and products, and a defence electronic system is itself a combination of many technologies and components. Defence electronics may be conveniently divided into a number of component and product areas:

Micro-electronics, including both circuit and component technology, are the basis of the revolution in electronics for both civil and military purposes. Micro-electronics enables the handling of large quantities of information and the performing of electronic processes at very high speed, with a high degree of reliability, within a small size and mass. Defence provided an initial stimulus in the development of semi-conductors generally, but is now benefiting from the pace and direction of innovation set by specialised civil producers, largely, but not exclusively, in Japan and the United States.

Opto-electronics is another generalised field of electronics technology. This underpins a range of detectors, sensors, optical information processors and transmission systems, and lasers for guidance and target illumination. Opto-electronic technology is increasingly incorporated into instrumentation, communications equipment and other man-machine interfaces. Other applications of this field can be found in infrared detection, surveillance and weapons aiming, following an insatiable requirement for higher resolution sensing and data/image processing.

Taken together, micro-electronics and opto-electronics have provided the stimulus for substantial improvements in established electronic systems, and for the development of new products:

Digital computers are a dominant element in contemporary weapons systems. A direct product of the advances in micro-circuitry, digital computers can be found in navigation, multi-sensor surveillance, weapon-aiming, missile guidance and other systems requiring high-speed data processing. Combined with developments in artificial intelligence and software, on-board digital computers will facilitate the development of military robotics and expand the range of 'smart' munitions. The digital computer enables the integration of several different functions vastly to increase the overall capability of a system. For example, its use in Ptarmigan provides a 'total and global' communications system for those involved in decision-making at all levels from platoon to national command centre. Increased processing power will also be necessary to handle multi-spectral sensing.

Radar was one of the earliest defence electronics systems. Many of the defensive and offensive applications of radar in detection, navigation, weapons aiming and proximity fusing, as well as electronic intelligence gathering (ELINT) were developed during the Second World War. Again, micro-electronics and computer processing have vastly increased the power and scope of the radar which is incorporated into numerous air, land and sea based weapons platforms and support facilities.

Wireless was the first application of electronics to warfare, and communications is still one of the most significant areas of defence electronics. Radio frequency technology, precision electro-mechanical engineering and again, data processing are at the heart of modern communications systems. Modern defence communications demand technological development of increasing complexity, flexibility and security. All of these developments have revolutionised the role of battlefield communications systems: indeed, they have become the 'glue' which holds together the concept of the 'force multiplier'.[5]

Acoustics technology, almost entirely related to underwater operations, has generated a range of active and passive detectors, range finders, homing devices, and underwater triggers. Such technology is integrated into a complex array of ASW and maritime surveillance systems involving air and seaborne units.

Millimetric wave devices, operating beyond the far infrared, may be used as sensors in a range of semi-autonomous and autonomous weapons. The use of this waveband will greatly extend the all-weather, day/night capability of such systems.

Navigation aids are essential for virtually all mobile weapons platforms. Self-contained inertial systems, virtually unassailable by hostile action and externally undetectable, are of importance in aircraft and submarine navigation. Satellite systems, such as GPS/Navstar, although vulnerable to hostile action, potentially offer very high three dimensional accuracy with global coverage.

The increasing commitment of defence forces to electronic technology has led to advanced **electronic warfare technology**. From the 'radar and beam battles' of the Second World War, this area has been expanded into a sophisticated interplay of technological ploy and counter-ploy. The main applications are still in airborne warfare, but the importance of battlefield communication, command, control and identification (C^3I) has produced land-based requirements for jamming, 'spoofing', electronic defence supression, multi-spectral communications, cryptographic equipment and so on.

Finally, **systems integration** links many of these various elements in specific combat and support functions. For example, although Airborne Early Warning depends upon a suitable airframe, its most critical elements are the radars, computers and other electronic devices integrated into an effective system. A modern combat aircraft or helicopter has an avionics 'fit' consisting of, *inter alia*, navigation aids, weapon-aiming and management, flight instrumentation, autopilot, a radar with several modes, sensors and detectors, integrated by a digital database. 'Fly-by-wire' electronic controls have also considerably improved the performance of military aircraft. The next generation of aircraft will also have computer-controlled 'unstable' aerodynamics, again with significant gains in performance. Other, but vastly more complex systems, are employed in naval vessels, air and missile defence, and for command and control. Further ahead, 'expert' systems, with increasing degrees of artificial intelligence will be employed in defence equipment.[6]

Many aspects of defence electronics are dependent upon software engineering and systems design. Indeed, software engineering 'has become such an essential element in the fast and cost-effective operation of large systems that it is now generally ranked, together with micro-electronics, as one of the key "enabling technologies" of the information technology industry.'[7] Inadequate software/processing combinations were, for example, contributing factors in the problems encountered by the Nimrod AEW and the spectacular failure of the United States Army's DIVAD. It is estimated that some £12 billion will be spent by Britain, France, and Germany alone on computer and software-based defence related equipment by 1991. Half the computing-related defence expenditure in the next few years will be spent on software development and support. As Dr. Chris Cain of Logica observed, 'software is becoming the critical factor. These days, hardware tends to be easier'.[8] The drive is one to develop higher level, standardised languages for defence equipment. The recent adoption by NATO of ADA will improve interoperability as well as solve a number of processing problems, including subsequent updating of programmes. However, the pressure is on to develop still more advanced languages, and failure to maintain national capabilities in software engineering will have profound consequences for the export potential of defence equipment, as 'fourth generation' software standards are set.[9]

The capability/cost dilemma

There is no doubt that electronics systems enable the contemporary armed forces to perform tasks which were beyond their capabilities two generations ago. There appears to be no technical limit to the possibilities offered by defence electronics and associated technology. Improved, reliable and secure capability does not come cheaply. The use of electronics has, in some cases, reduced the cost of new weapons platforms, and retrofitting existing platforms with new electronics can enhance considerably their capability and extend their operational life for a relatively modest outlay. Indeed, some defence analysts advocate the development of less sophisticated platforms, putting more investment into regular in-service updating of systems and weapons.[10] To some extent, this might help to reduce costs and confront more readily the pace of technological change. However, the need to maintain a state-of-the-art performance and consequently, increased complexity and development lead times, of electronics systems will continue to drive defence equipment costs upward.

This is exacerbated by the rate of change in electronics generally, and in the opportunities new developments promise the defence sector.[11] Increasingly, defence electronics equipment will need systems architecture which can respond to new developments without the cost of completely re-designing the product. Computational speed and memory have historically doubled every five to seven years. Considerably more capacity is now available on individual electronics components — 'systems on a chip' — than was the case in the late 1970s. This trend will continue as advanced manufacturing techniques and new materials come on stream. Self-testing and automatic re-distribution of function to delay systems degradation will be available in the next generation of components.

Recent advances in superconductivity were hardly imaginable five years ago and may be commercially viable within the next half decade. The implications which these will have for defence electronics in the next century can only be surmised, but clearly they could be profound. The British MoD has already announced an interest in using superconducting materials in extremely accurate inertial naviation systems for submarines. Superconductivity may also lead to a breakthrough in submarine detection by vastly increasing the sensitivity of sensor devices. Further advances in optical electronics are bound to have equally important consequences for signal processing, sensor fusion, pattern recognition and artificial intelligence — all fundamental military applications.[12] This technology will again lead to dramatic improvements in weapons capability. None of this will be cheap, however, and both basic and applied research, let alone full development programmes, will put still more pressure on defence costs.

This problem is hitting even the United States as one United States Air Force general put it,

> Sometimes we're between the proverbial rock and hard place. We absolutely depend on technology advances in electronics and avionics to hang on to the narrow capability advantage we currently enjoy, but some of these technical advances may become so very expensive that we will be on the verge of being unable to afford them.[13]

Clearly, the security demands of a Superpower, as well as its industrial and financial ability to meet them, are not the same as those of the United Kingdom. However, as a key element in Western defence against the Soviet Union, Britain's security and its ability to export weaponry is shaped by the technological standing of its major ally as well as its adversary. Britain will therefore face similar cost pressures. The dilemma is that while electronics is vital to a strong defence capability, the challenge for industry and government alike is to make that technology affordable.

Electronics has absorbed an increasing percentage of rising British defence expenditures. Since 1982 this has accounted for about a quarter of the defence equipment budget. However, the future for British industry is increasingly uncertain, affected by static export markets and the changes in British procurement policy which have been evident over the last few years. Hovering over the industry is the known decline in real terms defence expenditure — for defence electronics down from £2.5 billion in 1986 to £2.44 billion in 1987, with further falls expected — and the prospect of a more radical defence review affecting conventional equipment. Nevertheless, the British defence electronics industry is the most advanced and comprehensive in Europe, and in many areas, able to compete effectively against the best in the United States. As such, it represents one of the most important elements in the British industrial base.

The British defence electronics industry

The setting

The British electronics industry has been involved in defence work since the First World War. Indeed, the military demand for valves was a major catalyst in the creation of a civil wireless industry. In 1939, British companies formed a 'very healthy civil industry base', from which the fruits of new inventions such as radar, precision navigation, radio fuses and the like could be exploited.[14] During the Second World War, the radio business was transformed into a full scale electronics industry. After 1945, with little help from the state, a greatly enlarged industry had to make the transition to civil production. Some firms maintained and expanded their defence interests, while others aimed at an expanding consumer electronics market. The

Korean War re-armament programme provided a particular impetus to the expansion of defence work. By the mid-1950s, a quarter of all electronics work was for the military.

Since then, British defence electronics has evolved into one of the strongest and most comprehensive of its kind outside of the United States. Britain, uniquely in Europe, possesses a diversified electronics industry capable of meeting most of the national requirement for defence systems.

In broad terms, just over 20 per cent of British electronics ouput is directly attributable to defence, though this does not include components and some dual purpose technology[15]; 45 per cent of electronics R&D is funded by the government, the majority under MoD contract; and about 90 per cent of all government funded R&D in electronics is for defence. About two-thirds of radar, radio and other capital goods R&D are defence related. Government funding, as an absolute amount and as a balance of private and public investment, forms a larger element of British electronics R&D than in France, Germany or Japan. Although defence electronics is not a large employer, it does absorb significant numbers of highly qualified people. For example, in the General Electric Company's (GEC) defence-related divisions, 32 per cent of employees are qualified scientists and engineers (QSEs) compared to 14 per cent in its more civil orientated units.[16]

In some respects, and in some firms, defence work can be highly productive. For example, Racal's exports per employee are three times the national average. Generally, the British defence electronics industry has shown greater resistance to import penetration and demonstrated a better export performance than the electronics industry average. One-third of all British aircraft equipment turnover is directly exported, and a further 25 per cent is incorporated into aircraft, missiles and spacecraft which are also sold overseas. In 1986, the United Kingdom Electronic and Engineering Association (EEA) reported that defence electronics exports totalled £5.4 billion, representing some 47 per cent of all defence sales.[17] Historically, the British defence electronics sector may have been afforded considerable protection, but this still amounts to an impressive contribution to the British balance of trade.

The structure of the defence electronics industry resembles the proverbial 'iceberg', with a small number of large, diversified companies dominating the list of MoD contractors, but with a much larger number of firms providing important, even vital electronics goods and services. The sheer complexity of the electronics sector makes detailed analysis difficult. At the one end of the spectrum is GEC, one of Britain's largest industrial conglomerates; at the other are small, but highly capable specialist firms. Defence dependence can also vary considerably. For some large, diversified firms, defence electronics represents only a small element of their business, in the case of Morgan Crucible, 4 per cent of turnover; but for others, such as Cambridge Electronic Industries, with 30 per cent of group sales in the

TABLE 3.1
Major Electronics Companies' Defence Dependence

	Defence sales £1m	Defence as % of sales	% of Defence sales to MoD
GEC	1565	30%	55%
Plessey	495	35%	70%
Racal	414	37%	40%
Ferranti	340	60%	60%
Thorn–EMI	190	6%	65%
STC	140	7%	78%

Source: Wood Mackenzie & Co. Ltd. 1986

defence sector, it is a large part of a small company's activity. In some parts of GEC, defence work can reach 70 per cent of turnover, and overall, defence work comprises about 30 per cent of GEC's total operation. The degree of dependence on the MoD can also vary, from Plessey's 70 per cent to Racal's 40 per cent of defence sales. Matters are further complicated by the duality of many electronics goods and services, especially in components and software.

In practice, most defence work is separated from civil activities. The singular requirements of the military, especially that of 'operational equipment' demands a high degree of specialisation and a particular orientation towards the defence market environment. More important, firms working in this area must be 'defence qualified', able to meet MoD specifications and contract standards. This is an expensive process for a small firm, and many firms are unwilling to invest the time and money needed to reach 'defence qualification'. However, in the case of 'support' as opposed to operational equipment, the most stringent standards of performance and reliability may not be needed, and the need for either 'defence qualification' or for specialised defence electronics is questionable. Some aspects of electronics and information technology, particularly software, are 'grey areas', where the distinction between military and civil requirements cannot be readily distinguished. There may also be considerable advantage in using commercially available products which may not only be technically superior but also cheaper than specially designed defence equipment.

The 'Two Tiers' of British Defence Electronics

The 'top tier' of British defence electronics firms comprises six companies, GEC, Plessey, Racal, Ferranti, Thorn-EMI and STC-ICL. Table 3.1 details their defence sales and the proportion of these which are under contract to the MoD. Table 3.2 provides an indication of the range of products and their relative importance in each firm.

However, it is clear from this data that GEC and Plessey are the dominant actors in the British defence electronics industry. Together, GEC and Plessey account for over 70 per cent of the MoD's defence electronics contracts and

TABLE 3.2
Defence Electronics Product Segments (£ millions)

Product Segments	GEC	Plessey	Racal	Ferranti	Thorn EMI	STC
Avionics	400	25	25	20		
Displays		20				
Navigation Systems				70		
Weapon Control Systems	90			100		
Electro-optics	55			35	10	20
Electronic Warfare	175	80	115		10	
Communications System	250	200	230		50	50
Radar Systems	150	125	35	25	50	
Electronic Fuzing				10	10	
Guided Weapons						
Torpedoes, Sea mines	200					
Sonars		95		20		
Defence Space System	40		10			
Product Support				50		
Components					55	40
Software					20	30
Other	270			10		

Source: Wood Mackenzie & Co. Ltd. 1986.

are present in virtually all the major product areas. In 1985–86 the two firms' total MoD business was worth £1,034 million, or 16 per cent of the total defence equipment budget. (See Table 3.3). Such was their dominance, that the next largest defence electronics company, Ferranti accounted for only a sixth of that amount.[18]

TABLE 3.3
GEC and Plessey Share of the British Defence Electronics Market

a. MoD payments

	1982–83	1983–84	1984–85	£ million 1985–86*
Payments to major UK electronics companies†	1,215	1,467	1,707	1,360
(As a percentage of all equipment expenditure)	(19%)	(21%)	(22%)	(20%)
Payments to GEC and Plessey	877	1,070	1,244	1,034
(As a percentage of all equipment expenditure)	(14%)	(15%)	(16%)	(16%)

Source: MoD.

*Refers to payments made in the 10 month period April 1985 to January 1986. The percentages relate to total equipment expenditure in the corresponding period.

b. The United Kingdom market for civil and defence radar

	Total sales	GEC's sales	Plessey's sales	GEC's share %	£ million per annum* Plessey's share %	Combined share %
Civil primary radar	8.0	0.4	0.9	5	11	16
Data handling and display	2.5	0.5	1.1	20	44	64
Military ground-based 3D radar	14.0	1.9	8.6	14	61	75
Military ground-based 2D radar†	3.0	2.5	0.5(5.1)	83	17	100

Army tracking radar	14.0	14.0	0	100	0	100
Naval surveillance radar	18.1	16.8	1.3(0.3)	93	7	100
Naval tracking radar	24.8	24.8	0	100	0	100
Airborne radar	105.0	63.6	0	60	0	60
Data display and handling, including UKADGE	22.0	4.2	6.1	19	28	47

Source: MMC Study.

*Average annual sales over the period 1980–81 to 1984–85. Sub-contract sales between GEC and Plessey are shown in brackets, and include work for exports.
†Includes some development work on Army Surveillance radar.

c. The United Kingdom market for military radio and communication systems

	Total sales	GEC's sales	Plessey's sales	GEC's share %	£ million per annum* Plessey's share %	Combined share %
Army radio–strategic (Ptarmigan etc)	80.3	8.0(10.3)	72.3	10	90	100
Army radio–tactical (Clansman etc)	25.0	13.2	8.4	53	34	86
Army command, control and information systems	7.9	0	7.9	0	100	100
Battlefield surveillance systems	1.5	0.2	0.8	13	53	67
Defence strategic radio	6.0	2.4	1.2	40	20	60
Naval ship systems	39.0	7.2	9.6	18	25	43
Shore stations	3.0	2.0	0	67	0	67
Satellite communications systems	14.0	4.8	0.7	34	5	39
Satellite terminals	16.0	8.7	0	54	0	54
HF surveillance systems	0.5	0	0.5	0	100	100

Source: MMC Study.

*Average annual sales over the period 1980–81 to 1984–85. Sub-contract sales between GEC and Plessey are shown in brackets.

d. The United Kingdom market for avionics systems

	Total sales	GEC's sales	Plessey's sales	GEC's share %	£ million per annum* Plessey's share %	Combined share %
Airborne communications	31.0	12.2	4.7	39	15	55
Airborne navigation systems	82.0	10.4	0.1	13	0	13
Flight data systems	8.0	0	2.0	0	25	25
Aircraft defensive aids and ECM/ESM	50.0	38.0	0(4.4)	76	0	76
Airborne weapons systems	63.0	32.8	0.4	52	1	53

Source: MMC Study.

*Average annual sales over the period 1980–81 to 1984–85. Sub-contract sales between GEC and Plessey are shown in brackets.

e. The United Kingdom market for underwater defence electronics systems

	Total sales	GEC's sales	Plessey's sales	GEC's share %	£ million per annum* Plessey's share %	Combined share %
Surface ship sonar	14.0	0.6	12.7	4	91	95
Submarine sonar	10.0	0(0.4)	9.2	0	92	92
Helicopter sonar	8.0	0	1.7	0	21	21
Mines	1.0	0	0	0	0	0
Minehunting	2.0	0	1.5	0	75	75
Towed arrays	6.0	0	3.6	0	60	60
Sonar data handling and display	110.0	9.4	7.2	9	7	15
Torpedoes	138.2	137.6	0.5(2.7)	100	0	100
Launching systems	4.0	0	3.7	0	92	92

Source: MMC Study.

*Average annual sales over the period 1980–81 to 1984–85. Sub-contract sales between GEC and Plessey are shown in brackets.
Source: Cmnd 9867 (1986).

GEC is the largest MoD electronics contractor and is second only to British Aerospace (BAe) in total defence contracts awarded. With 165,000 employees, it is also Britain's largest manufacturer, with interests in a wide range of electronic and electrical products. It is so big, and its interests so diverse that performance has varied from division to division and from project to project. In recent years, a number of GEC's defence related sections have been the focus of controversy and dispute with the MoD over technical problems and cost overruns in major defence programmes. But despite these problems, GEC is a major force in both the British and the European defence electronics sector, and has achieved considerable success in the export market, winning a number of important American contracts against stiff domestic competition on quality and price.[19] GEC has recently re-organised its defence operation and is improving inter-divisional communication to improve the diffusion of R&D results across the whole company. Even in the view of its British competitors, GEC is recognisably a vital and irreplaceable element in the British defence electronics base.

GEC has sought to defend this position by expanding its role as a prime systems integrating contractor. A prime contractor requires a combination of size, capital resource and technical ability, three features which GEC has in abundance. A prime contractor has the most challenging tasks and this satisfies the firm's pool of scientific and managerial talent; it also represents some of the most value-added aspects of programme development and production. Above all, it enhances a firm's ability to control its commercial and industrial environment. GEC already has this status in respect of torpedoes, satellites and complete communications systems. Responsibility for guided weapons and other 'smart munitions' systems would offer similar benefits and returns. Beyond this, GEC believes that the pervasive role of electronics could even call into question the right of existing prime contractors to determine and to lead all contracts for major weapons platforms.

Plessey is the second largest British electronics defence contractor and has a broad range of civil and military electronics interests. Plessey also has an international reputation in the development and production of specialised micro-circuitry for defence and commerical uses, and exports over half its semiconductor production. Like many others in the United Kingdom electronics industry, it has put increasing emphasis on defence production through investment and acquisition strategies. In 1985-86, defence work accounted for 35 per cent of Plessey's turnover. About 70 per cent of £495 million in defence sales went to the MoD, and Plessey's MoD business has increased at an annual rate of 27 per cent since 1981. In many respects, only Plessey can be expected realistically to provide national competition for GEC, and for this reason, the MoD opposed GEC's 1985 bid to take over Plessey.

Of the top tier of British defence electronics companies, Ferranti is one of the more heavily dependent on defence. In 1987, 60 per cent of turnover was defence related, and over 30 per cent of sales were to the MoD. Ferranti's dependence on the British defence market has left it vulnerable to changes in MoD procurement policies. Ferranti's range of products were also thought to be particularly vulnerable to a wider use of standard commercial equipment in military systems. Its failure to win control of the Royal Ordnance Factory, and with it a broader defence base, left the firm open to increasingly powerful competition. These factors, and the prospect of cuts in the British defence budget, helped to reduce its share valuation by 60 per cent between 1982 and 1987. At one point, Ferranti appeared to be a prime target for takeover. Nevertheless, Ferranti was able to compete for a share of major British and European projects, such as the Eurofighter attack radar. The company has also fought back to increase its 1987 profits by 20 per cent and has merged with the American firm International Signal and Control. Although this has increased Ferranti's defence dependence to 65 per cent, the merger has broadened its range of products and more important, improved access to the US market.[20]

Racal is firmly established as an export orientated firm. Some 30 per cent of its turnover is in the military sector, and over 60 per cent of that is sold abroad. Racal has been one of the most rapidly growing of the British defence related electronics companies. During the 1970s, it moved into the top 10 MoD contractors and, with its acquisition of Decca in 1986, Racal doubled its defence capacity. In particular, Racal has been able to identify and take advantage of new markets, supporting its products with a high level of private venture R&D activity. This has given the firm considerable freedom to define its own specifications and substantial autonomy in marketing its products.

The last two firms in the 'top tier', Thorn-EMI and STC, with only 6 per cent and 7 per cent respectively of sales in the defence sector, and well behind the other four in terms of total defence work, nevertheless make valuable contributions to several key electronics sectors. Both would like to increase their defence activities. However Thorn failed to broaden its defence base through major acquisitions (in this instance a failed bid for BAe), and the shift to competitive procurement could have a particularly depressing affect on the range of products supplied by the company. STC, on the other hand, has a strong potential to exploit its commercially driven information technology capability.

If the top of the 'iceberg' provides a comprehensive range of military oriented goods and services, the full extent and quality of the British defence electronics industry extends into several hundreds of other companies. Most of these are again civil/military 'hybrids', with defence work having a varying degree of importance to their overall business. Similarly, electronics may only be part of a wider interest in civil and military high technology equipment.

Of these, one of the most significant is BAe. Although BAe is one of the largest MoD contractors and a key market for electronics equipment, it is also an electronics equipment manufacturer in its own right. It has recognised the importance of developing its systems and electronics interests to maintain its credibility as a major defence prime contractor and to act as an 'intelligent customer' in respect of electronics subsystems. As a BAe spokesman put it, 'any company having pretentions to be in modern weapons manufacture in 1986 isn't credible unless it has the whole of the electronics packaging technologies existing in-house.'[21] BAe has taken the lead in generating systems technology and coordinating work in the electronics industry for projects such as the Experimental Aircraft Programme (EAP) and European Fighter Aircraft (EFA).[22] BAe has invested in facilities for producing specialist integrated circuits and has considerable expertise in software. In addition to its own in-house capability, BAe has acquired a substantial share of Systems Designers, one of the top three British software houses.[23] Although it is unlikely that BAe has the resources or the inclination to become a major producer of subsystems, the general improvement in its electronics capabilities will, for example, provide the possibility of developing a complete guided weapon.

Smiths Industries is a rather more typical example of a 'second tier' firm. Of a 1986 turnover of £401.2 million, £159.6 million was generated by aerospace and defence. 62 per cent of Smiths' business is in overseas markets, and 40 per cent of its 1986 aerospace/defence output went to the United States. Smiths has long standing links with European firms through its work on the Airbus family, and also collaborates with Hughes on military systems. Dowty is another diversified equipment company, with some electronics work in both civil and military aerospace. Electronics/aerospace was worth £432.2 million of its £518.8 million turnover in 1986, and 65 per cent of its aerospace work was for the military. Dowty has also developed close links with Europe through various collaborative projects.

All the 'top tier', and the vast majority of British defence electronics firms, are British-owned. Nevertheless, foreign companies play a significant role, either directly or indirectly, in the 'second tier' of British defence electronics firms and MoD suppliers. These are not necessarily the largest of the electronics multinationals. Indeed, giants such as IBM and Honeywell are not major United Kingdom defence contractors. But Cossor Electronics, since the early 1960s an autonomous subsidiary of Raytheon, employs 2,000 people and is a important MoD contractor, especially for Identification of Friend or Foe (IFF) systems. Singer Link Miles (SLM), is another American owned firm with extensive and long established interest in the British defence market, specialising in highly sophisticated simulators for civil and military customers. DEC, a major computer manufacturer and significant American defence contractor, is investing heavily in British plant and R&D facilities in order to bid for MoD contracts in several computer/software areas. The increasing use of standardised equipment, instead of specialised military products, although it should benefit British firms such as STC, will also further encourage foreign companies to attack the United Kingdom defence market.[24]

Most important of all, Britain is largely dependent on overseas companies for components, especially generalised micro-circuits and processors. For example, in the Tornado some 45 per cent of its 'chips' are from American sources. British firms such as Plessey are important producers of state-of-the-art custom and semi-custom chips, and GEC has its own in-house capability. However, Britain has to import the vast majority of its standard chips for incorporation into defence and defence related equipment. Most of the supplying companies are American based, such as Intell, Motorola and Texas Instruments, but the United Kingdom MEL owned by Phillips, has received MoD funds for chip development. Foreign dependence is worrying many industrialists. American controls on the transfer of component technology may increase, not only affecting Britain's ability freely to export its electronics products, but could also force Britain to import more value-added products in the form of complete component based subsystems. This would have a depressing affect on profit margins and, ultimately, resources available for re-investment in R&D. Currently, Japan provides an alternative source of supply, but it too may become a competitor in the defence electronics market, and could withhold state-of-the-art component technology from British firms. Even if the Japanese do not become direct competitors in the defence field, British input costs would be vulnerable to Japanese pricing policies.

The British defence electronics industry is in a state of flux. This is due in part to normal, though increasingly acute technological and commercial pressures. Changes in the electronics business, with more capability and hence value-added activity being contained within the basic components, are squeezing some of the traditional areas of electronic sub-systems and sub-contract activity. Already some 70–80 per cent of the value of an airborne radar comes from the supplier chain, and we have been told that GEC subcontracts 90 per cent by value of Stingray components, buying in many 'world market' electronic items.[25] Huge sums are needed to keep in touch with the rapid evolution of component technology while some British firms are maintaining state-of-the-art chip development and manufacture, others will have to retreat further into specialised niche markets, or expect a drop in profitability and/or market shares. But British defence electronics firms are also being affected by the government's defence, defence procurement and R&D policy generally. In particular, the emphasis on competition and collaboration is having a profound effect on the British defence electronics industry, an issue which is discussed at some length in a later chapter.

Defence electronics and national R&D policy

In general terms, the British defence electronics industry appears to be in reasonable shape. This is something that cannot be said for much of the rest of British electronics. As Euan Maddock noted, 'in the past several decades the level of (the) civil platform has been subsiding, leaving the defence "peaks" standing ever higher relative to the national electronic engineering plateau.'[26] In this respect, the European Defence Committee (EDC) report of 1982 painted a grim picture:

> The United Kingdom's electronics industry has a number of technological and product strengths, but it is relatively weak in most of the businesses where world markets are growing fastest and amongst which are the best opportunities for growth in the future.[27]

A 1975 balance of trade surplus in electronics and information technology (IT) of £100 million had become a deficit of £300 million by 1980. In computers and IT, the gap was over £500 billion. Between 1980 and 1984, the general electronics balance of trade worsened from £181 million to £2,052 million. In the same period, import penetration increased from 37 to 59 per cent. In Maddock's view the inference was obvious; 'UK manufacturers have not concentrated on leading edge business, and in consequence the UK industry continues to lose its share of world market.' According to Susan Willett, in the early 1970s Britain had an industry with potential for 'transforming British industry and laying the basis of a new period of economic growth and national prosperity.' But, she continues, 'a decade later, nothing could be further from reality, the UK electronics industry is in a sad state of decline. The electronics industry, once hailed as the sunrise industry of Britain's manufacturing sector, has become increasingly dependent on the defence market in recent years.'[28]

To some critics, the causal link between investment in defence R&D and the decline of British electronics is clear. While reference is made to other factors in a complex arena of industrial decline and commercial malaise, defence dependency is identified as the main villain. The defence sector has encouraged the development of over-specialised products with limited commercial applicability. The loss of competitiveness on the part of major electronics firms is said to be due to their reliance on closed and risk-free public markets, primarily in defence. The defence sector has absorbed too many qualified personnel and has neglected the development of process technology which would have had a more general application throughout British industry. Levitt also suggests that the resources allocated to defence electronics have not been used very efficiently. He shows that productivity in defence-related electronics between 1976 and 1981 deteriorated at a rate of − 0.6 per cent when, at the same time, the average for the electronics industry as a whole increased by 3.6 per cent per year. In the components sector, where only 6 per cent of output was defence related, the gains were as high as 8.7 per cent.[29]

In his report for the EDC on defence electronics and the civil economy, Euan Maddock described the archetypal 'defence-dependent' enterprise. Such a firm, or autonomous division of a very large multi-product corporation, has been an established defence contractor since the Second World War, and its entire commercial and technological outlook is governed by the requirements of a single customer, the MoD. This type of firm was largely deficient in the entrepreneurial skills required to operate in the civil market. In any event, it preferred to work with customers who defined in advance the nature of their requirements, and paid, again in advance, for the necessary research and development. The defence market had its own uncertainties, especially in respect of changing requirements and the *deus ex machina* of changing government policy, but once the customer was satisfied technically, it tended to remain so for a relatively longer period of time. Civil markets were not only affected by an unpleasantly high rate of change, but the competition from established, stronger civil manufacturers, especially the Japanese, was too great. The safer course was to concentrate on the defence sector. Wider commercial business was seen in terms of exporting defence equipment. 'Non-defence' work was mainly the direct application of specialised defence technology in related areas such as civil aerospace and air-traffic control. In Maddock's opinion, the chances of such a company making a major contribution to civil industry, outside a few special cases, such as civil aerospace, were 'vanishingly small and even strong measures by the government (were) unlikely to have more than marginal effect'. Indeed, such measures could be counter productive if they inhibited the government's 'ability to carry out their defence obligations'.[30] In short, these defence dependent enterprises had become 'extremely efficient at operating within the defence market having developed managerial structures and operating procedures geared to dealing with the MoD ...'. However, it was 'precisely these management characteristics ... that inhibit[ed] the effective diffusion of high technology products in competitive markets.'[31]

Maddock also referred to companies, 'potentially the most important of all', which included those firms that had the greatest need for an 'injection of advanced technology'. They were not defence contractors, but were typically consumers of electronic products, or were undergoing change in their mode of operation due to electronic and information technologies. 'Most if not all of the techniques they require already exist within the defence contractors and establishments, but there is no coupling between those with the need and those who could supply.'[32] Even if the defence dependent companies should concentrate on supplying British defence needs, it was essential to ensure that the technology they generated is more generally available.

Maddock also wanted to see more active policies to encourage the smaller, more dynamic subcontractor. Where possible, the MoD should purchase standard equipment and services rather than highly specialised items tuned to military needs. The MoD should be sensitive to the commercial implications of its equipment, where necessary adjusting specifications to widen the commercial appeal of a product. He further recommended that government 'concentrate on raising the average national technology plateau, so that the difference between the civil and defence levels is substantially reduced'.[33]

In response, the MoD felt that it had many of Maddock's suggestions already in hand, and that the competition policy would provide greater access to new technology and provide more commercial incentives. But ultimately, while the MoD would look to help civil industry, 'the main purpose of Defence R&D was, and always should be, to support the Defence Programme'. The MoD also noted the general difficulty of encouraging 'spinoff'. Neither the Americans, nor the Japanese nor the Europeans had 'foolproof ways of transferring technology from one field to another'. Examples of successful spin-off were almost inevitably 'market-led', and as such, dependent on companies recognising market opportunities.[34] The MoD, perhaps rightly, clearly believed that it had done as much for the general good as it could within its own remit. The creation, promotion and protection of an electronics industry depends upon a complex of public and private factors operating both at a national and international level. In this context, defence procurement is only one factor amongst many which could contribute to success or failure in the stimulation and diffusion of technological innovation to the widest national benefit.

The British semiconductor industry represents a particularly good example of this problem. Britain has an international reputation for technical inventiveness in semiconductors, but most of the rewards and industrial growth seem to have occurred in the United States and Japan. During the 1950s and 1960s, the MoD was the major external source of funding for semiconductor research and remains an important sponsor of such research. MoD support has led to significant advances in a number of fields, for example microwave devices, optoelectronics, and novel semiconductor materials, in which British firms have maintained an international prominence. But, according to one highly critical study:

'In spite of the relatively high proportion of resources devoted to this specialist field over such a long period of time to produce military components, there is little evidence yet to suggest that the firms involved will fully exploit the technical achievements in the wider commercial arena to maintain that position of leadership.'[35]

The MoD had, *inter alia*, encouraged the development of a 'club' of semiconductor firms, consisting largely of established defence electronics contractors, to the exclusion of small, consumer orientated firms. This was in direct contrast to the United States, where the most significant developments in micro circuitry were made by small firms. The development of semiconductors for military programmes had also been delayed in Britain by changing military requirements. Under these circumstances, industry had been reluctant to invest in production facilities or in a commercial application of defence R&D.[36]

But the failings of the British semiconductor industry cannot be laid entirely at the door of the MoD. There are many reasons for Britain's comparative inability to extract commercial rewards from semiconductor research.[37] These include, *inter alia* the lack of readily available risk capital, inadequate domestic demand, low personnel mobility, and a general lack of managerial and entrepeneurial ability.[38] The British market for semiconductors in the 1960s, both civil and military, could hardly have given the kind of stimulus provided by the Pentagon, NASA and the American computer industry. Successive British governments have also neglected to provide suitable pump-priming policies for civil research. The DTI, for example, has only been involved to any great extent in semiconductor research sponsorship since 1970. Even then, there was poor coordination between it, the MoD and other quasi-governmental bodies.[39] Since 1980, Alvey and other programmes have encouraged a broader approach to micro-electronics, with more liaison and a better balance of funding between the MoD, the DTI and the research councils.[40] In the case of Alvey, the increasingly dominant role of the MoD and British defence contractors has caused some concern.[41] But of much more concern than any 'defence bias' is the absence of 'application-orientated' sponsorship along the lines of United States and Japanese programmes.

Commercial judgement has also led major British companies deliberately to opt out of general merchant chip manufacturing.[42] GEC argued, and still believes, that Britain could always buy the circuitry it needed from the lowest cost supplier to incorporate it in specific products. In general, this was a field where GEC perceived advantage in subcontracting, whereas more specialised, high value customised chips have generally been available from British suppliers. In this respect, Plessey amongst others, supported by the MoD, has maintained a particularly strong capability in custom chips. Its recent investment in new plant, costing £33 million (including £7 million from the government), will help maintain this position. Events in the international semiconductor industry also seem to confirm that the specialist 'merchant chip' manufacturer is being overtaken by the vertically integrated electronics company that provides an immediate market for new components and the capital base for increasingly expensive development.

In the view of some critics of British defence efforts, however, the general effect of defence dependence in the electronics sector has been bad for the economy as a whole. In the longer term, it may also have serious consequences for the quality of the defence industrial base:

> The erosion of management spirit is an insidious process. The retreat from the international market takes place gradually but has cumulative impact, making comeback doubly difficult. In time, it will affect manufacturing industry's ability to satisfy military customers because poor civil technology means poor military technology.[43]

It is difficult to refute the idea that the fruits of British inventiveness in weaponry appear neither to have been used wisely nor effectively in the civil electronics sector. The coincidence of a number of critical studies is, perhaps, a cause for concern. As Ian Davidson of the *Financial Times* put it, 'there can be little doubt that some of the facts to which they draw attention are worrying'. The Cabinet has at least begun to recognise that a problem exists. It has asked ACARD to establish a technical group (ACOST) to investigate how defence R&D can be used more widely in the economy, and how the 'enabling technologies' such as IT and electronics can be best disseminated throughout industry.[44] There are other signs that the government wants to adjust British R&D priorities to obtain a greater spread of commercial benefits. It is equally clear that the government wants to see private industry invest more of its own money in research.

However, the problem of Britain's relatively poor commercial performance in electronics is not necessarily a question of the defence sector absorbing too many resources, or the MoD and its procurement practices limiting the commerciality of British industry, or under-investment by British firms in civil R&D. A generalised neglect of civil electronics by successive governments may be at least equally to blame as an over-emphasis on defence needs. The Electronic Engineering Association's (EEA) recent submission to ACARD contained a strong defence of military R&D. An unjustified 'folklore', it argued, had built up suggesting that defence R&D crowded out valuable investment in the civil sector. The EEA warned that a reduction in funding would 'undoubtedly harm the highly successful UK defence industry', without necessarily leading to more resources going into civil electronics.[45]

Historically, the balance of policy may have been wrong, with the MoD apparently expected not only to provide an adequate defence policy, but a technology and an industrial policy as well. If the MoD could be blamed for killing the British electronics industry, there is, perhaps, a good case for asking what the situation might have been like without defence related activity![46] The MoD cannot make British firms seize such opportunities that do materialise. Equally, the broader problems of industrial sponsorship are not, nor should be, its primary concern. In this respect, the poor performance of DTI sponsorship of British electronics has attracted increasing criticism.[47]

The government too, has been attacked for its failure to intervene more extensively in electronics; to stimulate strategic research; to provide incentives for industry to invest in R&D; and to coordinate current research in industry, government establishments and colleges.[48] Concern has also been directed at the balance of research in the universities and the quality of technological education generally. In short, the weaknesses of British technology, and electronics in particular cannot be attributed to defence alone; it is a much more complex and, sadly, a more difficult problem to resolve than simply to re-distribute defence R&D.

The importance of possessing a strong, generalised electronics industry in support of a defence industrial base, however, is not in dispute. Electronics and associated information technologies have effected a profound and irreversible change in the foundations of national industrial and economic power. More significantly for national security, since the late 1960s, the speed and quality of innovation in civil electronics has tended to exceed that of the defence sector. In the United States, the Pentagon has warned that American security is being threatened by the erosion of the domestic semiconductor industry and unless the United States government is prepared to invest in strategic R&D, certain parts of the Japanese electronics industry may become *de facto* elements of the US defence industrial base.[49] Several British industrialists believe that the Japanese threat to American defence autonomy is serving to justify government intervention in a wide range of electronics, especially advanced micro-circuitry, which will also determine civil standards into the next century. In this respect, they argue that defence is again becoming a 'technological driver' for advanced components and software, a role which could only be equalled by an ambitious civil space programme. They also fear that because this is under a military heading, it will be easier for the United States to control the rate and scope of technology transfer.

Closer to home, the 1987 IEPG study recognised the value of a healthy electronics industry to Europe's defence industrial base:

> [Electronics] is a fast developing and intensely competitive sector of both civil and military industries — indeed in many cases the basic technology is identical, with only the applications being different ... Given the rapid pace of development and the speed with which the US (and Japan) can move from development to marketable systems, there is undoubtedly a major threat to European electronics industries. This threat is not merely to defence electronics, which normally constitute only a small part of the market, but to the entire market and hence to the continued existence of such firms. Due to the all pervasive influence and ever-growing importance of electronics this must be viewed as a very serious threat — indeed it is the most critical technology which has been considered in the survey.[50]

There is a clear danger that British and European defence electronics may face a general threat from the most advanced centres of electronic and IT development and production in the United States and Japan which could overwhelm both civil and defence electronics. It is essential that a 'value for money' approach to defence procurement appreciates this broader dimension. In this context, a preoccupation with short term savings to the detriment of long term strategic thinking undermines rather than strengthens national security.

4

UK Procurement Policy: Choices in Principle

The stages and modes of procurement

In order to identify realistic options for procurement and DIB policy, it is necessary to specify some basic elements in procurement. These are outlined in Figure 4.1 which shows procurement divided into four broad stages, of which the first includes research, general work into the 'enabling technologies' which could contribute to future systems and consideration of the feasibility of the concept concerned. The second is development, broadly defined as the process aimed at generating a specific system in a form ready for production. Development often includes a good deal of systems integ-

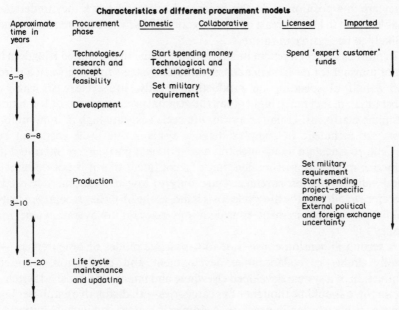

FIGURE 4.1
The Procurement of a Major Weapon System

ration work, in which existing subsystems, such as radar, navigation equipment, engines and so on, are made to work together. The third stage is the production of the system itself and the fourth is the maintenance and updating of the system once it is in service.

In practice, these stages can overlap. Certainly the gap between research and development can be blurred and in some rare cases it is necessary to complete development work after a system has begun production. This, however, is not thought to be good practice, often leading to substantial cost increases. Particularly in the case of complex weapons platforms, such as ships and aircraft, a system in service normally benefits from further development work as new, improved subsystems can be introduced.

In terms of funding, systems vary enormously in the relative volumes of money absorbed by the different stages. In most cases the research stage is the least expensive. However, it should not be overlooked that, in order to judge effectively what sort of system is likely to be available and would best meet a state's future, a considerable technical expertise is required. In buying defence equipment, governments need to be 'expert customers' and maintaining the knowledge base involved costs money. Clearly they need not rely entirely on their own expertise. They can purchase the advice of consultants and industrialists, both indigenous and overseas. But some sources of advice will be considered more authoritative and reliable than others. In the United Kingdom, one role of the Government's own defence research establishments is to provide expert customer advice to the MoD. They are in a position to do this because the research work they undertake enables them to keep abreast of what is going on elsewhere and to assess what is likely to be feasible in future.

In most cases development involves major sums. In the United Kingdom it is not unusual for development costs on some systems to be between a third and a half of spending on production. Lastly, life cycle costs can be substantial, in fact much higher than the original procurement cost for major weapons platforms. Even for a rifle, life cycle costs are high if ammunition costs are included. In complex defence systems, life cycle costs can be difficult to calculate in advance but a government particularly interested in value for money in procurement must be confident that it is not obtaining good value at one procurement stage only to lose it at another. It needs therefore to address the life-cycle costs issue, as the MoD has recognised in its public list of procurement considerations relevant to overall 'value for money'.

A second dimension consists of four possible modes of procurement — wholly domestic, collaborative development and production, licensed production of a system developed elsewhere and import of a finished system. Again these should be thought of as categories with distinctive emphases but some possible overlap in practice. A domestic system can include imported subsystems. In British warships and aircraft there are normally several subsystems which have been imported. Also, like other European states,

Britain has to import raw materials such as titanium and bauxite which have an important place in the construction of defence equipment. On average, the imported element in 'British' weapons is around 25 per cent of their final value.[1] Collaboration can become closely associated with licensed production and with domestic development. When Britain and France agreed in 1967 on a collaborative family of helicopters, two models, the Puma and the Gazelle, were designed and developed almost entirely in France while the Lynx was essentially a British product. France bought the Lynx as an imported item while the United Kingdom produced the Pumas and Gazelles it needed under licence. In the 1980s in the case of the AMRAAM/ASRAAM family in progress in NATO, AMRAAM is being developed nationally by the United States while the Europeans are developing ASRAAM collaboratively. Once development is completed, the Europeans are to procure AMRAAM, also through licensed production while the Americans will procure ASRAAM, through licensed production. But, despite overlaps, the distinctions have some significance.

Two important considerations are that, for the first two of these modes (domestic and collaborative development and production), a government must allocate funds for all four stages of procurement and must set its military requirement at an early stage before development begins. To use the latter two modes, (licensed or imported production) a government need spend research funds only to the extent it feels appropriate for it to be able to assess properly external offers of arms. Also it only needs to set its requirement and to commit extensive funds at the stage just before production, although the funds which then have to be spent may well have to contribute to the seller's original R&D costs. All procurement routes mean paying life cycle costs. Defence companies, like firms making durable civil goods, tend to see spare parts as a particularly profitable sector of their business. There can be different considerations at work with different procurement modes. Once the Americans took the Polaris missile out of service, it became much more costly to purchase parts just for the British system. West Germany has introduced some modifications to its imported F-4 Phantoms, not because it particularly wanted the changes, but because the United States was introducing them on its F-4s in Germany and it would have been more expensive for the Luftwaffe to have stayed with the previous version.[2] On the other hand, there can be economies of scale and technological advantages arising from association with the life-cycle activities of systems produced elsewhere.

Clearly a central element in procurement is establishing the military requirement. For states which are willing to fund development work, most probably by their own industry, this is a complex task, involving assessment of who should be considered as potential enemies, what an enemy's capabilities are likely to be at points at least 20 years into the future, how enemy capabilities can be countered in principle, what technologies will be available to the procuring state, and what the cost of any solution is likely to be. Not surprisingly, across NATO, industry makes a major contribution to the setting of requirements. However, governments clearly have a degree of choice in setting their requirements in that they can be select positions on scales going from optimistic to pessimistic as regards estimates of enemies potential and the likely costs of offsetting it.

Historically, national requirements have been settled first and then an effort made to base a collaborative project on a reconciliation or a sum of different requirements. This has caused many problems, including increased costs. From the mid-1980s in collaborative projects, more efforts were made for common requirements to be set as part of the whole cooperative process with national military staffs working together from the start. Both NATO, (through the Conference of National Armaments Directors (CNAD) machinery) and the IEPG (through its Panel 1 work) were trying to get states to work together on the setting of staff 'targets' which then serve as a basis for agreed 'requirements'.

On the other hand, states which are only interested in purchasing equipment can fix their requirement just before they place an order. 'Needs' have to be decided on the basis of what is available and a state may or may not have much choice. Providing a state can pay, there are possibilities for having equipment which is being bought 'off the shelf' customised to meet a specified need but, the more sophisticated the piece of equipment sought, the less flexibility a state is likely to have.

From the Armed Services point of view, all methods of procurement have disadvantages. In principle, national or collaborative development means Services can have equipment designed specifically to meet their preferences, although costs and the needs of likely export customers can involve compromises. But setting the requirement before development means technological uncertainty as to whether the equipment will eventually work to specification, and it involves the Services waiting a long time for equipment they have identified as needed to get into service. Buying off the shelf, on the other hand, means a relative certainty about what is being obtained and it means getting it sooner. It is also easier to feel confident about a requirement looking 10 years ahead than one looking 20 years in advance.

In terms of the four modes of procurement, there are significant variations in the nature of uncertainty associated with each. Fundamentally, the earlier in the life of a system that a decision to acquire it is made, the greater the uncertainty that its eventual costs can be accurately forecast. Developing complex military equipment is an inherently risky business, although governments can seek to reduce risk by delaying final commitment in legal and major financial terms until the technological problems associated with a project have been carefully identified and assessed. Historically, costs have tended to rise above estimates even during development. This is not just a British phenomenon but one found across the Alliance and there is some evidence that unscheduled cost growth tends to be greatest when defence funds have been increased and are in relatively abundant supply.[5] The basic relationship is that technology costs become more predictable the further into the procurement cycle attention is focused. But often it is only when a system has been in service for some time that its technological reliability can be assessed clearly and its life cycle costs clearly defined.

Technologically there is thus less uncertainty about the cost of imported weapons or of weapons made under licence since a decision in their favour can be taken at the production stage. However, imported weapons, along with collaborative projects in some ways, can have their costs substantially affected by exchange rate fluctuations as their prices are normally fixed in the currency of the exporting state. Britain's purchase of the Trident D–5 system has actually benefited by the dollar-pound exchange rates which have prevailed since the decision for the latest Lockheed missile was taken. However, the position would be quite different if the pound were to fall below about $1.40 when Trident spending peaks in the early 1990s.

Turning to the political aspects of uncertainty in the different modes of procurement, clearly only domestic development and production gives the maximum certainty of supply that is associated with a strong defence industrial base. A distinction needs to be made between the perspective of the national government and that of the Armed Services or industry. In the view of the latter, national government is itself a source of uncertainty since it can cancel projects. It may be felt that a government is less likely to cancel collaborative, licensed production or direct import arrangements because such a move might have international political repercussions. However, in this study it is the national government's perspective which is the central issue.

In the past governments have sometimes seemed reluctant to withdraw from collaborative projects, even when they have incurred substantial cost increases or other problems. The SP-70 (155 mm self-propelled gun) was a case in point. Increasingly, however, governments (and the British Government in particular) are deferring final commitment to a project until they are confident that precise and realistic performance targets have been set and can be attained at acceptable cost (see Chapter Five).

In broad terms, from a government's point of view, collaborative development means accepting interdependence with foreign partners while simple imports mean accepting dependence on an outside supplier, although some collaborative projects can be very asymmetric in the relative weight of each partner. In the case of raw materials, dependence can be reduced by having several possible sources of supply and by holding substantial stocks. Through licensed manufacture, a state can achieve a capacity to produce perhaps the whole of a system itself and may thus gain substantial operational autonomy as defined in an earlier section. In the event of crisis or war it could step up production of an item and of its spare parts, disregarding if necessary the preferences of the original supplier. Some licensed manufacture arrangements, however, involve the import of subsystems or major components.

There is therefore a broad central trade-off to be considered. Technological and economic uncertainty, while being an unavoidable feature of defence procurement, can be minimised by opting for a system which another state has developed and is in some ways proven. Political uncertainty, however, is greater the more that dependence is accepted on foreign suppliers and the domestic industrial base is neglected. In contemporary Britain, as reflected in the decisions to abandon the Airborne Early Warning (AEW) aircraft Nimrod and the Zircon satellite in favour of American systems, the government is probably more concerned about technological and cost uncertainty and less about political uncertainty, while industry naturally tends to support living with technological risk on the understanding that government will provide most of the funding.

The range of choices

The framework above, with the addition of more specific consideration of the outside world, can be used to illuminate the range of choices in principle which are open to government in procurement decisions. As a traditional armaments developer and producer, Britain currently tends to define its military requirements up to a decade before a system is needed. This means that a British or a collaborative development effort can be undertaken if preferred. When the United Kingdom considers a requirement at such an early stage, there are three possibilities which the MoD can encounter, assuming that all possible external suppliers are considered to be politically acceptable. These are that:

First, nothing meeting the UK requirement is in development or production elsewhere but other states may or may not be considering a requirement similar to that of the United Kingdom; or

Second, that a system broadly meeting British needs is already in production elsewhere.

Let us now consider the choices open in the event of all three of these answers.

In the event of the first course, the choices are —

☐ to fund a development programme in the United Kingdom (assuming that Britain has the technological capability).

☐ to fund a development programme overseas (on the assumption that a foreign enterprise will be more capable). This is quite rare but Defence Minister Younger has said that Britain spends about £200 million a year on R&D undertaken in the United States.[4]

☐ to search for foreign partners considering a similar requirement so that a collaborative programme can be set up.

☐ to decide that the requirement should be set aside given other higher priority claims on the defence budget.

In the event of the second possibility the choices are

☐ to commit the United Kingdom to buying the foreign system when it reaches the production stage. This is essentially what has been done by Britain with the Trident system.

☐ to set up a parallel British development programme to develop a national system. This is what happened with the British national commitment in 1977 to go ahead with the AEW Nimrod project.

☐ to link foreign and British efforts in a collaborative programme, as occurred, for example, with what has become the United Kingdom-Italy Tonal helicopter project;

☐ to decide that the requirement should be set aside given other higher priority claims on the defence budget.

In the event of the third course, the choices are

☐ to buy the foreign system already in production off-the-shelf or to arrange manufacture in Britain under licence. This is broadly what the British did with regard to MLRS Phase 1; or

☐ to set up a separate British development and production programme; or

☐ to decide that the requirement should be set aside, given other higher priority claims on the defence budget.

In some cases, because several states make weapons within NATO, it is possible that more than one answer will be received. In particular one system might be in production elsewhere while something similar elsewhere again might only be in development. There would thus be the possibility either of establishing a collaborative development programme with one country or making a straight purchase from another. Some Americans have said that the NH-90 helicopter programme will produce a system largely similar in capacity to the extant Sikorsky Black Hawk, although the European states involved deny this vigorously. In general, NATO states do not readily admit to developing something themselves which is already available elsewhere. They stress instead the unique qualities of their own system.

This short chapter has had two roles: first to describe the general shape of procurement policy and second to emphasise that an intention simply to procure from the best 'value for money' offer is not simply executed in a British defence context. An invitation to tender can yield offers of schemes at various stages of development which contain different levels of technological and cost uncertainty. Bids from foreign companies, or from the British subsidiaries of foreign companies, will probably involve the United Kingdom Government funding their development work. Politically there is a difference between buying a developed product from abroad and paying for a specific product to be developed. Given technological, political and economic uncertainty, deciding what represents best value for money is inevitably a subjective, judgemental process, depending much on the decision-maker's faith in the different sorts of commitment which are offered.

5

UK Procurement Policy 1979-87

At the best of times, the procurement of military equipment in the United Kingdom has to be taken very seriously. The Ministry of Defence spends over £8,000 million a year on equipment and, as with any cause for which every British citizen is paying an annual average subscription of around £160, the taxpayer is entitled to reassurance that the money is being carefully spent.

However, despite the odd shock about the poor management of individual projects, what has made the management of British procurement a really central issue in the last decade is that there has not been enough money to provide the Armed Services with the men and equipment they feel they need. There has not been enough money to keep everyone in the defence sector in work, let alone keep them happy. However, the Government, with some outside support, has put better management of equipment spending at the centre of its strategy of holding down costs so that Britain's current range of conventional and nuclear roles can be maintained. The management of procurement has thus assumed a pivotal position with regard to the shape of British defence policy as a whole.

Central to concerns about funding shortages are the rising costs associated with equipment. These are much discussed and are a problem for most states. Rising equipment costs represent a universal rather than a peculiarly British disease.[1] They occur in two forms. First there are anticipated cost increases between one generation of equipment and the next because successor generations tend to be more complex. Most items of military equipment are made in comparatively small numbers compared with many technological consumer goods in the civil economy and, while the real cost of some civil goods, such as colour televisions and word processors, has dropped considerably over recent years, the reverse has tended to happen with military equipment.

Second, defence equipment often ends up costing considerably more to develop and produce than had been expected. This can be for a variety of reasons. The price of important raw materials such as titanium and bauxite can go up suddenly, armaments firms may have to provide higher than average wage increases to hold on to their labour, technical problems in development can prove harder to solve that was foreseen, (which can leave sections of development teams idle while their colleagues take extra time to

70

TABLE 5.1
The Effect of Increasing Fixed Costs on Procurement

Assumed	Past Generation System	Next Generation System
Real Funds Available	£200m	£200m
Fixed Costs	£50m	£100m
Unit Production Cost	£2m	£4m
Numbers to be Procured	75	25

solve particular difficulties), items can prove harder and slower to manufacture than had been thought and project costs can increase because of bad management.[2] Unexpected cost increases in American defence equipment are often associated with the full development and production phases.[3]

A major source of anticipated and unanticipated cost increases are rising research, development and other fixed costs associated with preparing an item for production. Increasing fixed costs make it particularly important for a long production run to be achieved since ideally they should be spread thinly over a large number of units. Extended production also opens up possibilities for economies of scale (associated with a combination of more capital-intensive production techniques and learning) to be achieved. However, if the national market is only small, fixed costs have to be spread over few units and the overall cost increases. Table 5.1, assuming that real funds available in the defence budget remain constant from one generation system to the next, shows the impact of these considerations even when no allowance is made for economies of scale in production.

Because of planned and unanticipated cost increases, the British Government has accepted that many of the systems it is procuring and will procure are much more expensive than their immediate predecessors. The 1981 *Statement on the Defence Estimates* SDE contained a diagram showing how costs had increased in real terms between generations of selected systems.[4] Thus the Type 22 frigate cost three times as much as a Leander, the GR1 Harrier cost four times as much as a Hawker Hunter, the Lynx Mk.2 helicopter cost 2.5 times as much as a Wasp while the Warrior MCV-80 cost 3.5 times as much as the FV432 armoured personnel carrier. Similar data were presented to the House of Commons Defence Committee (HCDC) at the end of 1984.[5] All together, it has become conventional wisdom in Britain, indeed throughout NATO, that since 1945 defence equipment has tended to increase in price at a rate between 5 and 10 per cent above the rate of inflation in the economy as a whole. The Vredeling Report for the IEPG noted that 'the real cost growth from generation to generation of equipment can be more than 5 per cent each year'.[6]

The prospects for improvement — the pessimists

Responses to this situation vary and, to understand the nature and significance of British defence procurement policy, it is useful to present arguments in the form of a debate between two camps — the pessimists and the optimists. The pessimists feel that, if the government sticks to its defence spending plans, there will be a widening gap between funds available and the funds needed to maintain the current pattern of operating and capital expenditure. In an analysis in 1984, David Greenwood forecast that the 'funding gap' for defence would amount to £4,700 million by 1988/89. Included in his assumptions was that inflation in defence would continue to rise at its 'historic' rate of about one percentage point above inflation in the economy as a whole.[7] In early 1987 Mr Greenwood's belief was that the gap would be £5,000 million by 1990/91.[8]

Malcolm Chalmers, in a 1986 study, rejected the view that inflation in defence is inevitably higher than in the wider economy, but he argued that his anticipated real fall in the defence budget by 1989/90 of 6 per cent would all have to be borne by capital spending and that by the end of the decade the equipment budget would have declined by about £1,000 million (or 13 per cent compared with 1984/85).[9]

In broad terms the Labour Party tended to concur, feeling that Britain would be increasingly unable to fund its existing range of defence commitments. The particular villain for some analysts was the Trident nuclear programme. The Labour Party in 1986, following Chalmers' analysis, felt that the combined impact of Trident and planned budget cuts by the end of the decade would be to cut non-nuclear equipment spending by around 20 per cent.[10] Chalmers felt that, by then, the MoD would be having major difficulty in financing all its major programmes.

The pessimists argue that Britain needs to review fundamental elements in its defence policy in order to cut costs. 'No matter what happens at the next election we will end up with a major defence review' said David Greenwood.[11] For the Labour Party, had it won in 1987, cancelling Trident would have been a priority and a measure which would have liberated considerable funding for conventional forces. Others put at least equal emphasis on the need to cut back the Royal Navy and Britain's out-of-area capabilities. General Sir Frank Kitson, on the other hand, has said that the British Army of the Rhine (BAOR) should be redeployed with the British maintaining ground force support on the European mainland only in northern Europe, where it would need less armour.[12]

The prospects for improvement — the optimists

Funding gap problems of dimensions sufficient to force such a major reconsideration of British defence policy are not accepted, certainly not publicly, by the British Government who take the optimistic view. Some outside analysts concur and the HCDC is at least not yet ready to disagree completely, although on balance it comes down rather more on the side of the pessimists.

The British Ministry of Defence under Michael Heseltine and George Younger introduced a major campaign to improve procurement practices and so cut costs. An industrialist, Peter Levene, was appointed to head MoD procurement and to introduce appropriate reforms, many of them centering on making the Procurement Executive 'more commercially-minded' and making competition play a greater role in bringing down prices. It was not the view of government that these reforms would be a panacea. Indeed it was accepted that 'hard decisions' on priorities would still be necessary. In 1986 Defence Minister George Younger told the House of Commons that the 1985/86 budget restrictions meant that the planned Type 2048 towed array sonar had had to be abandoned, that funding for the LAW anti-tank mine had been cut and that a reduced number of GR5 Harriers might have to be procured. He also looked ahead to future likely slowdowns and cancellations at the level of individual systems.[13] But he did not see the need for any major rethink on the basic shape of defence policy.[14]

At the heart of the Government's strategy was an aim to flatten or even reverse the established curve which shows the trend towards increasing equipment costs. Clearly there are other elements in the Government's cost saving schemes. There has been an effort to make the operations of the services more efficient so that, for instance, sailors are shore-based for a smaller proportion of their time and more training takes place in operational ships. There has been an effort to coordinate training better among the three Services. Staff throughout the official defence community (civilian and military) are being made subject to responsibility budgets to encourage them to use money with optimum care. The individual service staffs have been weakened and emphasis placed on coordinated central staffing with more people doing what are popularly known as 'purple' jobs in Whitehall.[15] General Kitson would go much further down this road, not just in the interest of saving money.[16] But procurement remains the area in which most money can be saved, because it is there that so much money is spent.

In this field the Government has sought to introduce a major range of measures whose emphasis is on changing the means by which weapons are bought rather than explicitly on buying from foreign sources.[17] The overall aim centres around the appealing but rather elusive, even subjective, concept of 'value for money'. In applying value for money policy, according to MoD documentation, officials are expected to integrate consideration of over 50 relevant factors concerning the short, medium and long term. The main headings under which the factors are listed are Status of the Firms Involved, Equipment Offered, Immediate Cost of Acquisition, Delivery, Operating Costs, Product Support, Replacement Arrangements, and 'Strategic and

Structural'. How in practice these factors can be integrated is a matter for debate.

Introduction of competition

The MoD has introduced more widespread competition into procurement, wherever possible getting bids from several companies for a contract. The proportion of contracts being awarded on the basis of competition has been considerably increased by value and by number. In 1985–86 cost-plus contracts represented only 8–9 per cent of those awarded by MoD. Formal competitive action involving tendering by two or more companies accounted for 39 per cent of contracts. For 25 per cent there were elements of competition and 27 per cent were of the incentive type, with government and industry sharing the benefits of any performance below a ceiling price.

Thus cost-plus contracts, traditionally used on a widespread scale by MoD, have been rejected and are being used only where there is no alternative. This should mean that they are used only for risky and uncertain early development work. Where possible, existing cost-plus contracts have been renegotiated but many remain in operation and will do so for years to come. The preferred substitute is for fixed-price contracts agreed after competition.

Privatisation

In part to reinforce the competitive contracting policy, and in part because of the Government's overall faith in private enterprise, several state-owned defence enterprises were privatised on the grounds that this will bring more effective management. British Aerospace, the Royal Dockyards at Devonport and Rosyth, the Royal Ordnance Factories, the naval shipyards of British Shipbuilders, and Rolls-Royce are all examples of major enterprises which were privatised winning substantial defence contracts. Elements within the services, such as catering within messes, have also been reallocated to the private sector.

Selling to the MoD

More firms are being encouraged to compete for defence contracts. The government has published a document, *Selling to the MoD*, giving detailed advice on how to seek defence contracts and since 1986 has produced a fortnightly digest of its contracting intentions, the *MoD Contracts Bulletin*, so that firms can see if there is work in which they might be interested. For a range of reasons, many small firms believed that it was difficult for them to win subcontracts from the big prime contractors. In 1986 a special office, the Small Firms Advice Division, was set up in the MoD.[18] In cases where major contracts are handed to the 'national champion' companies which are in a position of virtual monopoly within the United Kingdom, the Government is requiring the extensive use of competitive subcontracting and is committed to monitoring how far this occurs. The House of Commons Public Accounts Committee has been told that, in cases of single sources of supply, 'prime contractors were required to let subcontracts, which could be 70 per cent or more of the value of the main contract, by competition'.[19] However, the national champions, such as Rolls-Royce and BAe, will not have to change their subcontracting patterns substantially as a result of these measures. BAe starts from the position that only about 30 per cent of a modern aircraft's cost is derived from the production of the fuselage and in the case of Rolls-Royce

> about 30 per cent by value of the Supply Group's expenditure is incurred on in-house manufacture. The remaining 70 per cent is incurred in external purchases including raw materials, forgings, castings and finished parts .... The company's policy is generally to manufacture only those components which have high added-value or whose performance is critical to the overall performance of an aero-engine.[20]

BAe and Rolls-Royce are, however, among the major firms which have made presentations at the Society of British Aerospace Companies which were designed to help firms interested in becoming subcontractors to bid effectively.

The Conservative Government has sought to widen the DIB to involve more small firms 'with their qualities of enterprise and willingness to innovate' on the grounds that this would make it easier for the MoD to implement its policy of maximising competition in defence contracting.[21] Thus equipment price increases would be kept down. In addition to the publication of the brochure already referred to above designed to assist firms who wanted to sell to the MoD the government has contributed to 'Meet the Buyer' seminars organised by bodies such as Chambers of Commerce.[22]

More exploitable equipment

Indirectly related to competition, the Government has said that where possible simpler rather than over-complex equipment should be specified. This should have the effect of meeting another stated government preference, that of making equipment which will be successfully competitive in external markets, particularly in the Third World. The Government has taken on board, though not yet clearly acted on, the suggestion that bidders should be encouraged, not just to give a price for the stated requirement, but also to show savings from developing 'something less ambitious but more easily attainable'. Ferranti moved ahead on this by offering its Blue Vixen radar being developed for the Harrier as a candidate for the EFA radar. According to one American study, 'achievement of the last few degrees of performance tends to raise costs by 30-50 per cent and Sir Frank Cooper has observed that the last 10 per cent of performance generates 30 per cent of the costs and a higher percentage of the problems.[23]

Use of commercially available equipment

Still in connection with simplicity, in 1982 the Government made an appeal for the Armed Forces, wherever possible, to use equipment which was already being manufactured for civil purposes. Requiring a militarised version of a piece of equipment already performing a parallel civil function was rejected, not on grounds of cost, but on grounds of availability during wartime.

> It would not be open to us to expand industrial capacity dramatically to meet defence needs during an increase in tension; the complexity of modern manufacturing processes and the sophistication of the material to be used militate against this.[24]

This significant statement raises several questions. If expanded production of military goods will not be possible, why will expanded production of civil goods such as Land Rovers and word processors be of significance? Does the government mean that the surge capacity of a DIB, the capacity to increase supplies at times of tension or war is of no relevance to the United Kingdom? Alternatively, should Britain look for stocks of items which are hard to manufacture, such as combat aircraft and their spares, to carry it through a war, while assuming that it will be possible to increase production of straightforward items such as many sorts of ammunition, hand guns and so on? There is no clear government position on these issues, indeed the 1982 Government reference to the value of an emergency production capability is an isolated one.

In reality it is hard to perceive that the emphasis on simpler, more exportable equipment has yet had much effect and the capacity of the Defence Export Services Organization to influence requirements remains small. Moreover, the HCDC in its 1987 report on the Falklands Conflict warns particularly against the deployment of simpler but essentially under-equipped warships.[25]

The Cardinal Points scheme

The MoD has sought to improve the design and running of projects, by introducing, for instance, a Cardinal Points Requirement scheme which gives only the essential performance parameters required from a system. This contrasts with earlier practice and extant American practice of building many design and other detailed features into a requirement. Under the new arrangement, industry should have far more scope to design equipment to do a specific job using as many or as few innovatory principles as it thinks necessary. Generally, the Government believes that involving industry more at the early stage of a project will improve procurement performance. A major change of emphasis occurred in warship design where formal predominant responsibility was transferred from the Navy's warship department at Bath to industry.

Learning from the past

Other management and procurement changes included direct lessons from the Nimrod experience, such as abandoning progress payments being made on a time schedule and linking them instead to technical progress achieved. On national and collaborative projects, Britain became ready to commit itself to the full development stage only when a project was defined in detail and fully explored in technological terms, so that the risks of cost overruns should be minimised. Such overruns traditionally stemmed from clarifying and changing requirements once development had begun and the difficulty of overcoming unexpected technological barriers. However, it seemed that the relevant decision-making body, the MoD's Equipment Policy Committee, had a poor record of judging technological risks and feasibility and it was suggested by an internal MoD report, publicised in 1988, that further decision-making structure changes were needed. These included giving individual project managers more responsibility and linking them directly to the Controller level. This would involve omitting the four intermediate levels currently in existence.[26]

Better information systems are being introduced to facilitate MoD supervision of the progress of all projects by the Procurement Executive Management Board. Not least because of past experiences with torpedoes and the AEW Nimrod, the MoD is concentrating on acting as a customer rather than on taking responsibility for a project's development, and is emphasising the need for a single industrial prime contractor for projects. Changing specifications while a project is under development is being discouraged and, within the PE, contracts staff have been made directly responsible to project managers. Measures have been introduced to ensure that fixed-cost contracts are drafted so as to be legally watertight. The Government is experimenting according to the product both with placing large orders (so that a company can justify investments in productivity) and with placing limited orders so that periodic competitions can be held to keep a manufacturer trying to hold down costs. (Large orders tend to be referred to as batches and are justified in similar terms as multi-year procurement projects in the United States. Smaller orders, on the other hand, are often described as 'tranches'). There have also been efforts on occasions to hold separate competitions for the development and production phases.

Major managerial changes

Early in 1988, as evidence grew about the MoD being induced to sign equipment contracts which gave GEC-Marconi in particular a chance to earn high profits, Peter Levene reportedly proposed major managerial changes. These would involve bringing in more long-term and better paid project managers, instead of relying upon short-term appointments, particularly of Service staff. It is at least arguable that, in the 1980–87 period, the MoD appeared rather more ready to subject industry to radical change in terms of competition policy, than it was to shake up the Procurement Executive, and in particular to disturb the role of military officers in running projects.

The Government has indicated increased reluctance to develop a system in the United Kingdom if an equivalent is already available from a suitable external supplier. However, it is often looking for licensed production in Britain of such major items. The potential gains from implementing these and other changes have on occasions been asserted to be substantial. In introducing the emphasis on competition, Michael Heseltine said that he felt that savings could amount to 10 per cent of procurement spending. The median savings from competition claimed by the MoD for the six cases it cited in the Statement on the Defence Estimates of 1984, 1985 and 1986 came to 20 per cent.[28] By 1986, however, the MoD was being rather more modest and accepting that it was, in fact, rather difficult to measure precisely the gains from competition since so much depended on the estimate made at the beginning of a project. A large 'saving' could be made by making a high initial cost estimate and subtracting from it the cost of the lowest bid eventually being made. More realistic initial costings reduced the volume of 'savings'. Nevertheless, the Ministry clearly feels that it has begun to make savings on procurement, and there is no reason to doubt that some equipment is being bought for considerably less than it would have been under older arrangements. Peter Levene said in 1986 that there had been cases of 30 per cent savings where additional purchases of equipment in service had been made through competition. He told the HCDC that he still hoped to achieve his target of saving 10 per cent of the procurement budget within five years although he doubted that he would be able to prove it.[29] He was reported in May 1987 as hoping to save 10 per cent on buying spares through the implementation of tighter procedures. The 1987 Defence White Paper reported further savings from competition, varying among the individual projects cited from 16 per cent to 50 per cent.[30]

In the late 1980s waste remained present in procurement and savings were therefore available, at least in principle. The House of Commons Public Accounts Committee (PAC), building on the work of the National Audit Office, looked at 12 major projects where the average cost overrun, from the base at the start of full development, had been 47 per cent, involving £938 million. For all projects which had begun full development between 1979 and 1985, it found that the average cost overrun to date was 28 per cent.[31] The Committee did not assess the degree to which it felt the total expenditure could have been avoided but it was critical of traditional MoD management practices and highly critical in particular of the running of the Nimrod project. Earlier in 1986 it had suggested additional steps for improved procurement although it recognised that advances had been made.[32] In 1988, further authoritative assertions of waste emerged, although many cases related to the era before the Levene regime applied.[33]

Alongside competition, the other pillar of the Government's procurement strategy was collaboration, particularly but not exclusively with European states. Broadly defined, this not only included joint development of projects but also the idea of *'contre achats'* where two countries agree to buy already-developed defence equipment from each other. In the mid-to-late 1980s, Britain bought the Goalkeeper short-range ship defence system and sold Spey marine engines to the Netherlands. In October 1986, France bought a British naval navigation radar and Britain purchased a French mine clearing system. In 1987 Britain and France instituted a series of bilateral conferences designed to identify opportunities for modest off-the-shelf purchases from each other.

Britain has long practised collaborative development and production but traditionally it has done so with some reluctance. Then, especially under Michael Heseltine, the Ministry of Defence became a public enthusiast for collaboration. This is reflected in political and bureaucratic terms as well as in actual projects with which Britain is involved. Ministers spoke regularly of the need for collaboration and MoD civil and military staff were actively encouraged to seek out collaborative solutions to equipment problems. Reflecting this, the government is involved in a series of projects including the EFA, the Trigat missiles, ASRAAM and AMRAAM, and the Tonal and the EH101 helicopters. It is also a participant in many of the projects being arranged with the United States under the Nunn-Quayle amendments to promote transatlantic armaments collaboration.[34]

In principle the great economic advantages of collaborative projects are that they enable fixed costs to be spread over more units of production and production itself can be arranged in a more effective way because more units are to be made. Historically, savings have often been difficult to calculate. Insofar as they have proved identifiable, they have sometimes appeared less than might have been anticipated. Collaboration, however, does not stand still and, although many remain sceptical, it is reasonable to believe that the management of collaborative projects will continue to improve with experience. It can be claimed that Tornado was at least as well managed as many national defence projects. Ian Mackintosh has observed that, 'while all budget breaches are to be deplored, Panavia and its main contractors have clearly done a better job in this respect than many earlier military development programmes of lesser size and complexity, including several which were not burdened with trans-frontier problems of liaison and administration'.[35] In the civil field Airbus Industrie has shown that collaboration is compatible with commercial success.

The relationship of competition and collaboration is not always clear. As things stand at present, on many collaborative projects there is virtually only one possible British leader — Westland on helicopters, British Aerospace on combat aircraft and missiles, Rolls-Royce on jet engines and so on. Moreover, the *juste retour* principle, coupled with the allocation of subsystems to participating states, means that countries are guaranteed chunks of work. The scope for competition in a project is thus reduced. As noted in the previous section, in the case of the radar for the EFA, there are two competing consortia for the contract, with Ferranti and GEC as rivals in the United Kingdom, but with AEG as the only German possible participant in either grouping. In general, competition is possible to arrange within collaboration, but it is sometimes difficult and it often involves subcontractors as opposed to main contractors. On occasions, however, it is possible to proceed through competing consortia, as is the case with MLRS Phase 3.

As noted, the calculation of savings from competition is not easy. It is even more difficult with collaboration, with the absence of any real equivalent to a collaborative project rendering problematic any methodology for calculating savings. There is, of necessity, reliance on estimates from groups which may have vested interests. Bearing this in mind, in the case of the France Rafale, French sources estimate that its cost could be reduced by between 10 and 20 per cent if it could become a collaborative effort. However, unless substantive foreign sales are made, it could prove to be as much as 50 per cent more expensive than the EFA in the light of figures given by the French MoD to the parliament.[36]

The Government's support for collaboration, particularly within Europe, extends beyond the military sphere across the spectrum of high technology. The British Government participated over the range of European Community schemes including Esprit, Race and Brite and it supported the French Eureka initiative. However, in 1987 it was markedly more reluctant than many of its European partners to provide funding for international civil collaboration and the consequence was that the Community's five-year framework proposals had to be cutback. Lack of government support for British participation in collaborative space projects led to the resignation of the Director of the British National Space Centre, Roy Gibson in August 1987.

Currently, collaborative projects account for about 15 per cent of British defence equipment spending. About 80 per cent is devoted to national projects and 5 per cent to foreign purchases. Overall, an increased role for collaboration in relation to national projects should help to hold down costs. As a rough calculation, if the share of collaborative projects can be increased to 50 per cent, as Sir David Perry, the MoD official in charge of collaboration, has indicated could occur, and if the cost advantages of collaboration compared with a national effort are between 10 and 20 per cent, then the savings from the additional collaboration should amount to between 3.5 and 7.0 per cent of the equipment budget.[37]

However the government has also accepted that work done in the military sector should and could contribute to the economy as a whole. To increase the civil application of findings from military R&D, the MoD considered ways of making sure that civil opportunities were identified and exploited. It promoted the establishment of a new company, Defence Technology Enterprises (DTE), to identify research output from the Government's R&D centres which is of interest to civil industry and to promote the diffusion of that research. By March 1986 it was said to have identified 200 technical ideas which looked commercially promising and one technique, a computer program called Malpas, which checks complex software, had been transfered to the civil sector. A year later, about 25 ideas had gained small amounts of financial backing from companies and clearly DTE made real but not dramatic initial progress. In early 1988 the Government announced that the facilities and staff at the RDEs would be made available on a commercial basis to private industry and in particular to small firms trying to get started with research and development.[38]

The SDE in 1987 emphasised the growing links between the research establishments and the civil sector in collaborative activities and said that

> we shall be encouraging our suppliers to think more broadly about the relationship between their military and civil markets, and we shall be very willing to join them in identifying changes to our defence procurement processes, consistent with our defence requirements and the achievement of value for money, that would make it easier for them to achieve success in the latter as well as the former.[39]

While the sentiment is clear, the cynical observer will note that the reference to 'defence requirements' and 'value for money' actually mean that the MoD is not committed in the statement to doing anything.

Preliminary evaluation and the limits of competition

What emerges from the above is a straight disagreement about what can be achieved. On the one hand were those who believed that the rate of increase in procurement costs could not be reduced significantly. Money, even hundreds of millions of pounds, may be saved but it would prove insufficient. Some authors did not expect procurement policy changes to have much effect unless foreign (explicitly or implicitly American) companies were allowed to compete freely for British orders.[40] On the other were those who believed that equipment cost increases could be brought down to the extent that no major element in British defence policy needed to be questioned.

Historically, there is nothing new about increased equipment costs generating budgetary pressures and the pessimists can point to these increases as one of the factors contributing to the series of defence reviews which have brought about a steady concentration of the British defence effort, away from a global and towards a European emphasis. The optimists take comfort in the fact that Britain has managed to adapt incrementally to new pressures and that industries have survived major changes in procurement such as the cancellations of the TSR2 and the AFVG aircraft. There is no doubt that the post-1979 increases in defence spending meant that many difficult issues did not have to be faced and the optimists may hope that something similar will come along again before funding shortages get too bad.

One of Gavin Kennedy's arguments is that defence spending will in fact be increased in real terms because governments will, in the end, prefer to keep it at a constant percentage of gross domestic product. With GDP rising at between 2 and 3 per cent a year, he calculates that 'economic growth will force the government to raise real defence spending in order to maintain a constant D/GDP ratio. The fund gap is exorcised'.[41] The force of this argument is not enhanced by Britain's being way out in front of any other major European state in terms of the percentage of its national income it allocates to defence. The argument would lose much of its weight (about £4 billion of defence spending in current terms) if government allowed the D/GDP ratio to fall to a floor of 4 per cent. Moreover, there is no major British political party which feels that defence spending should be increased and higher defence expenditures are not favoured in opinion polls.

A potentially significant factor offering support for the optimists is the recent decline in the relative price effect (RPE) with regard to defence equipment. The RPE is the difference between the rate of inflation in the defence equipment sector and the rate in the economy as a whole. In 1985/86 the rate was in fact negative, that is defence equipment inflation was less than inflation in general. Should this continue (and such a negative rate has occurred only three times in 11 years), it would be a favourable development for government policy.[42] The shape of the curve of future needed resources would change drastically. MoD evidence does not make clear the extent to which the reduced RPE somehow reflects procurement policy and the extent to which it just reflects inflation in the economy as a whole. A rather different but nevertheless relevant point for those who feel a budgetary crunch can be avoided is that officials have noted that defence expenditure on specific projects often proceeds rather more slowly than had been anticipated.[43] With more collaboration possible, this trend could be accentuated.

Looking forward, the Government's commitment to greater efficiency is unlikely to be questioned in principle and the PAC has made clear that there are improvements to be made. But what are the constraints on what can be achieved by the government's present line on competition in particular?

An initial consideration is that the government is currently stressing that its competition policy is a means of improving the process of industry, in how well it performs. Peter Levene, speaking at the Royal United Services Institute for Defence Studies (RUSI) in March 1987, was keen to point out the cases when application of competition had stimulated companies into more effective performance and better sales.[44] The MoD asserts that there is no reason to suppose that increased competition should have an adverse effect on the volume of MoD business or employment in British defence industries, providing they can continue to offer the right products at the right prices.

Hence improvements in international competitiveness should offer opportunities for increased overseas orders and consequent increases in employment.

There is something, perhaps much, to this argument. The competition and value for money ethos which the Conservatives brought in, significantly coupled with a readiness to put a ceiling on spending, did have an effect on industrial attitudes and performance. Industrialists and financiers in the late 1980s saw defence as a shrinking market in which no one had a birthright to a contract. In the five years after 1983 the defence industry undoubtedly received a short, sharp shock which stimulated performance. Redundancies were announced, new manufacturing facilities introduced, greater readiness shown to enter civil markets and more export success registered.

In the longer term, however, competition is bound also to have an impact on the structure of industry, driving out the less successful companies in different sectors. There has long been emphasis on competition in American defence procurement but there is awareness there that, for competition to remain possible, at least two firms in a field must be regular winners. In an era when higher costs mean that fewer systems are being developed and are replaced at longer intervals, maintaining a range of firms becomes difficult. The number of military airframe companies in the United States is still declining and the surviving firms are having to collaborate with each other. In areas where there is ease of entry, the disappearance of losers is not important because new firms can replace those pushed out. But ease of entry is not the case in many defence areas where the products involve advanced and often specialised technologies which are integrated by established design teams. The Government would like to have introduced a competitor to Marconi Underwater Systems (GEC) for torpedo manufacture. Given that GEC subcontracts 80 per cent of Stingray production, this might be feasible, but it would be more difficult to find an alternative company to develop torpedos. BAe is the obvious candidate, although it has had little direct experience of what are essentially underwater terminally-guided missiles. When government establishments were in charge of torpedo development, they had a long record of delays and cost overruns. Had Shorts not been awarded the Starstreak contract, it is doubtful if the firm could have remained in the ground-to-air missile business except, perhaps, as a subcontractor. Once out, it would not easily have been able to get back in at some future date. In the United Kingdom and other major armaments producing states, ease of entry for new firms is made more difficult by the weighting that is often given in awarding contracts to whether a company has a solid reputation for delivering relevant defence goods to cost and on time. Another potential barrier to entry is that the MoD looks to companies to have sufficient capital backing to be able to absorb losses should fixed price contracts go wrong.[45] A 1988 report digesting the views of a senior industrialist said that

Fixed price contracting puts a premium on getting the technology decisions and specifications absolutely right perhaps five or six years before the equipment enters service and, coupled with the trend towards extracting more R&D money upfront from industry itself, favours the bigger companies. In the long term there will be an inevitable reduction in the number of equipment and systems companies themselves, and the bigger firms will find it easier to survive than the smaller ones.[46]

Currently the government feels that in many areas there are several potential producers within the United Kingdom and thus this is scope for competition. Data presented earlier indicates that this is broadly valid but the government has acknowledged that competition policy cannot be applied with absolute strictness. This was apparent in the award of parallel two AOR ship contracts to Harland & Wolff and Swan Hunter, although the Government hinted strongly that it obtained the best competitive price for both.[47] A similar thing occurred with the award of separate Type 22 frigate contracts to Cammell Laird and Swan Hunter, although on that occasion there was an extra cost of £7 million.[48] In the United States, where there is considerable formal emphasis on competition, it is apparent that contracts get spread around to keep a range of companies in operation in an area. The division of cruise missile responsibilities between General Dynamics and Boeing is a case in point. An evaluation of the United States policy on fighter engines of having Pratt & Whitney and GE compete against each other is significant: 'this has resulted in some notable competitions, and better performance and reliability guarantees than the Air Force has ever enjoyed. The arrangement, while painful for the competitors, ultimately benefits both since it guarantees their survival'.[49]

Moreover American industry argues that, when competition and cost-cutting policies are pursued with persistent vigour, the effect over time is to damage the national DIB and thus security: militarily important, innovatory projects become unattractive because of the risks and firms are driven out of the defence sector.[50] British industry is far from this point and in the past the MoD has been too optimistic about many technological risks. Yet Levene overtly acknowledged this broad area of concern and it is worth quoting his views when asked about procurement decisions possibly endangering future industrial capacity or expertise.

> We also work very closely with the DTI to take their views on this sort of thing and we have meetings with DTI to discuss both the general and the specific. It is very important for us; it is not very clever if we adopt a policy which knocks everybody out of the business and we end up with only one firm to chose from in any one area. Of course we look at that. Our prime aim is to get value for money but we must not overlook the points you have mentioned.[51]

In jet engines, combat airframes, tanks, nuclear submarines, and a few aircraft subsystems, including ejector seats, there is very limited scope for competition within the United Kingdom. Over the longer term, as the technological content of weapons increases, there may well be more fields in which a state such as the United Kingdom will be able to sustain only a single producer, if that. In the NATO Europe region it might be appropriate to have only a couple of companies. The best current example is the jet engine sector where General Electric, Pratt & Whitney, Rolls-Royce and perhaps Snecma are the only companies in the world with a capacity to develop major military and civil engines alone. However, even the largest three are driven increasingly to collaborate among themselves and with others to form still bigger entities to handle individual projects.

Effective competition policy needs careful implementation and regular review. Not to be overlooked are trained personnel necessary to make a policy such as that of the present government work fully. More competition requires qualified civil servants able to assess more bids. Some companies are tending to put in three bids in response to requests for proposals, one of which does not quite meet the requirement but offers a cheap price, one which meets the requirement, and one which offers more than was asked for but at a slightly higher cost. The MoD currently does not have a surfeit of qualified engineers and financial experts and the RDEs are being reduced in scale. If there is excessive delay before decisions are reached, prices offered can become dated. Industry itself can and does help with the assessment of technological problems and possibilities but there are limits to which industry can be expected to judge in its own case, and to which one firm will be happy to be monitored by a possible competitor. As noted earlier, Government is having to turn more to specialist systems houses for help in assessing offers.

One element in the new approach to procurement is the effort to award separate contracts on occasions for development and production. Moreover, companies are sometimes being given awards for only a tranche of production so that a competition can be held for the next tranche. There can be specific problems attached to trying to have these separate competitions. Logically, government should and does own technological knowledge which it has paid for with its own development money. But, as is known from American experience, there can be major problems attached to trying to discern, which developments in a particular system were funded by the government, which were funded by company R&D funds, and which were possible only because the company brought its own major background knowledge to a project. Naturally, the government feels that hard bargaining can produce a fair deal in this field.[52] However, companies are not readily going to give away their own intellectual property. Participation in two stages of competition is least appealing to smaller companies and to subsystem and components suppliers which are mainly interested in production only.

Some industrialists perceive that elements in the Services and MoD might be less enthusiastic than their ministers about the reduced role being sought for cost-plus contracts. In the past the ministry-industry relationship has been marked by an informality which, while having disadvantages, meant that both sides could show flexibility. Under the new regime, however, companies accused of falling down on fixed price contracts might well resort to the law and an enforceable fixed-price contract requires that very clear terms are set for its completion. Certainly the MoD will have to strengthen its legal support, as industry is doing, to make sure that suitably precise contracts can be drawn up. For complex systems, where the Forces themselves may be uncertain about their precise requirement, this may not be easy. Fixed price contracts will also make it harder to amend a contract once it has begun whereas under the present system, if cost-plus is being used, changes can be brought in easily on an informal basis.

Lastly there is the consideration of how 'value for money' is being interpreted in practice. The publicised guidelines of 1983 allow for the decision-maker to be guided by a host of considerations, including, reliability, the life-cycle costs of equipment and implicitly but not explicitly the health of the United Kingdom DIB. However, industrialists are inclined to feel that the initial acquisition price tends to emerge as the single most important factor (although the MoD's own Guidelines say it should not). It is the most tangible element and decisions about equipment tend to be made by accountants rather than engineers, the only ones who can judge reliability and life cycle costs. Peter Levene has hinted that life cycle costs, despite their importance, began to be addressed seriously only from around 1987.[53] Moreover, the Treasury is seen as having an important voice and its concern is with holding down spending this year rather than long-term savings. Thus, although the decision-maker can refer to 50 or so considerations in principle, cheapest acquisition price tends to be the only important one. A company perception that this is the case can lead it to neglect reliability and life cycle costs in order to keep down its price.

Looking to the future

Managing defence procurement in the United Kingdom presents major problems since the funds available will be relatively fixed (unless Gavin Kennedy is proved right) while the historical tendency is for costs to rise. In looking to collaboration, competition and associated measures such as privatisation and reforms within the MoD to ease the budgetary pressures, the government is seeking to hit a target which other allied countries have found elusive.

Nevertheless, given the sought after savings from improved procurement techniques and collaboration which the government feels are possible, it is understandable why the MoD feels that it might avoid a wider defence review in the immediate future. Much depends also on other factors, including the rates of increase in servicemen's pay which are needed and on the extent to which further 'salami slicing' on operations and training can be introduced without provoking too much of a response from the Services. A continuing low price for fuel would help to keep down demands on the defence budget and the cost of Trident will be much affected by the dollar exchange rate against sterling.

However, a continuing problem remains the ratio of R&D to production spending. John Nott highlighted this as a major problem in 1981. Overall the ratio is around 1:2 and for some systems it is much less.[54] Sir Frank Cooper has said that individual projects with ratios of between 1:1.3 and 1:1.8 are not uncommon.[55] Such ratios mean that substantial fixed costs are being spread over only a limited number of units of production. It is this aspect of industrial inefficiency which is particularly problematic for Britain. Nott observed that, while high relative R&D costs are not necessarily undesirable in every case, 'despite the cautions, the present ratio remains one which, if sustained, will lead us to bankruptcy'[56].

The various elements in government declaratory policy offer the possibility of producing a ratio nearer 1:3 since increased collaboration should reduce R&D costs, and systems based on Cardinal Points Requirements or on optimum cost/sub-optimum technical performance should be simpler to develop. By actually giving export considerations a greater weight in drawing up requirements, instead of tending to gesture in this regard, the Government could again keep R&D costs under scrutiny at the same time as keeping production costs down by having longer production runs. Reducing the relative weight of R&D would also have the advantage of helping to release scientists and technologists from the military sector to the civil, a target in which the Government is interested and to which the Labour Party is committed.

With its emphasis on competition and collaboration in procurement, British procurement policy is broadly in line with the IEPG Report on improving the competitiveness of Europe's defence industries.[57] The Report's Independent Study Team consisted of distinguished Europeans, experienced in armaments development, production and procurement, and it was chaired by the former Dutch Defence Minister and European Commissioner, Mr H. Vredeling. The Report could help to shape the procurement policies of, not just the United Kingdom but West European states in general.

The Report had recommendations covering all aspects of procurement. To select just a few, it argued that national defence ministries should seek the best 'value for money' products within Europe rather than preferring and thus protecting national firms. In terms of British procurement, this means that the United Kingdom was being asked to give preference to West European firms in general rather than just British firms in particular, on the clear understanding that British industry would get reciprocal access to the markets of others. The Report did not make clear the precise processes by which barriers were to be broken down and it put the burden for arranging change within government machinery on the shoulders of defence ministers in particular. It says that the time is not yet right for pan-European defence companies to be established but argues for more collaboration between existing firms, preferably in competing international consortia. Rather than have each collaborative project incorporate the principle of *juste retour* (under which each participant state gets the value of work equal to the value of its purchase), the report suggested that projects should be bundled together and work shared out on the basis of a group of projects. This idea of inter-project compensation should mean that fewer inefficient contractors have to be selected just to give a state its appropriate work share. Balancing the books across projects to make sure that every state is equitably treated in the end, was one of the tasks proposed for a new permanent IEPG staff. The study group also recommended that the coordination of defence research should be improved so that less money is used on generating the enabling technologies which are later applied in defence systems. The IEPG was recommended to strengthen its Cooperative Technology Projects scheme. Finally, the report endorsed the need to involve Europe's Less Developed Defence Industry in defence manufacturing and suggested that work should be directed to them.

The Report's authors were anxious to suggest modest changes which had real chances of being implemented, yet they recognised that even these required a good deal of political effort and commitment, particularly from defence ministers. Not surprisingly, those familiar with the practicalities of procurement saw the importance of bureaucracies in policy implementation. Thus the Group said that 'the most essential prerequisite to any remedy is a willingness by Defence Ministers personally and actively to oversee the preparation of the required procurement policies and practices and, on a continuing basis, their implementation'. It went on

We recommend that governments agree formally to two points of principle:
a) that they are prepared to adopt a policy of competition across Europe.
b) that they will not distort the market directly or indirectly.
Governments should ensure the translation of these points of principle into action by instructing their procurement staffs accordingly.

The Report was presented to National Armaments Directors (NADs) at the beginning of 1987 and at the IEPG Ministerial it was formally welcomed. It is understood to have been read by ministers personally and reactions to it were favourable. However, no dramatic follow up action was taken and the report was passed back to the NADs for work on how it could be implemented. Particular reservations concerned the idea of setting up yet another European staff, yet there is a case that such a staff could play a useful accounting role as well as prompting governments to live up to cooperative commitments. Certainly no other European organisation staff could play such a role at present and it is hard to see how the IEPG's existing secretarial arrangements, using a few personnel in national ministries, could be adapted to many more extra tasks.

The Report, which basically called on states to move towards a West European free market in arms and to accept the consequences in terms of inter-dependence, could only be implemented with some difficulty. It meant a tricky balance of collaboration and competition and there are many problems of national resistance to be overcome. At present, governments frequently reveal their specific procurement intentions only to a restricted national group and so the potential for competition within Europe is often non-existent. The Report called for information on planned contracts to be made widely available so that any appropriate European firm can bid. As noted, Britain has led the way in this respect.

This section concludes that MoD procurement policy overall has had a favourable impact so far on the performance of British defence industries, where complacency is now rare. The Vredeling Report suggests that the route taken by the United Kingdom might be one which the rest of Western Europe might reasonably follow. However, British policy will prove harder to implement in the longer term, especially if competition reduces the number of credible domestic suppliers in many areas. Moreover, that policy is ambiguous on the role of foreign suppliers. The next two chapters will consider how procurement policy has operated specifically in the electronics sector, and the policy of the government over foreign suppliers to the MoD.

6

Defence Procurement Policy and the Electronics Sector

Whereas the previous chapter considered the nature and impact of the Government's procurement policies in general, the following pages consider their specific application in the electronics sector.

Competition

The sheer number of subsystems incorporated into a modern weapons platform means that competitive procurement affects a large number of electronics firms. This is accentuated in Britain by the range and quality of the defence electronics industry where, compared with many European countries, a relatively high degree of domestic competition is feasible. As Peter Levene observed, in electronics 'there are few areas where we can't have competition'.[1] The government has sought to encourage 'unqualified' companies to gain a foothold in the defence sector through deliberately opening up the non-operational equipment defence market. The MoD has also made it clear that where a prime contractor, or major subcontractor has an effective monopoly of domestic supply, and where an overseas purchase is ruled out on policy grounds, the 'lead' company will be expected to institute competitive tendering for subsequent subcontracts which will be 'policed' by the MoD. As Peter Levene put it, 'we want to ensure the maximum number of bidders bid on subcontracts'.[2]

Of major importance, in order to maintain or to enhance the prospects for domestic competition, the MoD has been prepared to influence the structure of the British defence electronics industry. In this context, GEC's December 1985 bid for Plessey was particularly significant. The merger would have brought about a radical change in the structure of the British electronics industry as the two companies each supplied between 25 and 30 per cent of the total British ouput of electronic capital equipment and components. The bid was based on the fact that size appeared to be associated with success in the telecommunications industry and that a merger would produce a stronger, rationalised electronics capability. GEC also argued that a single, large company would be better placed to participate in collaborative ventures, and to attack overseas markets in either civil or defence fields.[3]

However, this after represented a serious challenge to the MoD's competition policy. As we have noted earlier, together Plessey and GEC accounted for 73 per cent of the MoD's defence electronics contracts. The MoD considered that 'the existing areas of monopoly or product dominance enjoyed separately by GEC and Plessey would tend to be enlarged as the merged group strove to maintain and expand its market share further by acquisition'.[4] Although GEC argued that many of their respective defence technologies were complementary rather than competitive, the two firms had been involved in a number of important competitive awards. More importantly, the MoD asserted that the merger would pre-empt future competition in areas where this could become desirable, such as multi-function and three-dimensional radar, and sonar and mine warfare technology. In the MoD's view 'the loss of potential competition between GEC and Plessey would be a significant feature in the competition, in relation not only to cost but also to the availability of choice between technical solution'.[5]

The MoD conceded that in some overseas competitions involving GEC and Plessey, the British Government had been forced to adopt a 'neutral' position, but felt that this had not in the past prevented either company from achieving success in export markets. The MoD conceded that there could be some advantage in rationalising electronics R&D, but this would be offset by the loss of alternative technical ideas that might be generated by two independent and competitive entities. Separation would also have benefits in a collaborative context. If competition was to be encouraged in international programmes, it was important that a strong and comparable British contribution was present in any international consortium bidding for major equipment contracts. If GEC/Plessey provided the British element in one consortium, in many cases, it might be difficult to find a comparable British participant to join America or European firms in any other.[6] The MoD was backed by other firms with an interest in defence electronics, such as BAe, Racal, and Thorn who feared that the new company would dominate the market. The merger was also resisted by Plessey, who felt that it was technically and financially capable of maintaining its place in British and overseas markets.[7]

The GEC bid was only supported by the DTI and some civil telecommunications users. The DTI believed that

> The MoD already had the means to preserve the competitiveness of United Kingdom defence equipment markets, partly by demonstrating to their contractors that they were prepared to buy abroad to encourage competitive bids by the United Kingdom-owned contractors and partly by encouraging the contractors themselves to seek out the most competitive components and sub-systems throughout the world.

The MoD agreed that all things being equal, international competition could balance any loss of domestic competition, but there were political limits to the feasibility of such a policy.[8]

In the event, the Monopolies and Mergers Commission (MMC) found that the merger was undesirable on the grounds of lessening competition in defence. Although the MMC did not think any 'precise reliance' should be placed on the MoD estimate that lost competition would cost between £540 million and £840 million over 10 years, it did accept the MoD's general economic argument that the merger would lead to increased defence equipment costs. The MMC questioned the contention that bigger would in fact be better for British electronics research generally. The only advantage in a merger would be the rationalisation of System X telecommunications development.[9]

In its evidence to the MMC, the MoD appeared willing to encourage the entry of firms into new areas of business, and cited torpedos as one possibility. Since 1972, GEC has been the main British torpedo manufacturer, and the MoD suggested that it might like other British firms, including Dowty, BAe, and Plessey to compete for future torpedo contracts. However, as GEC has invested heavily in new plant and test facilities, a new entrant would probably need some help to match these capabilities. Although BAe has claimed that 'underwater defence systems' represent a 'potential growth sector,' and cited the danger of creating a monopoly, it is unlikely that either the home or the export market for torpedos could sustain two British companies. There is some danger, therefore, that an excessive commitment to competition could lead to unnecessary and commercially wasteful duplication. However, in other areas, such as the MoD's encouragement of small software houses, intervention to stimulate competition might be beneficial.

Potentially of much greater significance is the fact that a number of American firms have spotted opportunities under the new regime to enter or to increase their share of the British defence market. Some, such as Cossor, are already well-established British-based MoD contractors. But DEC, for example, is increasing its defence interests in the UK, believing that competition policy will benefit large, well resourced companies irrespective of national origins. The question is whether this marks a significant trend in British defence electronics, or is simply a selective attack based on a narrow range of specialised activity. Many of the new, or potential entrants have spotted niches in the British market, particularly in software, which may prove to be of a short duration. The long term success of Cossor, for example, in securing a British monopoly of a major systems area, is unlikely to be repeated. Increased American activity in the defence sector could, however, be backed by an expansion of United States investment generally in British electronics.[10]

Although the defence sector still retains some obstacles to the unrestricted penetration by overseas contractors, British defence electronics companies cannot afford to relax. The British civil market has already been dramatically affected by freer market conditions. Since the onset of telecommunications deregulation and BT's privatisation in 1982, a balance of payments surplus of £18 million on telecommunications equipment had become a £75 million deficit in 1985.[11] Other factors will have contributed to the decline, but a truly open market inevitably exposes national industry to the most vigorous overseas competition. This may have a salutory affect on efficiency and competitiveness, but a too chill wind can destroy rather than prune an industry. In the defence sector, the Nimrod might still be viewed as a special case, containing an element of *pour encourager les autres*, but continued pressure to reduce defence costs could increase the vulnerability of some firms to overseas competition. Over the longer term, competition policy could have profound consequences for the structure and operation of the British electronics industry.

The convergence of civil and military electronics is also working to the advantage of established but non-defence specialist companies. For example, commercial computers now have the power, reliability and security needed for military use at a much lower unit cost. Similarly, commercially available radios are competing effectively against specialist defence equipment. There is, then, a major threat to many specialised, high cost defence products, which in Britain are the province of Ferranti, GEC and Plessey. DEC's two recent British defence contracts for network computers and associated software are classic examples of commercially available systems bought for use in 'benign' military environments.[12] BT has also achieved a 'defence milestone,' in winning a contract to manage part of the GEC united communications system for the RAF. In this case, Thorn and Plessey were the losers. Gresham CAP and Dowty, in a consortium based on software expertise, overcame a Ferranti 25 year monopoly in winning a £100 million contract for a Royal Navy submarine command and control system. As *Jane's Defence Weekly* noted, 'commercial systems technology is leading (military technology), the price is often lower and the reliability can meet many defence requirements. The traditional defence computer specialist companies have a major battle to keep the giants like DEC from eating all of the defence market.'[13]

The future for the British defence electronics industry is likely to be riskier, though potentially more lucrative, than it has been in the past. The survivors should be able to achieve a higher level of profitability and could reap the rewards of emerging technology and new, electronically dependent weapons systems. Wood Mackenzie feel that, while the future of the British defence electronics industry is assured, the 'glory days are over,' and that 'value for money' procurement will lead to a rationalisation within the industry. Indeed, some City analysts believe that too much domestic competition could even affect GEC, undermining its home base, and making it less competitive in international terms.[14] The international trend is towards larger and more vertically integrated firms, able to sustain the increasing financial demands of component innovation, process engineering and systems development.[15] The pressure to rationalise national capacity will not disappear, and despite the MMC's findings in the GEC/Plessey case, the advantage of rationalisation for the wider interests of British electronics remains an open question. The plain fact is that, even together, GEC and Plessey are dwarfed by their European and World competitors.[16]

Industrialists have observed that the foundation for current competition amongst British firms is based on past generations of R&D expenditure, most of which came from the defence budget. They recognise that there has been too much 'feather-bedding' in the British defence electronics industry, and largely welcome the new environment of commercially driven procurement. However, they also expect the government equally to be aware of commercial requirements; to pay more than lip service to 'exportability' in defence specifications; to ensure that the attitudes and actions of officials are attuned to a 'hands off' role in fixed price contracts; and that government does not entirely abandon its role as a sponsor of high risk, long lead-time technological research.

To be fair, the government has never equated competition with the lowest common denominator of technology or simply a question of price. 'Value for money' procurement does have a qualitative dimension.[17] The danger is that more strategic issues, especially possible changes in the structure of industry to improve British industry's ability to take on foreign competitors, will be lost in a parochial concern to maintain domestic competition. Unless the Plessey/GEC affair is to be repeated for other prospective mergers which might threaten to reduce competition in the United Kingdom, increasing emphasis will have to be put on internationalising both production and competition.

One consequence of the MoD's opposition to the GEC/Plessey merger was that it has deterred other companies from considering similar domestic re-alignments and takeovers. However, helped by a weak dollar and the prospect of improving access to American civil and defence markets, several British firms, including GEC, Ferranti, Smiths and BAe, have bought into American electronics companies. This does often mean accepting restrictions on the transfer of technology outside the United States through the appointment of 'blind trusts' or Pentagon appointed proxies on the American subsidiary's board to filter out sensitive technical data. The MoD has claimed that its attitude towards the GEC/Plessey merger did not preclude other domestic mergers, but officials are reportedly quite happy with what is felt to be an unexpected bonus. As one procurement official observed,

if, as a result of their expansion abroad, we have a number of UK companies which regard the MoD as a customer of substantial but not overwhelming, importance, then they can afford to take a more relaxed view of MoD contracts, and so can we.[18]

There is, then, through overseas mergers and acquisitions, some prospect of both resolving any structural weaknesses in the British electronics industry and, at the same time, increasing the scope for real competition in defence equipment contracts. This may also be achieved through international collaboration between companies, but for the British electronics industry, there are a number of potential problems, especially if collaboration is with European companies, due in part and some what paradoxically, to its very strength and overall competence.

Collaboration

As the British domestic market narrows and becomes more competitive, safety for many established defence contractors will be considerably aided by links with American or European firms. Indeed, as collaboration has become the norm for major weapons platforms, British electronics companies have been obliged to find European partners in order to participate in international nal programmes. For the government, collaboration may also increase the scope of competitive procurement and subsequent savings in defence costs. However, in Britain, collaboration and competition are compatible because of the diversity of the British electronics industry. Usually, when British firms cooperate with the Europeans, they face a limited number of national partners. In Germany, the industry is dominated by AEG and in France by Thompsons.[19] Both the French and German governments have sought to strengthen their electronics industry through encouraging, or at least not opposing, mergers. These 'national champions' are put forward in collaborative programmes, and consequently, Thompson and AEG seem to be present in some guise in every collaborative project involving the French and the Germans. This is well illustrated by the competition to supply the EFA attack radar. Ferranti and GEC are members of two different consortia bidding for the contract, and one British firm will lose out in the eventual decision. As the designated German contractor for the Eurofighter radar, AEG will be a winner whichever consortium wins the competition.[20]

In the past, collaboration, certainly with European companies, has had a mixed reception from British electronics firms. The very strength and breadth of the British electronics industry compared with its continental colleagues has caused problems when the principle of *le juste retour* has been applied, and when 'downhill technology transfer' has occurred. In general, the electronics industry believes that it has come a poor third behind the British aero-engine and airframe industries in collaborative programmes. The MRCA/Tornado programme was a case in point. The Germans, using American technology, claimed a considerable (but 'fair') share of the aircraft's equipment contracts. This was much resented by some elements of the British electronics industry. There is some feeling that collaboration, 'blended with competition' has led to a situation where European firms have built up their technology through partnership with British companies and are now in a position to compete for MoD work.[21]

On the other hand, collaboration has produced commercial gains for British companies. Notwithstanding the problems associated with the Tornado, the programme has generated considerable business for the British electronics industry, and will continue to do so into the 1990s. More importantly, when the MRCA programme was started, the industry was suffering from the twin blows of the TSR2 and the AFVG cancellations. Without the MRCA, the industry, certainly the avionics sector, would have faced major difficulties. The airframe industry, often grudgingly, has had to accept that a share of a successful collaborative programme is significantly better than a full share of a cancelled domestic project. The electronics industry is now experiencing the cost and market pressures which drove the aircraft industry into collaboration during the 1960s.

Nevertheless, European collaboration, at least in its present form, still tends to cause particular problems for the British electronics industry. For example, in the case of the Eurofighter (EFA) project, some British electronics firms were concerned that their interests generally would not be given the same weight in the international negotiations as those of the prime contractors. There was also some feeling that the MoD was not as helpful as it might have been in supporting British bids for contracts. British electronics firms were especially aggrieved that, unlike their European colleagues, the British MoD did not give any credit for private venture R&D in the EAP when contracts for EFA were being considered. Eurofighter's tight timescale and possible American pressure for 'interoperability' may also imply off-the-shelf purchasing which could benefit American, or European subsidiaries of US firms. There has also been some concern that Eurofighter production contracts might be put out to competitive tender, and that developers' design rights will be severely constrained. Again, British electronics firms would be particularly affected by errosion of their property rights.[22]

Europe is not the only arena for collaborative and other forms of international partnerships. Several British firms have developed links with American industry. As the British defence market is slowly opened to foreign competition, the government favours 'teaming' — in which the overseas company reaches a preliminary agreement to cooperate with a domestic firm to compete for MoD business. For example, GEC is working with both Rockwell and Bendix in bids for two MoD contracts. The GEC/Rockwell partnership also landed a $1.85 billion order in 1987 from the United States Department of Defense (US DoD) for a secure radio system. The 1986 Plessey/Westinghouse agreement could bring Plessey an extra 5 per cent growth a year beyond 1990, and £1.5 billion of additional orders up to the end of the century. The two companies had been discussing joint ventures for a number of years. However, the decision to put the British AEW tender out to competition catalysed talks between Plessey and the Americans. Where talks had been useful but guarded before the AWACs deal, they became much warmer and more productive thereafter. But it is clear that the Americans were also attracted by the quality of Plessey's technology, especially in the results of its long term investment in component design and manufacture.[23]

However, the main thrust of collaborative project work with both civil and military implications, along with various 'pre-competitive' joint research initiatives, such as Esprit and Brite, is with European partners. Along with the Eureka initiative, these schemes have generated dozens of large and small collaborative projects involving electronics companies. Even Plessey, its link with Westinghouse notwithstanding, recognises the need to 'collaborate in Europe as competition and costs become more intense.'[24] Such 'pre-competitive' cooperation in basic technological concepts may certainly generate new ideas, products and processes which could be used in civil and military applications. Its long term impact could be even more important for the British and European electronics industry.

The electronics industry does not easily lend itself to permanent collaborative formulae. Where possible, cooperation is based on clearly defined modules which limit specific technology transfers to the interfaces between modules. European collaboration in defence electronics has been *ad hoc*, and has not produced the same kind of consistent and continuous contact that has often been achieved by the airframe companies. It is unlikely that 'Airbus' or 'Panavia' consortia will easily be formed amongst the electronics companies. The greater number of British companies bidding for joint ventures has caused European firms to complain that cooperation with the UK is difficult. Working with different partners obstructs the creation of the depth of relations to run an effective international programme.[25] Some British industrialists are also sceptical of efforts to stimulate long term European cooperation. There will have to be radical changes in the policies of major European producers and customers to achieve any really substantive shift away from nationally based electronics industries.

In the past, collaboration in electronics has tended to follow agreements to cooperate on platforms, but increasingly, firms are beginning to take the initiative, looking for partners in anticipation of a major collaborative venture. However, as costs and systems complexity continue to increase, more permanent relationships may yet emerge. If such networks between European electronics firms do evolve, major advances could be possible in the operation of a European defence electronics market. The emergence of a truly European defence industrial base, in which the British electronics industry would play a major role, is one of the issues addressed in the conclusions. However, it should be clear that the future of British electronics, for defence or for commercial use, will, at some point in the future, lie in a stronger and more comprehensive European dimension.

Movement towards more elaborate forms of collaboration may well call into question certain aspects of domestic competition policy. There may yet be a need for British 'national champions' to compete more effectively for shares of a limited number of large European programmes. In this respect, the desirability of domestic competition may not sit so easily in the context of stable collaborative networks. Some industrialists even consider that competition and collaboration are fundamentally irreconcilable if British firms are to play a leading role in international programmes. As the main source of competition, technically and commercially, is increasingly from the United States and, sooner or later, the Japanese defence electronics industry, a regional approach may be the only realistic strategy for Europe. In this event, it makes long term economic sense for British firms to have a dominant place in a European industry. This in turn, will mean that government has to play its part in supporting the R&D base necessary to maintain Britain's leadership in defence electronics.

7

Government Attitudes Towards the Defence Industrial Base

This chapter considers what the British Government has said with regard to the DIB as such, ie about the desired shape and scope of British defence industrial capabilities. It explores the circumstances under which the Government buys British and why. In years past, however, buying British was a near automatic choice.

Background 1945–1979

After the Second World War, the fundamental British trend was to reorientate industry back to civil production and to have the Armed Forces rely on existing stocks of equipment for a decade. However, defence production was never completely given up, indeed investment in it was considerably stepped up under American pressure at the time of the Korean War. It seems likely that British economic recovery was damaged substantially as resources were diverted to defence which would otherwise have gone into the promotion of exports.[1]

Britain stayed on the path of self-sufficiency in armaments production, developing most significantly its own nuclear and thermonuclear bombs and three types of aircraft (Victor, Vulcan and Valiant) to deliver them. In 1960, however, Britain dropped out of the ballistic missile sector when it cancelled the Blue Streak project. It opted to buy the stand-off Skybolt missile from the United States and, when this project was cancelled by Washington, Britain negotiated the purchase of American Polaris missiles in 1962. Britain, with some help from America, built its own submarines to carry the missiles and its own nuclear warheads.

In the 1950s Britain had developed and produced its own combat aircraft, in particular the Canberra, the Hawker Hunter, the Buccaneer and the Lightning. However, in the 1960s the preference for a British product went badly wrong. The TSR2 project had to be cancelled in 1965 because of expense and technical problems. Britain turned to the purchase of an American aircraft, the F–4 Phantom (which was equipped at considerable expense with Rolls-Royce engines) as well as to collaboration, initially with

France on the Jaguar. From the end of the 1960s, collaboration began with Germany and Italy on the MRCA Tornado. Away from aircraft and nuclear delivery systems, Britain tended to rely on the output of its own defence industries although it did participate in other collaborative projects such as the Martel anti-ship missile, the Anglo-French family of helicopters (Lynx, Puma and Gazelle) and the towed FH–70 field gun. It became involved at rather a late stage with the Franco-German Milan anti-tank missile and became a licensed producer of it in the late 1970s. Notable national products included the Rapier anti-aircraft missile, the Chieftain tank, the Hawk trainer and the anti-submarine warfare (ASW) Nimrod aircraft.

From the late 1950s government took a major role in reshaping defence industries so that they would become more able to survive in an age of high R&D costs and advanced technology. In particular the formation of large 'national champion' companies was brought about in aerospace, shipbuilding and jet engines. In 1959 the Government engineered the merger of five engine companies into Rolls-Royce and Bristol Siddeley, and a dozen airframe companies into the Hawker Siddeley Group and the British Aircraft Corporation. In 1966 Rolls-Royce took over Bristol Siddeley and was nationalised in 1971 as it went into liquidation. British Aerospace and British Shipbuilders were formed by mergers and nationalisation in the Aircraft & Shipbuilding Industries Act of 1977. The belief was that big firms, although holding a monopoly in the United Kingdom could survive best in a global competitive environment and GEC, through takeovers, emerged as a giant electronics company. The production of land armaments had always been dominated by the government-owned Royal Ordnance Factories.

This was the structure inherited by Mrs Thatcher's first Administration in 1979, a structure which reflected not just a commitment to strategic autonomy and the existence of firms making a wide range of defence equipment but also to government intervention to shape and control industry.

Explicit and implicit policy

The concept of policy is that of a set of values, reasoning and prescriptions which can serve to guide officials dealing with individual issues and cases. There is no guarantee that officials will in fact follow policy guidelines in their day-to-day duties and some analysts see the implementation of policy as being as much of a problem area as policy formulation.

A feature of the argument below is that there is no clear government policy on the desired shape of the DIB. There are official observations made in the SDEs and elsewhere on the subject and there are individual procurement choices which represent implicitly government policy. However, there is not any great coherence in the composite picture which emerges from these sources. At least one expert observer has seen short-term expediency and lack of properly worked out policy as a feature of UK defence policy in general, and of defence industrial policy in particular.[2]

UK DIB Policy Outlined

One apparently central statement about British defence industrial policy is the observation that 'we need a strong defence-industrial base, as was illustrated vividly during the Falklands crisis.'[3] Although in context this comment was made not as a main point, but as a rider to an argument which stressed the value of competition in British defence procurement, it indicates that the British Government prefers to buy its defence equipment at home.

Clearly British firms have traditionally received preferential treatment regarding defence contracts. The MoD has often acknowledged this openly, saying that one long-term aim of procurement policy is 'to maintain and stimulate British industry, especially in areas of high technology which are important to the whole economy.'[4] The 1981 SDE said that:

> the Government will use the purchasing power of the defence budget to give the maximum practicable support to British industry . . . It will be our abiding aim to secure, through our decisions in the procurement field, the maintenance of those vital areas of British expertise which best serves our Forces' needs and which offer the best future opportunities in terms of new technologies, their applications and marketing potential.[5]

Significantly, the reasons listed for buying British did not include the political, strategic or operational autonomy which that might bring. Instead the emphasis was on economic considerations, on the consequence of buying British in terms of jobs, foreign exchange, greater national R&D spending, improved prospects for arms exports, import substitution and the increased capacity to obtain worthwhile roles in collaborative projects. The only military point was that buying British increased the freedom to shape equipment to the British Forces' own needs.

Yet although it sees itself as contributing very positively to the national economy, the MoD still insists that its prime job is the procurement of military equipment needed by the British Armed Forces, not the promotion of economic health in the United Kingdom. As was observed in 1981,

> the procurement budget . . . cannot be used specifically to support industry in its civil markets. The defence industrial base was created to satisfy the equipment needs of the services and not vice-versa.

Although advantage should be taken of common interests between the civil and military sectors, 'the size and shape of the defence industrial base ultimately depends on the formulation of defence requirements.'[6]

In general, the autonomy arguments regarding the DIB and the use of force have tended to fade in recent years as it has increasingly seemed to be the case that Britain would not be fighting in future wars except with the support of allies, and that future conflicts would involve only equipment and stocks in being rather than additional production. As noted in the previous section, the exhortation to the Services to use equipment made for the civilian sector where possible, on the grounds that it would be more easily produced in wartime, was an isolated case. In general, mobilising industry for war seemed unlikely and the overall coalition orientation of British policy was a reflection, not just of the decline of the task of imperial defence and of the rising importance of NATO and the NATO area to Britain, but also of the growing importance of the European Community and European Political Cooperation in UK foreign policy. Even out-of-area military activities seemed likely to be pursued, if at all, only with at least the political support of European friends. The situation in 1965 had seemed rather different to the Plowden Committee established to review the position of Britain's aircraft industry:

> Today the main defence argument for having a domestic industry capable of supplying major weapons systems is that it provides a measure of independence in British foreign policy, especially in circumstances where we might have to consider using force. Without an industry of our own, our policy would be in the hands of the supplying country which could always cut off supplies, including spares.[7]

Lord Plowden did, however, qualify the argument by pointing out that Britain would probably be relying on allies, including the United States whose views were already taken into account in the formulation of British policy. Moreover, he concluded that collaboration with Europe was the way forward for the British aircraft industry.

What were the perceived implications of the Falklands Conflict? One interpretation of the statement which opened this chapter could be that the Government felt that the United Kingdom should maintain a wide-ranging DIB to provide operational autonomy, to allow it to fight future, small scale, wars without participating allies. Support for this interpretation can be drawn from Defence Minister Younger's responses to the House of Commons Defence Committee (HCDC) when he said that 'there are some items of equipment, and I think particularly of small arms ammunition and that sort of thing, where we would always wish to have some capability here'[8] and from Mr Heseltine's comment, after he had resigned from the Ministry of Defence, on the prospect of generally buying more cheaply from the United States — 'it would be, in my view, totally unacceptable as a judgement . . . in the strategic concept that you should never allow the strategic control of your defence requirements to be outside your hands.' The MoD acknowledges its concern with 'the long-term defence manufacturing and design capability of the country' but it is not apparent that there is a clear view as to what that capability should be.[9]

However, the relevant sections of the Government's public analysis of the Falklands Conflict did not mention the autonomy-dependence dimension. *The Falklands Campaign: The Lessons* pointed mainly to the utility of the United Kingdom DIB as a means of quickly modifying equipment.

New operational demands were satisfied in record times through the ready availability of a broad spectrum of scientific and engineering expertise in the Ministry of Defence research establishments and the comprehensive resources of the United Kingdom's defence industry. The Campaign demonstrated the value of a broadly based national defence industry, and the benefits of an in-house research capability.[10]

The document listed examples of what had been achieved including the rapid development of a helicopter-based AEW system using the Searchwater radar, the development and production within 10 days of a man-portable radar jammer, the accelerated introduction into service of the aircraft carrier *Illustrious* and other equipment, and the adaptation of aircraft for in-flight refuelling. The HCDC, however, did address the issue when it looked back on the Falklands Conflict after five years and, while noting the costs of independence, accepted that even the US might not be a wholly reliable source of future supply.[11]

However, recognition by the Government of some of the security dimensions of the national DIB can be found among the strategic and structural longer term considerations which the MoD has said should be taken into account in procurement decisions.[12] These include 'Safeguarding of vital sources of supply,' 'Length of the supply chain and its vulnerability to disruption,' and the 'Effect of procurement on price, availability and competition for future supplies (eg arising from dumping or artificially depressed quotations) including, as appropriate, supplies for other public purchasers.' The Government has, however, not made clear how it has weighed and treated these considerations in practice. Is there a general sense, for instance, that the Atlantic is treated as an acceptably invulnerable supply chain? An earlier chapter included the observation that initial acquisition price in practice dominates other value for money considerations and is likely to continue to do so if the government needs to hold down equipment costs in order to avoid the need for a review of Britain's five defence tasks.

Whatever the relative weight of economic, military and political considerations, the implicit evidence points firmly towards a policy of support for the British DIB at the expense of external competitors. Using the values of arms imports as an indicator of protectionism, Britain seems to be much less protectionist than France or the United States (which spends only 2 per cent of its defence equipment budget on foreign equipment) and rather more protectionist than the Federal Republic of Germany. Japan, which makes about 90 per cent of its own defence equipment, also shows a clean commitment to home products and is willing to pay a substantial premium for them.[12] Maintenance of Japan's DIB is an explicit element in its security policy.[13]

The premium for support of the British DIB

The preference for British products is not unconditional. The 1980 SDE included an overt statement of government policy of support for the British

DIB. It did so, however, in a qualified way and it is worth quoting the document at some length.

> Para 735. . . . By providing most of the equipment the Services need from our national resources and through collaboration, we keep to a minimum the proportion we buy from abroad. Sales of British defence equipment abroad contribute to the balance of payments and generate further returns for the nation on the capital invested in research and development.
>
> Para 736. The ability to develop and produce arms is thus an important national asset. It ensures supply; it enables British Service requirements to be met in an appropriate and timely way; it provides domestic employment; it can be paid for in our own currency; it enables us to collaborate, where that is our preferred course; and it offers the prospect of securing foreign exchange through sales. Above all, because of its contribution to our defence, it helps maintain our national security. The government therefore intends to give full support to British industry in providing these benefits. In return we look to industry to develop and produce equipment of the desired quality, in the quantities required and at the time expected, in a cost-effective way.

The 1981 SDE took this further, saying that British industry could only hope to hold its place in British procurement if it offered 'competitive products at the right quality and standards, on time and at the right price.'[14] The SDE pointed to the need for defence costs to be cut wherever possible and indicated that British goods might be bought only if they were the cheapest available. The statement suggested that the Government would pay no premium for British goods. Particularly under Mrs Thatcher, the British Government has certainly felt, not just that it should pay the minimum possible premium for buying British, but also that often it had had to pay considerably more than this. To improve the situation, the MoD, particularly under Michael Heseltine, introduced a series of measures designed (summarised in the previous section) to secure an improved performance from British defence industries. As with the Boeing E-3A AWACs, where necessary the MoD was ready to buy from abroad.

The breadth of the DIB

In the face of rising costs of domestically-produced equipment, the Government has faced the question of how wide and comprehensive the British DIB should be. To this issue, which is tied in with the priority to be given to NATO standardisation in British procurement policy and to the place of European collaboration in British policy, it has not given clear or consistent answers. Decisions have been taken on an *ad hoc* basis with regard to collaboration and foreign purchase.

The British tradition is that of possessing a comprehensive range of defence industries which have the effect of providing strategic if not operational autonomy. Even in fields where the United Kingdom has sometimes bought from abroad, such as missiles and combat aircraft, the governments of the 1950s and 1960s maintained Britain's long term capacity to produce desired items by devoting resources to research. Historically Britain's commitment to defence R&D has been greater than any of its European allies and as we have seen defence accounted for three-quarters of total government R&D spending in the late 1950s.[15] The volume and range of British defence research spending has diminished proportionately in recent years as budgetary pressures have begun to be felt and staff levels have been cut back at the government's seven specialised R&D establishments. Yet, as the Council for Science and Society Report pointed out in 1986, about a fifth of the MoD's R&D budget still goes on research, as it had in the 1950s.[16] In the early 1980s Britain spent a greater proportion of its Gross Domestic Product on defence R&D than even the United States did.

Back in 1976, defence industrial specialisation was not looked on with any great interest; indeed, the MoD seemed anxious that collaboration should not mean that Britain's strategic autonomy in armaments would be lightly compromised. This was the message between the lines in the observation that, when looking at collaboration, one of the things to be kept in mind was 'the preservation of adequate design and production capabilities.'[17] The 1981 SDE, while pressuring British industry to be competitive with its external rivals, nevertheless indicated that the British Government wanted to maintain at least a capacity to develop and manufacture all types of defence equipment.[18]

A year later, however, budgetary pressures meant that any commitment to a comprehensive DIB had been forgotten. A clear statement of intent was given in the 1982 SDE:

Para 431 . . . It is no longer open to Government to maintain the current level of R&D spending across the present wide field. Selections will have to be made, and we shall need to consider reducing the range of our defence industrial capabilities and concentrating on a more limited range of weapons technologies.
Para 432. The implications of developments of this kind also need to be faced. To a greater or lesser degree, specialisation requires that the participants rely on the judgement of others in designing, developing and producing weapons systems. Industrially, withdrawal from certain sectors would be virtually irrevocable and would involve industry itself in a difficult period of adjustment . . .
Para 433. The potential rewards are, however, great . . .

Industrial specialisation had been pointed to publicly in 1981 by the then Defence Minister John Nott as the only way out of Europe's problem of rising equipment costs. However, he anticipated that it would be very difficult for governments to negotiate who should do what. His expectation was that specialisation would come about, if at all, though a process of attrition and elimination in which only some companies would survive an increasingly harsh commercial environment.[19] Considerations of specialisation, however, seem to have been put aside with his departure. Michael Heseltine had great faith in collaboration as a means of preserving British defence industrial capabilities and his evidence to the HCDC is instructive.

I do not know that I have ever asked for military advice as to what it is essential to retain, but, if I am in the position of responsibility for maintaining the defence industrial base, which I am, I do not doubt that on the list of capabilities there would be air platforms, there would be sea platforms, there would be helicopter platforms, and I cannot believe there would be any doubt about that.[20]

However, the 1982 Value for Money in Defence Procurement document was more open-ended, and it is worth quoting since it points up the absence of any clear government stance towards the United Kingdom DIB.

We will accordingly be considering the procurement source for new requirements within the following framework:
a) importance of the project in absolute terms to the Services, and the military need for and benefit from the associated indigenous industrial capabilities, whether at the system or component level;
b) affordability, having regard to the effect on cost of the likely size of the MoD demand, the potential export market, and the prospects of sharing the R&D costs through acceptable collaboration and/or joint ventures with Industry, founded on confidence of achieving a viable market share. The feasibility of product improvement and the availability of suitable commercially developed products are also relevant;
c) the extent to which non-UK sources are likely to be available to meet Service needs at acceptable cost (initially and whole life). This should be considered in terms both of whole and sub-systems and components and address questions of security, eg in relation to software, and ease of modifications in emergency. Such considerations should also cover possible political restrictions on use for sales and/or national interest considerations;
d) the relevant position of UK industry compared to overseas sources and whether, and how, industrial competitiveness will be improved, including the extent to which opportunity can be taken to further the aim of securing the alignment of industrial capacity with likely levels of requirement.

The considerations above will not always point in the same direction; and some aspects will be of greater relevance than others at different times and to different projects.[21]

Thus the Value for Money document committed the government to nothing specific. However, competition was a key element in overall procurement policy and scope for competition is clearly increased the more that foreign firms are allowed to bid.[22] The government has tended to hint that, in general, it intends to restrict competition mainly to British firms. Yet its fortnightly publication of contracts to be put up for tender is obviously available to foreign companies representatives in the United Kingdom and, by cancelling the AEW Nimrod project and buying the E-3A AWACS system, the government has signalled a readiness to buy from abroad when it feels that British industry cannot provide what is needed. It also chose Harpoon as a surface-to-surface weapon in preference to a sea-launched version of Sea Eagle. A decade ago it would have been unthinkable that a British Government would buy a Brazilian trainer aircraft for the RAF, yet this Government has bought the Tucano for licensed manufacture by Shorts.

While there is as yet no explicit commitment to open up the British market further to either European or American firms, there is a sense that preference for British suppliers has been slightly reduced, at least for the time being. Peter Levene told a British audience that

We buy British whenever it is sensible, economic and consistent with our international obligations to do so. We buy from overseas when the advantages of cost, performance or timescale outweigh the longer terms advantages of procuring the British alternative. Foreign firms — or British firms for that matter — are not invited to tender to act as stalking horses.[23]

In the first half of 1987, foreign firms were encouraged to bid, for instance, on ASR 1238 dealing with a short-range, air-launched anti-armour weapon, although they were encouraged to find a British partner. Among the reported reasons why the United Kingdom was not interested in an off-the-shelf purchase was that it would make the spreading of costs over several years more difficult. In another case, BMY of the United States was allowed to bid against Vickers and the ROF of the UK for a system to fill the gap left by the cancelled SP–70. American, British and French companies were invited to bid for a laser designator pod for Tornado in May 1987. Foreign firms were involved in responding to a tender for a helicopter radar warning receiver for the British Army. Finally nine companies, including two from the United States, were invited in October 1987 to bid to supply sonar systems for the Type 2400 submarine.[24] It might be concluded that, beyond ships and combat aircraft, the MoD would consider foreign bids for almost any system.

In 1986 there were signs that the MoD was again taking specialisation seriously, although the burden of responsibility was seen to lie mainly with the companies. Defence Minister George Younger said that firms supplying MoD should seek to broaden their horizons since, as defence goods became more sophisticated, it was necessary to look for a wider market than just the British Forces. The tenor of his views was that firms had both to specialise more and to look more to external markets if they were to survive in an age of growing technological sophistication. However, these were viewed as issues for the firms rather than as matters of governmental concern.[25]

Then in 1987 came a Cabinet decision to limit the scale of defence R&D. It is not yet clear in which fields Britain will concentrate but work has begun within the MoD to consider such questions as

☐ in which areas of defence need does the United Kingdom have a particularly strong capability which should be further built up?

☐ in which areas could Britain buy from abroad without losing the capability to develop future systems itself?

☐ in which areas does the United Kingdom have capabilities which are also held by many others? In such areas Britain might decide to buy from abroad and neglect the British R&D base.

☐ which technologies and systems can the United Kingdom not buy from abroad?

A study on this last issue was undertaken earlier in the 1980s and it found that only a small number of items, some of which obviously concerned nuclear weapons, were not available from elsewhere. The updating exercise, which will perhaps be undertaken every four or five years, it understood to be generating a similar list to the previous study.

Many MoD statements do not distinguish between buying from European states and the United States. They refer only to 'allies.' However, in part the British concern with specialisation is tied to the idea of Britain being an element in a relatively comprehensive European DIB. This DIB would be sustained in the main through collaborative projects and the British Government, or at least elements in it, have given some support to the idea. Thus the 1980 SDE, while accepting that the easiest route to NATO standardation would be the purchase of American equipment and conceding that some military equipment would be bought from that source 'when appropriate,' asserted the value of a European DIB:

> the Government considers that it is appropriate to retain in Europe, where we offer major expertise, a development capability for modern weapons systems, and we intend to strengthen European equipment collaboration.[26]

The MoD, particularly under Michael Heseltine's leadership, showed support for the idea of maintaining the West European DIB. This was signalled most explicitly by the MoD support (until being overruled by the Cabinet) for the 1985 European national armament directors' recommendation that ministers should reaffirm their 1978 commitment if possible to procure only helicopters largely designed and produced in Europe.[27] In the event, this recommendation was rejected by the Cabinet but the MoD under George Younger remained committed to European collaboration for many of the items needed by British forces. However, under Younger, Britain ceased to be such a driving force behind the IEPG when that body turned its attention to the Vredeling Report, to European cooperation at the research stage in Cooperative Technology Projects and techniques for strengthening the competitiveness of European defence industries as a whole.

Although Britain remained committed to European collaboration, it was not clear whether, in collaborative projects, Britain needed to specialise in some fields or could neglect others. Indeed British policy lacked any sectoral dimension; the only indicators of the sectors which the Government felt unnecessary or undesirable for Britain were the procurement decisions on individual pieces of equipment such as the Boeing AWACs.

The American dimension

Direct purchase, collaboration and the licensed production of foreign weapons involves Britain with the United States as well as Europe. British officials and some politicians often see defence projects with America as a source of advanced technology. A contrasting view, on the other hand, is that working with the Americans can tie British companies into a position of permanent inferiority and that they will not be allowed to exploit freely technology they acquire from the United States because of the extra-territorial application of United States law. This was one item of concern raised by the SDP-Liberal Alliance in the Nimrod AEW cancellation debate and the issue held up the final conclusion of the AWACs contract.[28]

Varying perceptions of the utility for British industry of working with the United States in a sub-contractor position accounted for some of the disagreements over both the Nimrod cancellation and the Westland crisis. In Parliament, after the cancellation of the AEW Nimrod Project, Denzil Davies, Labour's defence spokesman, emphasised the importance of AEW technology, saying that the cancellation was

> a bad decision, because ultimately a country can only defend itself on the basis of its industrial and technological base. The Secretary of State has dealt a heavy blow to that high technology base.[29]

The Defence Minister disagreed, feeling that the British defence industry as a whole could absorb the blow and having some confidence that Boeing would generate high technology jobs within the United Kingdom. Similar sentiments of disagreement about an industrial sector could be observed during the Westland crisis with participants varying substantially in the importance they attached to the continued survival of an independent British helicopter manufacturer.[30]

Under the Conservative Government, American defence industrial interests have been welcomed to Britain. Not only are British firms with substantial foreign ownership, such as Westland, treated as normal elements in the British DIB, but so also are companies which are subsidiaries of foreign companies. Cossor, with responsibility for the manufacture of British IFF equipment, is in that category. Cossor is a subsidiary of Raytheon and has been since the early 1960s. Paccar, which took over the struggling Foden truck manufacturing business in the early 1980s, is an American firm making civil and military vehicles in the United States. In the Westland and Land Rover crises of 1985, the Government made clear that it was happy to see American business buy into the British DIB in the expectation that the firms concerned would become more efficient and effective organisations. The Government's preferred choice of company to take over the running of the Devonport Dockyard was a consortium of which Brown & Root, an American firm with a 30 per cent holding, was the leader. Other prominent foreign companies in the British DIB are the American Singer Link Miles (SLM), which makes simulators, and MEL, which is a Philips electronics subsidiary. The United Kingdom places no specific restrictions on these companies, unlike the United States which requires a foreign-owned defence company to be overseen by a board of trustees whose composition is agreed by the government.

Finally, in procurement awards to British companies, the British Government has no formal concern with the foreign and in particular the American content of 'British' systems. The United States Government, in contrast, has positively to give permission for the foreign content of an 'American' system to rise above a set level (15 per cent). As a consequence, some major British projects are incorporating a good deal of American technology as a means of keeping down costs and technological risks.[29] The discernible danger is that British producers, while ostensibly 'acquiring' American technology, might, in fact, not obtain either the capability to manufacture such equipment or the development expertise behind it. British firms might be drawn to being technology assemblers and fall further behind with their own expertise. Extensive use of American components and subsystems, including software, could in the medium term lead to British, and even European firms as a whole, losing capabilities in such important sectors as air-to-air radars and advanced seekers on missiles, unless specific action is taken to cover the possibility. The possibility is recognised by officials but there is little inclination to identify sectors where the loss of a capability is thought worth avoiding.

Conclusion

The first of Mrs Thatcher's two Administrations broadly preferred not to develop explicit interventionist policies to protect or promote the British DIB. The Government's emphasis was on securing improved performance from equipment suppliers, particularly through competition and collaboration, and on occasions it was ready to turn to overseas suppliers. In line with its general philosophy of the benefits of competition for industrial performance, it preferred a 'hands off' policy and, despite its influence through defence contracts on corporate fortunes, it wanted to minimise its responsibility for corporate strategies. It drastically reduced government ownership of defence industries. The Westland affair presented the Government with some difficult choices and, as Lawrence Freedman has pointed out,

> the Government's difficulty was really in trying to find a middle ground between taking and not taking a view on the future shape of British defence industry . . . The Government could not bring itself to say that a British helicopter manufacturer was dispensible; but neither was it prepared to commit substantial resources to its preservation.[30]

In general, the Government has tended towards a stance that says that current procurement policy will strengthen the DIB by making it more competitive in world markets. It has been more reluctant to acknowledge that procurement policy might diminish or narrow the British DIB. Yet in 1981 it had pointed out that:

> It may be false economy to opt for a cheaper foreign product if the result is to weaken or lose altogether British industry's own producing capacity in that line. We would then be dependent for future generations of equipment on foreign suppliers and on their ideas of what to produce and when, and how much to charge.[31]

Yet it is not clear how these vital and sensible considerations have been used in practice. Reference to them by the Government is not apparent since

1981, presumably because low acquisition prices have become central to the goal of avoiding a major defence review.

British declaratory policy throws little light on the role of the British DIB as regards crisis or war, although occasional, off-the-cuff observations by ministers indicate a preference that the DIB should give them some freedom of action. But Britain has no stated policy on reducing vulnerability to external suppliers by holding set stocks of imported raw materials, subsystems or components. A preference for a specific surge capacity in British defence plants seems to have been limited to some ROF factories and this seems to have disappeared with the sale of the ROF to BAe.[32] However, as we have already noted, a preference has been expressed for the services to use civil products when possible as these could be made more easily in wartime. The capacity of Britain's dockyards to ready ships for war has been reduced by the decreased labour availability in dockyards brought about by privatisation. In a parallel area, the Government has shown little else but complacency for the declining British, indeed NATO, merchant fleet. Yet the position in the Alliance as a whole here is a matter for concern if the Alliance sees a capacity to bring large numbers of men and material across the Atlantic as an important element in its deterrent posture. The most common British assumption is that Britain will be involved only in wars to be fought with weapons in service, despite the fact that even the Falklands Campaign did not fall into this category.

While the Government did not publicly address the dilemmas of DIB policy to any degree, the House of Commons Defence Committee, while reaching no distinct conclusions, considered the issue of the DIB explicitly in its reports on both the Falklands Conflict and the Westland affair.

Its analysis of the latter is noteworthy.[33] It begins by noting that concern with the DIB is spread between two departments, the MoD and the DTI. 'Although it is the responsibility of the Ministry of Defence to identify those assets which make up the defence industrial base, the priority to be attached to these assets in relation to the rest of industry is a matter for the Department of Trade & Industry.'

It went on:

The objective of maintaining the defence industrial base has two main aspects. First, there is the wish to secure for British industry and the economy as a whole benefits of defence contracts, such as higher employment, foreign exchange earnings, overseas sales, the development of high technology capabilities, and the maintenance of skilled design teams. Second there are 'strategic' objectives — security of supply in times of tension and war and the need for indigenous firms ready to give national requirements the highest priority and be responsive at times of emergency. The second set of objectives is the particular concern of the MoD, although as the largest single customer of British industry it has a good deal of influence on the first set of objectives. In terms of Government responsibilities, however, the first set of objectives is primarily the responsibility of the Department of Trade & Industry.[34]

Yet, when it came to views available to the Committee, a prominent MoD official implicitly argued that procurement from the most competitive source in the NATO Alliance, regardless of national boundary, was the proper way forward and the DTI Minister held that the defence interest was only in getting the right equipment at a reasonable price. The Committee noted 'We do not agree with such a narrow definition of defence interests.' Defence Minister Heseltine was alone in arguing that it was 'essential' that the United Kingdom should have an indigenous helicopter industry, the Industry & Information Technology Minister thought it 'important,' while a senior service representative felt it 'desirable.' The Committee, noting the unsatisfactory relations between the MoD and the DTI, came out at the governmental level in favour of Mr Heseltine. While it acknowledged that the commercial interest of Westland might lie in links with Sikorsky, it felt that membership of a European consortium 'might in the long term have served the broader defence interests of the United Kingdom.'[35]

The HCDC took up the issue of the DIB again in its 1987 report on the Falklands. In this report, while acknowledging the costs of securing independence of action, it raised questions about the reliability of external suppliers, including the United States. Although the assistance which Britain received from the United States during the campaign was described as 'very timely,'

> there can be no guarantee that this would always be so; it seems likely that, for example, where British requirements were competing with those of the United States armed forces, our needs would be accorded a lower priority, and might be met more slowly. It is not inconceivable that at some future date the United Kingdom might be involved in operations where the suppliers of essential items of equipment did not wish to be seen to assist us in any material way.[36]

These authors are unaware of any governmental response to these points.

8

Options for UK DIB Policy

As previous chapters have shown, the present Government has developed a clearly articulated and positive policy on procurement, based on the concept of 'value for money' and making extensive use of competition and collaboration. However, its policy towards the DIB has been implicit rather than explicit, and lacking a clear expression of what sort of DIB the government felt that Britain should have. Thus this chapter discusses a series of options which involve choices of priorities or targets. They are not all totally compatible, although many are interrelated, and the government could be expected to have a stance, not just about those which it wishes to endorse, but also about the volume of resources which should be used to support any one option. Some have already received qualified endorsement from government. Others are unlikely to be adopted in any unequivocal form, but they nonetheless merit identification if only to illuminate the nominal choices open to the government.

Broadly we see a pattern of choice as having the following logic. First the MoD could choose to ignore the national origin of military equipment and seek unqualified value for money. Alternatively, it could positively discriminate against British equipment. Both these possibilities are discussed initially in the following paragraphs. Thirdly it could choose to have some policy to discriminate in procurement in favour of British goods. There are then two possibilities — to support a comprehensive British DIB, or to work for some kind of partial base. If the latter is selected, there are various criteria which could direct the shape of the British DIB. One would be that the United Kingdom could contribute those capabilities particularly relevant to a comprehensive European DIB. Others, which could be implemented so as to be compatible with support for a European DIB, would be to have Britain make

- [ ] only that which could not be bought from overseas; and/or
- [ ] that equipment where the British technology was internationally competitive;
- [ ] that which involved militarily critical technologies;
- [ ] that where there were good civil industrial spin-off prospects;
- [ ] that which provided limited autonomy for British forces.

These options are laid out in diagrammatic form in Figure 8.1 and will be discussed individually.

113

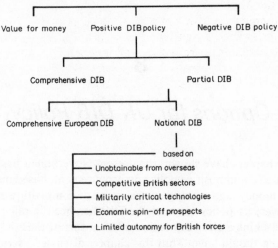

FIGURE 8.1
British Government Options

However, it is significant that the appeal or otherwise of any option is a function of its direct consequences and the indirect effects it may generate in terms of responses from other relevant actors, including British industry, industry in other allied states, and other NATO governments.

In the late 1980s, British and foreign industry were clearly responding to Britain's procurement policy. Some companies were diversifying away from defence, corporate acquisitions and disposals were frequent with some defence acquisitions being outside the United Kingdom, and some production was being directed abroad to parts of the world where labour was less expensive. Many more inter-company collaborative links were being formed and in general the arms industry could be seen to be becoming more internationalised. Overall, government policies, particularly in NATO states, represented a basic element in the environment of defence companies, constraining and directing the viable choices open to firms.

Option 1. 'Value for money' as the sole procurement criterion

The MoD could opt to procure equipment on the basis of what offered best value for money, regardless of its source. Some analysts, endorsing this view, have suggested for instance that, within the confines of a fixed budget, the services should be given a free hand in equipment purchase to buy what they felt was most useful.[1] As seen above, some officials in the MoD and DTI would like to take much less notice of the source of a piece of defence equipment.

The appeal of the straightforward 'value for money' approach is that it suggests that British forces might be better equipped and/or equipped more cheaply if the MoD, instead of being able to enjoy only the benefits of competition among British companies, could also gain from competition involving British and foreign companies. As one academic put it, by buying British, 'the government are in effect sacrificing the gains from international trade by preventing the Armed Forces from 'shopping around' and buying their investment off-the-shelf from the lowest cost suppliers in the world market.'[2]

As a general approach to defence procurement, clearly this assumes the shelf contains what is required, but it also takes little account of security of supply or of the possible need for increased supply in times of crisis. Vice Admiral Jeremy Black, when Assistant Chief of the Defence Staff (Systems), observed that 'buying military equipment off-the-shelf is not like buying a tie because the shelves are not replete with the right goods in the right time-scale, customers are second in line after the producers' nation has taken its quota, and once a monopoly has been established, they may not be cheap.'[3] Also the services may not be best equipped in business terms to judge the best deal in the light of reliability and life cycle costs. Determination of such costs is not easy for any party. Interestingly, the academic author quoted above apparently believes that the services, to whom he would like to hand more responsibility for equipment procurement, have an 'insatiable appetite for technologically sophisticated and costly new weaponry.'[4]

However, because of domestic political considerations, no British Government is yet likely to put as a central plank in its policy a commitment to buy defence equipment from abroad on a large scale, even on grounds of apparent value for money. In a state with a balance of trade surplus and full employment, that might be acceptable, although in fact it is not an approach even adopted by Japan, which, as we have seen, pays a major premium to have almost all its defence equipment made inside the country. All major and even minor arms producing states favour their own industries. Thus using the simple value for money criterion would make political sense only if it could be shown that other relevant governments were reciprocating (and so giving British industry a chance in their markets.)

Also, under this option, unless only equipment already in production was to be bought, the British Government might increasingly find itself in the politically more vulnerable position of regularly placing development contracts overseas.

Recognising the reality of domestic politics, the present government's commitment to competition is implicitly qualified. Particularly in shipbuilding, it has accepted not just the need to buy British but also the need to spread orders around the yards and the country, albeit on the best terms possible. Admittedly, there were hints that a change might be imminent in 1988 when the MoD explicitly considered ordering four Type 23 frigates from a single yard in order to secure economies of scale. When foreign items were bought, the government normally sought licensed production or offset arrangements, neither of which necessarily keep prices down. The Labour Party's official 1986 statement on defence, while promising many procurement changes, still said that 'a Labour government will ensure that Britain's defence equipment is overwhelmingly purchased from British companies.'[5]

Of course, the British Government could choose not to pay directly for the development of new equipment, but only to buy (from the shelf) items which had already been developed by companies. A unilateral decision to that effect would leave foreign companies normally getting their development work funded by their governments while British companies had to seek private capital backing. British companies would have to be allowed a higher profit margin than is permitted under present arrangements, given the risks they would carry. Such a stance might not be popular with British forces, when they found themselves under pressure to choose only from equipment in service elsewhere. The possibilities of their having 'customised' equipment would be much reduced. The British Government could also not be sure that it would not have to pay indirectly for development by being debited with an R&D surcharge.

In order to be successful in the British market, foreign companies would certainly try to win the help of their own governments, for instance in the form of hidden subsidies. Companies with a large protected domestic market as a base would be at an advantage compared with British companies. American companies in particular would be in a position to offer one generation of loss-leader products to drive British companies out of business, although European defence companies, which generally operate on the same sort of scale of British firms, would be less able to do this. It should not be overlooked that a rational aim of business on a free trade system is to eliminate effective competition and that there is a tendency towards natural monopoly in many defence sectors since advantages of scale can be built up more or less indefinitely.

A buying from the world market approach would require the United Kingdom to adopt mechanisms to invite bids from a wider range of firms than at present and it would probably mean that more companies' offers would need to be evaluated. All this would cause problems within the British procurement system which has much lower manpower levels than it had a decade ago. However, it could be argued that, with the 1983 'value for money' factors for procurement choices not including any explicit preference for British companies, with more foreign firms being invited to bid for contracts, and with the MoD virtually encouraging British firms to acquire foreign partners when they compete for contracts, the British Government is moving implicitly rather than explicitly towards this policy.

Thus it is worth emphasising two fundamental points about encouraging international competition in the British defence market place. The first is that opening up the British market makes much more economic and political sense if reciprocal action by other countries gives British companies an opportunity to compete there. The second is that open competition in defence equipment within Western Europe is for the moment more appealing than competition between the United States and individual European countries, despite the optimism sounded by Defence Minister Younger in the summer of 1987.[6] United States firms have real advantages of scale and will continue to possess them until firms in Europe can operate to serve the European market as a whole. Moreover, protectionism is deeply built into the psychological make-up of American military and procurement officials as well as into the legal framework of American defence procurement. Sales to the United States are possible and valuable, but they are largely of specific niche products.

Option 2. Negative DIB policy

A radical possibility would be for the government to decide that the development and perhaps even manufacture of military equipment is bad for British society as a whole and it should therefore diminish substantially. This prescription could be backed by combining the views that the arms business is a buyers' market (that the purchaser can obtain what is needed almost at the marginal cost of production) and that the resources devoted to defence manufacturers hinder the ability of British industry to compete in civil markets. The logical conclusion then becomes that Britain should opt out of defence production as far as possible. Clearly these arguments are not easily compatible with the commonly expressed view that the prosperity of the south of England is boosted substantially by the defence sector.

The overall political acceptability of this option is also clearly questionable. There are security issues related to whether the world arms market will remain in favour of the buyer should Britain and perhaps one or two other countries no longer compete in it. One aspect of British DIB policy is the extent to which it establishes a precedent for others such as Germany and Italy to follow. It is even debatable if the current market so favours the buyer. Would the United States have released the APG–65 radar for West German F–4s had it not known that West Germany was involved with EFA which will also need a radar? It is clear that the United Kingdom obtained a favourable deal regarding the AWACs which it decided to buy in 1986 because it still had Nimrod as a possible option. Then there are also questions about the capacity of the British economy to adapt to a diminution in defence employment at a time when defence spending would not be falling. With current levels of unemployment in Britain it would be optimistic to assert that those leaving the defence sector would easily find work, especially if they were, for example, from the shipbuilding industry. This is not to say that it might not be easier to reduce unemployment if rather more engineers and scientists were available for the civil sector of if more R&D money was available for civil research.

Then there would be the consequences for the balance of trade. Those who assert the economic harm of defence production anticipate that a British economy liberated from the burden of defence work would grow rapidly. This is debatable but, even if the point is accepted for the purpose of argument, there would still be an awkward transition period when the United Kingdom would be without defence exports, defence imports would be rising and new exports had yet to win markets.

A more moderate version of this option might be to buy only foreign equipment but often to arrange its licensed manufacture in Britain. For those who believe in the inherent production inefficiency of the British defence industries this would generally involve paying a premium. Yet, in specific instances, British industry has shown a capability to produce systems under licence at least as effectively as the original supplier. Two examples would be the Sea King helicopter and the Milan anti-tank missile. Significantly, the British aerospace industry believes it would have been cheaper in terms of life cycle costs, had Britain decided to buy the F–18 and to have produced it under licence in the United Kingdom rather than to have bought it built by McDonnell Douglas, the more so once life cycle costs were taken into account; the United Kingdom would supply spare parts more cheaply. However, it is doubtful if a capacity for licensed production which is not much more expensive than direct purchase from the developer can be sustained over the long run without the licensees having their own development programmes to enable them to stay abreast of technological advance.

Licensed manufacture would give some kind of capability to expand production in crisis or war and there would be less operational reliance on the overseas supplier. This could be further reduced if the imported parts were pre-stocked in some bulk in the United Kingdom, although this too would have a cost. Thus some British operational autonomy could be maintained but there is no doubt that a policy which aimed at increasing stocks substantially would be expensive. It could offset any savings from procuring equipment abroad.

Even with this option, the British Government would need to allocate defence R&D spending to the level necessary to maintain its expertise as a customer. Just what this level would be would depend on the range and depth of expertise which the government wanted to keep in the light of its procurement plans. Currently, its spending on the RDEs of about £750 million a year is inadequate for the export customer role. Only about one third of the RDEs' budget is devoted to research and the government is increasingly shifting the burden of judgement on equipment to industry.

Discriminating against the British DIB as a general principle could never make sense to those who believe that British industry is comparatively good in the defence sector, which is often marked by high technology, low volume, customised production, and rather weak in high volume, low technology areas. However, discriminating against British defence firms could only have any chance of support when the rest of the British economy was in splendid shape, and when the uncertainty of relying on outside suppliers was diminished in significance because the real dangers to British security were thought to be minimal. Neither of these conditions was present in 1988.

Thus a reasonable conclusion is that the British Government should discriminate in some way or ways in favour of the British DIB. All countries which have the choice open to them in fact support their own defence industries to a greater or lesser degree. The issue then becomes what should be the precise nature of the British commitment to its defence industries. Here we can initially identify two extremes — the choice between supporting a comprehensive or a partial DIB.

Option 3. A comprehensive British DIB

Aiming for a comprehensive DIB providing Britain with operational and strategic autonomy is a theoretical possibility. Such autonomy is sought in the Soviet Union and the United States. French policy too still seems, in many ways, to be directed towards at least a considerable measure of strategic autonomy. At least as late as 1981, the British Government used words which suggested this as a desirable goal for the United Kingdom.[7]

However, the economic costs of maintaining a comprehensive DIB, even one defined as 'thinly spread over everything' would clearly be enormous, unless for some reason it proved possible to substantially downgrade the technological demands made by British military requirements because of a drastic change in British security needs.

In practice, Britain abandoned any aspiration towards a comprehensive DIB long ago and has moved out of development and production work in fields such as ballistic missiles. What Britain has sustained, through its extensive research efforts, is a broad expertise in enabling technologies which means it could move back into many areas if it so wished and should the resources be made available.

It is clear that, whatever political party holds office, the United Kingdom's future DIB will, of necessity, be partial in its coverage. What are needed, therefore, are criteria to suggest the nature of its limits.

Option 4a. Britain in a comprehensive European DIB

A reasonable, if ambitious, case can be made that the British DIB should contribute to the need of Western Europe as a whole to have a wide-ranging DIB, providing operational and strategic autonomy, with the capacity to produce competitive products for sale in world markets and able to act as an equal partner to American industry in collaborative projects. The concept of the European DIB is associated also with ideas concerning a perceived need for more European defence cooperation, for a stronger European pillar in

NATO, and for the countries of Western Europe to prepare for the day when the United States commitment to NATO may weaken considerably or disappear. The British DIB's contribution could be determined by the need to maintain competition in Europe in specified fields, by specific areas of British capability such as aero-engines and even, if a protracted conventional war in Europe is envisaged at any stage, by the need to locate manufacturing facilities in areas away from the frontier with Eastern Europe.

The primacy of the European, rather than the national, DIB has implications for collaboration. Until the end of the 1970s it could be said that European states collaborated in order to maintain or build up the comprehensiveness of their DIBs. Some collaborative arrangements were made less efficient by the requirement that all partners retained expertise and capability across all or many aspects of the project, even though this resulted in some wasteful duplication of effort. Collaboration itself is a technique which the Government has correctly embraced for spreading R&D expenses, for generating a large initial market and for generally limiting what it needs to pay for new defence systems.

The British Government, committed to European collaboration as a means of making EC industry as a whole more competitive with that of the United States and able to collaborate with it on an equal basis, can be said to have adopted this option implicitly. It has, for instance, endorsed the Vredeling Report on measures to improve the competitiveness of Europe's defence industries. However, since the departure of Michael Heseltine, Britain has adopted a more low-key posture in the IEPG and, partly as a consequence, that body has lost some of its momentum. Moreover, the commitment to collaboration in parts of the British Armed Forces is stronger than others, if the incidence of collaboration is a guide. The Royal Navy is involved in few collaborative projects and appeared initially as a hesitant participant in the NFR-90.

It is clear that emphasis on British support for the strength of the European DIB does not exclude the possibility of collaborating with the United States as well. From a British point of view, collaboration with Europeans will often (but not always) be easier than collaboration with America. Collaboration with the United States should work better if Britain has other European partners. British behaviour is compatible with these statements since Britain has more collaborative projects with Europe than with the United States and there are several European partners in many transatlantic defence projects with British involvement.

Collaboration with Europe is easier because, in addition to the relative political closeness of European states, even the largest European industries are of similar weight to their counterparts in the United Kingdom. They cannot dominate a project against British interests. Within Europe, technology transfers flow more easily than they do across the Atlantic, and the United States, with authority divided between Congress and the Presidency, is not always a reliable partner in collaborative schemes, as the British experience with the Harrier over the years has shown.

Most important, there is in Western Europe a framework of commitment to free trade in general within which defence could be accommodated, given political will on the part of governments. The changes associated with the establishment of a single European market by 1992 involve the abolition of national protectionism in public procurement. While there is a legal case that such protectionism need not be given up in the defence sector, in the longer term the overlap between civil and military goods will make the maintenance of any distinction hard, for instance in the field of computers. Moreover, the single European market will make it easier for all companies, including those with strong defence sectors, to operate on a Community-wide basis and even to become European rather than national companies.

The lesson of the past decade is that, for successful collaboration with the United States or to sell individual systems to it, European states' solidarity about their reasonable interests is helpful. It is not a likely coincidence that the United States became more ready to team with Europeans and to buy their products once the IEPG developed. In the 1980s the IEPG countries made clear that they preferred collaboration to buying defence equipment from America and that they expected the 'Two-Way Street' in defence equipment trade to approach parity. Among other measures, they established a programme of Cooperative Technology Projects in order to strengthen the research base of Europe's defence industrial capabilities. In the atmosphere created, transatlantic defence cooperation, much of it involving British companies, grew considerably.

Option 4b. Concentrate British production on what cannot be reliably bought from overseas

It is almost incontestable that Britain should continue to develop and produce equipment designated as central to British security which cannot be obtained from somewhere overseas. The MoD has tried to identify such equipment, much of which concerns nuclear warheads and encryption technologies, and periodically reviews its list of the items concerned. There is a degree of disagreement within government on this issue, particularly between those who look at what technologies may be available. Nigel Hughes, Director of the Royal Signals and Radar Establishment at Malvern (RSRE), observed in 1988:

> Not all technology developed by other nations is available to us, as they regard much leading-edge technology as of major significance to their 'national security.' For example, the US Very High Speed Integrated Circuit (VHSIC) programme was specifically declared at the outset as being for the strategic benefit of the US national defence technology base and few products from that programme have been released to Allies. Even where such products may be released, controls may be exercised over sales of resulting equipment to third parties. It is for these reasons that I emphasize the

importance of maintaining an international inventory of available and exploitable technology . . . detailed professional knowledge, rather than glossy brochures, is required for the building of reliable technology availability data bases.[8]

Clearly, the MoD could also take its basic analysis further to consider which terms are available from only one state and which are available also from only one company. If the possibility for competition is thought important and if the United Kingdom wishes to limit its vulnerability to a cut-off in supplies, it may choose to produce at home that which otherwise would be available only from one external supplier state.

Additionally, building on Nigel Hughes' argument, this option suggests the need for the MoD to continue a fairly wide British R&D effort so that, should new and vital technologies emerge elsewhere which were not accessible to the United Kingdom, Britain would be able to develop its own versions. Hence this option is related to the option below which suggests that the British DIB could be focused on military technologies predicted to be central to future weapons systems.

Option 4c. Aim at a DIB comprising only those United Kingdom sectors which are, or could reasonably become, internationally competitive

This would involve the government paying a relatively small premium for a British DIB. First, several points must be acknowledged which make basing policy on international competitiveness problematic. One is that, among the bigger firms, different sections of the companies often perform better than others (in part because they may have been allocated the best people). Another is that the evidence from the National Audit Office and elsewhere suggests that efficiently-run programmes depend as much on the role played by the MoD as they do on industry. In global terms, defence industries tend to be as effective as the supervision over them. A third point is that it is not easy to measure international competitiveness. The capacity to export successfully is one guide but, in defence, overseas sales can be a function of how much effective government backing a company enjoys and the extent to which its products are geared towards export markets rather than national forces. Companies can be commercially competitive and successful in world markets without possessing the advanced technological capabilities needed in equipment to reinforce deterrence in Europe. With these reservations on the nature of competitiveness, it is clearly desirable that the British defence industry should be as competitive as possible with its counterparts in other states.

Aiming at an internationally competitive DIB would mean a procurement policy in many ways similar to Option 1 of making British industry compete against foreign opposition with the British Government ready to fund development in the United Kingdom when it felt that the British bid was best. However, it could also mean government undertaking separate assessments, independent of any single project, of individual firms or of technological areas, to decide if some companies were worthy of temporary protection while their strength increased. In the late 1980s, as part of an effort to decide how best to use reduced R&D funds, the MoD generated internal studies of the defence industrial areas in which the United Kingdom appeared technologically strong. As Vice Admiral Sir Jeremy Black told the RUSI in March 1988:

> In our blueprint we will wish to retain capability in high tech areas and to prevent our becoming the metal bashers of NATO. In particular, we will wish to encourage development in the UK in those areas of technology in which the UK is a leader, and to ensure that we maintain a research base to support that leadership. In cases when our lead is less strong or doesn't exist, the priority for research is lower.[9]

If competition is necessary for efficiency, and often in the defence sector it would seem to be very helpful, a case could be made that the British DIB should be sustained only in those areas where there is scope for internal British competition. This would mean the United Kingdom encouraging foreign bids when there could not be effective competition within Britain. The Government has in fact followed this line on some projects and is clearly tempted by it. On the other hand, a preference to keep open the possibility of purely internal competition alone was clearly shown when the Ministry of Defence opposed the GEC-Plessey merger.

But another element of such a policy would be that the government would not favour British industry in those fields of most advanced technology where the necessary resources mean that there is only one British firm in being. Thus the 'national champions,' such as British Aerospace in aircraft and Rolls-Royce in jet engines, could lose their favoured status. The government has not been willing to do this and has instead insisted on national champions using competitive subcontracting where possible. Clearly there can be conflict between the option of an internationally competitive DIB and the preference for internal competition in fields where the national market is limited and the financial and technological demands placed on companies is great. In some defence areas, national markets barely support the existence of even one firm.

Then the logical action for the United Kingdom would be to encourage the emergence of a single West European market for defence equipment. In such a market, there would be scope for at least two companies in all spheres save perhaps jet engines. Thus it would be possible to have intra-European competitions. However, the logic of this situation is also that fair competition could most easily be envisaged between defence firms which had a European rather than a national character. If Britain wanted a new helicopter, it would be easier to choose objectively between two competing 'European' companies with British elements than between a 'British' and a Germany company.

The IEPG has recognised that integrated European 'defence firms' are some distance away, although at least one leading industrialist, Plessey's Chairman, Sir John Clark, has said that such firms are feasible and desirable.[10] Some transnational defence companies do exist to a degree (Philips and United Scientific Holdings are two cases in point) with many major multinationals having defence sectors. Pilkingtons and GKN are two major suppliers of the MoD which, in their activities as a whole, have more than 50 per cent of their employees outside the United Kingdom. Also, some of the big British companies concerned with defence, most obviously BAe and GEC, are looking to expand their activities overseas (often in the United States, given the value of the dollar in the late 1980s). Thus the multinational defence company, with a clear base in either the United States or Europe, could be a phenomenon of more importance in the future.

However, until the European market exists and the European defence company becomes common, the government will have to make use of other techniques to stimulate industrial efficiency.

One such technique, being used for instance in the case of the Alarm missile, would be to make British manufacturers compete on world markets, even if they were automatic choices at home, by limiting payments for research and production tooling on the assumption that a volume of exports would be achieved.[11] This is common French governmental practice. The British Government is believed to have accepted that, when companies put their own funds into a project's development and accept the risk of a fixed-price contract, they should be allowed greater profit margins at the production stage (if they can keep down their costs). This approach could be used also in collaborative projects where it may be difficult to have substantial competition within the project itself. Perhaps Tornado costs would have been held down with more rigour in the early stages of the project if the companies had realised that, even with an initial order for around 900 aircraft, exports would still be needed to enhance corporate viability. One possible disadvantage of this approach is that companies naturally keep the proprietary rights associated with development work they have funded. A government can then find that the most commercially interesting technologies have been funded with the company's share of the development programme and that the government may be called to pay for the use of those technologies in other systems. Certainly companies see knowledge ownership as a real advantage of their contributing to development expenses.

Option 4d. Building an DIB around future key defence technologies

Another focus would be to concentrate the DIB on key enabling technologies which were expected to provide competence in those systems of decisive importance in future war. To a degree the MoD already tries to give priority in research to technologies which can support a range of future systems.[12]

There are bureaucratic problems involved which the MoD is trying to overcome. In particular, 'individual desk officers [in MoD] tend to be concerned with a particular area of application and no one individual will instinctively wish to sponsor an area that benefits so many others.'[13] Today, materials technology concerned with armour, sensors, data processing, software and aerospace propulsion technologies appear among the strong candidates for support on grounds of their military significance. It is widely agreed that the force multipliers of the future will involve technologies for C^3I and battle management coupled with the capacity to direct weapons accurately against high value targets. Nigel Hughes of RSRE, discussing the analytical technique of illustrative weapon system design, said that:

> it has already shown us the value of such technologies as: guidance and control, target detection, recognition, identification and homing, advanced structural materials, reduced radar cross sections, high energy directional warheads, command, control and information systems etc, and this informs the military customer on the priority he should be attaching to sponsorship of work on research and technology.[14]

The American aerospace industry has highlighted eight key technologies needing future attention and funding: advanced composites, VHSICs, software development, propulsion systems, optical information processing, artificial intelligence and ultra-reliable electronics.[15]

Overall, the identification of future key military technologies does not appear an impossible task and the UK need not aim to be comprehensive in its ambitions. Capacity in just several key areas would give Britain useful bargaining power to obtain the necessary technology imports in collaborative programmes to cover areas of relative weakness. But, to quote Nigel Hughes once more,

> an element of UK unique technology is needed even to win a place at the international collaboration negotiating table. An element of UK unique technology is also needed to barter for real information on internationally available technology . . .[16]

Option 4e. Aim at a DIB which particularly benefits the civil economy

Going further than the Government's known preference that more civil advantage should be taken of the British military R&D efforts, a specific choice could be made that the DIB should be shaped to encompass those technologies which are of particular civil significance. While spin-off from the military to the civil sector is often thought to be limited, there is no doubt that in some significant cases it does occur. Some particular sectors might be aerospace, sensors, data processing, some elements of communications and machine tools. Encryption is finding more civil applications, particularly as electronic movements of money proliferate. As a specialist example, Pilkingtons have begun to apply their military laser expertise in the development of new surgical techniques and equipment.[17]

Any such option implies that the British Government would prefer its defence suppliers not to be too dependent on defence business. Spin-off from the military to the civil sector is more easily conceived if both sorts of product are made by the same firm. Yet despite the fact that some firms which are largely dependent on MoD contracts are sometimes criticised for uncompetitive and inflexible practices which they reveal when they try to compete in the civil sector, there is a feeling in industry that certainly in the past MoD officials have preferred companies to be dependent on defence contracts. Such dependence was seen as ensuring that companies would be sensitive to MoD wishes and the MoD could be sure its business was receiving the attention of the best people in a company.

The government's preference to get more civil spin-off from defence R&D is reflected in its concern to open up the RDEs to industry and in its promotion of the establishment of Defence Technology Enterprises (DTE). Also, to advance the development of aerospace activities on the Farnborough site, it is setting up the Farnborough Aerospace Development Corporation. The MoD is participating in the inter-departmental Link programme which is meant to promote the advance of scientific programmes into commercial products and services. The Advisory Council on Science and Technology (ACOST), the Government's new advisory body announced in a July 1987 White Paper, has been charged with keeping under consideration science and technology priorities for both civil and defence R&D.

Yet at present the Government appears to want mainly to ensure that the volume of defence R&D is not so great as to damage civil industry. It could go further to promote defence contributions to the civil sector. A decision could be reached to promote the production of defence goods whose manufacture depended on modern techniques of computer-aided engineering, experience of which could perhaps be profitably used also in the civil sector. This would, however, not be the case if CAD/CAM was still used often in defence work primarily for what one industrialist called bringing 'efficiency to the interminable re-design process, caused by specification change.'

In general, looking for civil spin-off would mean directing defence funds to enabling technologies capable of a range of applications similar to the financial support given by the United States Department of Defense for research into VHSICS, VLSICS and superconductors. Signal and data processing would be strong candidates for support, kinetic energy armour piercing ammunition would not. Gansler has suggested, for the American economy, that the civil benefit from military development spending could be increased by placing less emphasis on major projects and more on components, technologies and process techniques, which could be relevant to the civil sector.[18] Such a policy thrust would clearly require government to undertake explicit studies of future likely military-civil links and of future key civil technologies. Until about 1985 the Conservative Government was reluctant to address the question of which technologies would be crucial in future economic advance, feeling that answers were best left to industry. However, it did establish the Alvey programme, which had a clear military element, and it encouraged British participation in European Community Framework schemes such as Esprit. From the middle of the decade it went further, in particular by upgrading the ACARD Committee to become ACOST, which was planned to be chaired on occasions by the Prime Minister. It also encouraged industry to establish the Centre for the Exploitation of Science and Technology (CEST) organisation. Thus, although the Government would not commit itself to responsibility for the identification of critical civil technologies, it moved to accepting that it should establish frameworks in which industry, with inputs from government, collectively would consider such issues. Industry itself appears confident that key civil technologies can be identified.[19]

To encourage civil spin-off, as a procedural approach, the MoD could introduce a preference in awarding contracts to companies which generated a designated share (perhaps 60 per cent) of their income from civil work and which had demonstrable internal mechanisms for ensuring that the expertise derived from defence projects could be transferred across to the civil sector. The establishment of such mechanisms, which already exist in some companies, could be made a condition for certification as a qualified MoD contractor in addition to the features which are currently sought. Formal MoD-industry consultation on spin-off issues could be increased and take place before decisions on individual projects are made. To calculate which technologies are the best candidates for civil and military advance, the government, presumably through ACOST, must clearly take account of trends and opinions in the rest of Europe, Japan and the United States.

It is too early to assess the eventual impact of ACOST on defence procurement but, clearly, increasing the weight of the civil spin-off dimension would give the Department of Trade & Industry a bigger voice than it has traditionally had on defence equipment issues. Within this general area, the HCDC would like to see governmental consideration of an interdepartmental Aerospace Board to look at the civil and military sides of that industry.[20]

Option 4f. A DIB to secure partial autonomy for British forces

A different emphasis would be to direct the DIB so that at least some British forces could undertake specific operations for a given period of time (perhaps three months) without foreign support. Domestic manufacturing facilities, stocks of finished products, components and raw materials would have to be explicitly designated. This would be most obviously relevant to

British units specifically designated for action outside the NATO area. Such forces include 5 Airborne Brigade, 3 Commando Brigade Royal Marines and the RAF Air Transport force, as well as elements of the Royal Navy.

The general notion of force autonomy is clearly of some appeal since ministers have indicated a preference, for instance, for British self-sufficiency in the production of some ammunition. Operational autonomy for a short war could in principle be achieved through stock-piling, although this would probably be a costly approach, certainly in terms of equipment with a degradable chemical content.

Consideration of fields of desired British autonomy must also include assessment of the advantages of an independent British arms exports policy. If a state seeks a free hand with arms supplies, it clearly needs to have the firms manufacturing in its territory to be under its authority. This raises the question of which firms are to be considered as 'British' and thus part of the national base. One approach, that adopted by the United States, is to treat as foreign any firm which is not beneficially owned in the host state. However, a European firm can set up a defence subsidiary in the United States and have it supervised by a United States Government approved board of trustees. The United Kingdom takes a different line with regard to companies like Cossor, which is owned by Raytheon but is formally treated as British. Discrimination against foreign-owned companies, if it occurs, is concealed, although one reason why the Sperry Corporation sold its British subsidiary to BAe was that it felt that it was not in favour with the British Government. Significantly the United States under President Reagan sought to exercise extra-territorial control on the overseas subsidiaries of American companies.

Freedom of manoeuvre with arms supplies also means that there is a need for wariness of reliance on external suppliers for subsystems. One reason why there was reluctance to accept American offers of a radar for the European Fighter Aircraft and why the French developed their own air-to-air missile instead of participating in the NATO AMRAAM/ASRAAM programmes was the fear of desired European exports being prevented by an American refusal to allow American subsystems to be included. Licensed production can help get around some of these issues, as can the validation of a piece of equipment so that it can use, for instance, more than one radar, engine or other subsystem.

Conclusions

These are the broad options which can be discerned as open to the Government with respect to the British DIB. Some are of more obvious appeal than others. Others appear feasible only in principle and would generate considerable political opposition should an effort be made to introduce them. The preferences of the authors clearly show through to some degree but always colouring the attraction of any choice is the wider range of values and beliefs about the future which any analyst or decision-maker must hold. Thus this study concludes with some observations about such values and beliefs.

9

The Future of the DIB: Political Considerations and Priorities

It must be acknowledged that DIB policy is a difficult area for the British Government publicly to address. It involves issues marked by complexity and risk, where different government departments have varying concerns; it means addressing uncomfortable issues concerning the circumstances in which the state may wish to use military force, and it threatens to absorb many resources. Any policy which aims to sustain even limited British strategic or operational autonomy will have a cost. Moreover it is threatening in international political terms because it raises questions about whether Britain should work closest with Europe rather than the United States, or whether it should neglect its European partners in favour of large-scale cooperation with Washington. Also explaining official reluctance to address the DIB is the fact that, because of the complexity of the issues concerned, there are no easy answers which can be presented to the public in a simple form.

In the 1980s, attention was drawn to the British DIB by a succession of pressures and events — the persistently growing cost of defence equipment, which made collaboration more appealing, the publicity drawn by problematic national projects such as the Nimrod, AEW, the Westland crisis (which then had in its margins the possible Land Rover sale), the Falklands Conflict and the Government's privatisation of many companies with major defence interests. Yet the Government did not devote much public attention to the question of what the basic shape of the British DIB should be. Of central significance was the Government's public concern with value for money and its implicit need to hold down the rate of increase in the costs of defence equipment. By the mid-1980s, once the Government had decided to lower the level of real defence spending, the role of 'value for money' in procurement had become more than just an exercise aimed at avoiding waste of the taxpayers' money or a means of maximising the fighting efficiency of British forces; it had become a significant element in a campaign to keep costs down so that fundamental questions about the future roles of British forces (a 'defence review') could be avoided. In practice, emphasis on value for money apparently led to, not just improved performance by industry, but also less commitment to buying British, a perceived tendency to define value for money in terms of low initial acquisition prices and little inclination to identify what sort of DIB the Government might like to see, let alone to devise a strategy for sustaining it.

Clearly this interpretation is contentious. Supporters of the government's approach, with its emphasis on competition, would argue that the effect of competition was to make companies more efficient and able to compete in the world as a whole, in short to strengthen the DIB. As noted earlier, this point has real if partial weight. The impact of the Government's procurement techniques and defence spending cuts on many parts of the British DIB has been to stimulate the emergence of leaner and more competitive companies which often are no longer willing to rely on military markets. Companies like Thorn and Pilkington were clearly keen to expand their civil work and the strategic plans of many major corporations aimed to reduce the weight of defence work in their turnover.

The limitations of the Government's approach, however, were apparent in the Westland crisis, because the emphasis on competition alone gave the government little guidance as to what it should do. Another interesting case, which drew less attention, was that of VSEL and the Trident submarines. No other British shipyard had VSEL's submarine capability and expertise and no meaningful intra-UK competition could be held. On the other hand, it would have been politically unacceptable to have seriously considered a foreign submarine builder for Britain's independent nuclear deterrent. The government had to make the best contractual arrangement it could with the only possible supplier. A third instance revealing the limitations of government policy arose when GEC sought to take over Plessey. The British Government was divided between its eventual choice of forbidding the move, which left the MoD with more scope for domestic defence electronics competition, and permitting it, which should have helped the new company to compete in worldwide civil and military markets. It chose in the event to forbid the merger, although the two companies were later able to merge their telecommunications interests.

Policy consistency and coherence in an area such as the DIB, with its wide-ranging implications, can only be achieved in a framework of views about how the environment for British economic and security policy is likely to evolve. Therefore this essay concludes by looking at some of the questions, which constitute the more important items in that framework.

The political bases for DIB policy

On the defence front, of central relevance is whether, in the long term, NATO will need to have an explicit capacity to wage sustained conventional war in order to give weight to its deterrent posture.

In the past, there has been little pressure for such a capacity, indeed its presence would have been thought to undermine the real essence of NATO's deterrent, the threat to resort to nuclear weapons. However, there are signs of change. Public opinion in the West is divided on the desirability of heavy reliance on the nuclear option and it seems likely that many sectors of European opinion would have confidence in a NATO posture of 'No Early First Use.' Then there are the stances of the Superpowers. Under Carter and Reagan the United States indicated that it wanted to reduce the role of nuclear weapons in Western defence. The SDI, the 1986 Reykjavik summit and the INF Treaty of 1987 to abolish nuclear missiles with ranges between 500 and 5000 kilometres were all signs of American reservations about nuclear forces. Moreover, a Soviet analyst wishing to show that the United States would not in practice use nuclear weapons for the defence of Western Europe would have no difficulty in assembling appropriate supportive quotations from prominent Americans who had held high office. Within Europe, West Germans across the political spectrum in the late 1980s were favourably disposed to the removal of short-range nuclear weapons once the longer range INF had been negotiated away. These weapons would be in principle easiest in the nuclear category to use in a future war since they could be directed at armed forces, although obviously it would be a difficult decision in practice to escalate a war to the nuclear level. Political stresses in NATO in 1988 were apparent on the nuclear issue and the Spring NATO summit could do little more than smooth them over.

The United States and the Soviet Union have accepted in some ways that protracted conventional war in Europe is possible. Soviet doctrine has recognised that a European war need not necessarily go nuclear and, on the other side, the United States has accepted that protracted conventional war could occur. In America the assumptions used by the National Security Council to direct the shape of the strategic materials stockpile say that the United States needs to be prepared for a war that begins in the Middle East and spreads to Europe and the Pacific. The war, it is said, could last in this form for three years. The Americans stockpile the raw materials which their armed forces would need for equipment in that three year period, although they do not stockpile to take account of European forces' needs.[1] The implications for Western Europe of such thinking are clearly extensive. They involve questions relating to the location of industry, the vulnerability of supply lines and manufacturing facilities, the need for stocks, the recognition of the value of surge capacity, and planning for the mass production of basic equipment as opposed to the small scale production of sophisticated items. There is evidence that the Soviet Union does take specific account of such factors in its defence policy.[2]

On the other hand, if the need for a conventional war-fighting capability is rejected, the significance of the European DIB as a whole is much reduced. The British Government tends towards this position, even though the two states best placed to shape the war (the United States and the Soviet Union) may have different ideas.

A further central defence question is what sort of operational autonomy the United Kingdom needs for its conventional forces. On what sort of outside support, and from whom, should Britain plan to rely should it decide to deploy its armed forces overseas or to send arms supplies to areas of conflict? This is clearly a question of enormous complexity where there are many possible relevant scenarios. But there are basic questions which could be addressed. Should Britain view the United States or Western Europe as reliable sources of supply for British out-of-area activities? As seen earlier, the HCDC has expressed doubts, particularly about the United States.

Another area where this issue arises is that of subsystems and component supplies for British defence products available for export. Should Britain rely on a single external supplier, for example for an air-to-air missile for the EFA or engines for the EH101? Given the Government's emphasis on holding down prices, and encouragement of British manufacturers to seek overseas subsystems, it would appear that the Government calculates that the United States will not interfere meaningfully with British export plans. Historically this would seem to have been the case, but the Americans have certainly interfered with the planned exports of other states using the United States subsystems.

Consideration of the likely need for British autonomy directs attention to related foreign policy issues. Phrased in perhaps a rather basic form, one question asks whether Britain's future lies most appropriately as an independent entity seeking to maximise its freedom of action, or as a junior partner of the United States or as an active member of a Western Europe association of states which collectively seeks to influence the world.

Despite Mrs Thatcher's appearing as almost an instinctive Atlanticist, the direction of British policy for some years has been towards Europe, and for solid reasons. As a state commanding substantial but nevertheless limited resources, the United Kingdom in isolation is likely to have only occasional impact on the United States and the Soviet Union, especially if its views are not supported by its major European partners. Yet with Western Europe Britain has already experienced considerable convergence of interest and judgement, and, most markedly after the 1986 Reykjavik summit, has been able to influence the United States.

This does not mean that Britain or any other European state should deny the centrality of the United States to NATO. It means instead that, if transatlantic relations are to be healthy, they must probably be based on sufficient European solidarity to ensure that America is not automatically dominant. On the armaments front, where the Europeans have been relatively solid since the beginning of the 1980s, transatlantic relations are stronger than for some time and the Europeans are selling successfully to America. On the other hand, despite the 1987 commitment of ships by several European states to keep open the Straits of Hormuz, which would have been unthinkable even three years earlier, the possibilities for concerted European action in foreign policy terms appear limited. European Political Cooperation has been successful in stimulating consultation and even common stances on some issues, but foreign policy action seems likely to remain predominantly a national responsibility.

A final political point is whether DIB policy can be seen only in simple defence terms. Obviously one perspective is to view defence as an activity discrete from other areas of government, to see the military protection of territory and the utility of military power as a separate, even predominant field of government activity. In this view, the role of procurement policy is to obtain the weapons most appropriate for the armed forces' needs at the lowest possible price and in a manner which assures the availability of future supplies of equipment. This perspective is given added weight because defence is organised within a specific government ministry with a massive budget and a staff dedicated to defence considerations. This perspective asserts that the defence budget should be spent on improving the country's defence, its military capabilities and little else.

However, a contrasting perspective is that government policy can best be viewed as a single entity. While it is true that different ministries with their own particular foci are maintained to spread workloads, their concerns overlap extensively. It is therefore reasonable that any one ministry should take into account the problems of the rest of government. In this perspective, procurement policy should take into account considerations such as employment, the balance of payments, foreign policy and wider national technological potential.

Put crudely, the first viewpoint is narrow, appealing in its way to the ministry official seeking a defined area within which to work, with clear, singular terms of reference and values.[3] The second view is roughly that of the statesman, concerned in broad terms with the overall good of the nation and, more pragmatically, perhaps with re-election. However, the second perspective is also that which most clearly reflects the challenges of the real world. The intellectual tidiness of the first perspective is useful for routine matters but, when major issues arise presenting substantial opportunities as well as dangers, it is the common and overlapping concerns of ministries which come to the fore. This needs to be taken into account when choices of DIB and procurement are considered. It obviously points to the conclusion reached by Gansler for the United States that defence procurement should be used where possible to reinforce American overall industrial strength and to produce civil spin-off from defence R&D.[4]

Governments, on occasion, do argue that 'value for money' (implicitly based on cash prices) will be rigorously enforced as the only relevant procurement criterion. Such a stance presses companies to keep their prices down. But inevitably other considerations intrude. For example, some British Aerospace officials feel that, once Short's had put in a reasonable bid for the RAF trainer contract, there was little chance that Short's would lose, given that work for them would provide needed jobs in Northern Ireland and might open up possibilities for wider British exports to Brazil. It is at least arguable that it is not in the national interest to have notable discrepancies between living standards in different parts of the country. If arms contracts can help to moderate this problem, they are likely to be considered for the role. In reality, almost every government in the world, including the Japanese, recognises the political and economic consequences of its arms spending and takes them into account. In some states, such as Belgium, the Economics Ministry has a major role in procurement choices, and offsets and licensed production have become a very common feature of arms import choices by governments.

These discussions lead to a further fundamental question about the consequences of defence equipment spending in the United Kingdom for the national economy. Some assert that the current DIB is too large and is bad for British economic growth overall. Others claim that the British DIB makes a substantial contribution to national well-being.

Before passing any firm judgement in this area, it is worth recalling that Norman Clark, a British economic analyst, has observed that 'there are certain things economic analysis does not do very well and one of these is to shed much light on the process of economic growth.'[5] Considerable caution should be exercised before any great weight should be attached to claims about the negative effects of defence spending in general and defence R&D spending in particular on the British economy.

Such issues need to be located in the narrower debate about just what is included under the 'R&D' heading and the wider debate about 'what's wrong with the British economy?' Assertions that the British defence industrial effort is bad for the economy as a whole often argue that Britain spends disproportionately more than its industrial rivals on defence R&D. The British aerospace industry, on the other hand, led by Ivan Yates of BAe, has worked out that about £1 billion a year of what the Government calls R&D spending is devoted to systems or project engineering which involves little or no innovatory work. Thus it is claimed that this should not be classified as R&D spending given the Frascati definitions of R&D used by the Organisation for Economic Cooperation and Development (OECD).[6] The logic of this argument is not that Britain spends too much on defence R&D, but that in real terms it spends too little on R&D in general.

Against the charge that the defence sector is less efficient and productive than other parts of British industry, and less successful at turning its R&D expenditure into sales, the Electronic and Engineering Industries Association has retorted that the defence sector generates more sales per unit of R&D than does the pharmaceuticals sector, often cited as one of more successful parts of the British economy.[7] There is a consensus that Britain does not put enough effort into civil R&D, but disagreement as to whether this is somehow a consequence of defence activities.

The Conservative Government coming to power in 1979 clearly felt that

Britain's major economic problems lay in a tradition of ill-judged intervention in industry, outdated industrial relations and the restrictive attitudes of work forces. There is a continuing element in Conservative thinking that the heart of the problem has little to do with defence and that improvements will come as people learn to rely more on their own efforts to shape their lives and as free market forces ensure resources are used more effectively. Other strategies and tactics suggested from outside government to promote economic growth make reference to the continuing need to increase public spending and investment, the lack of tax incentives for company research and training schemes and the shortage of skilled personnel, especially engineers.[8] Reference is also made to the reluctance of British financial institutions and companies to invest in high-risk but potentially highly profitable technology projects, even when the MoD has funded relevant basic research which needs to be further developed and applied.[9] A study by Henry Ergas of the OECD stressed that Britain did not so much spend too much on defence R&D as manage its overall R&D effort badly.[10] Some prominent British industrialists believe that too many British companies just do not appreciate the importance of R&D effort and technological advance.[11]

Of the many elements which determine a country's overall economic progress, it would seem reasonable to conclude that current British defence equipment spending is simply not a major factor either way in Britain's economic troubles.[12] Defence is not thought a particularly pertinent factor by many academic economists, consequently the majority of economic analyses of the British economy do not deal explicitly with the defence sector. It can be noted in parenthesis that a recent study of the impact of the defence budget on the United States economy concluded that the influence of defence is small.[13] A publication from the Economic and Social Committee of the European Community opened with the following observation:

> There is broad agreement on the reasons for Europe's difficulties with the new technologies. The main causes are identified as the lack of a large unified market, which is necessary if production costs are to be brought down; the compartmentalisation of the public purchasing market; the duplication of research work; the failure to exploit research findings in processes and products; and the insufficient contribution of small firms as a result of numerous bureaucratic obstacles such as the lack of risk capital and many other factors. In short the European dimension is lacking.[14]

There is much here that is pertinent to the defence sector but nothing to suggest that defence efforts in themselves are seriously damaging to economic advance based on high technology.

The British situation may have been different in the immediate post-war years when Britain's needs were different and its defence spending proportionately much higher. But today talk of the scarcity of engineers caused by the demand from the defence sector must be treated with some scepticism. Government engineers are often not paid at attractive rates, even with the special pay increases which are occasionally introduced. Any shortage of engineers in the United Kingdom has not pushed their salaries to astronomical levels and, in fact, the best paid professionals in British industry appear to be accountants. A BAe view was that the company's activities, far from taking engineers from the civil sector, actually help to train them. Young engineers come to the company and are willing to work for modest salaries for the sake of being involved with highly advanced, exciting projects. They tend to leave in their early 30s for positions in the civil sector where their experience means that they can earn higher salaries and hold positions of greater responsibility in smaller organisations.

Overall, it would be economically disruptive for the United Kingdom to increase markedly the human and financial resources it devotes to defence. On the other hand, it would be optimistic to expect that the British economy could quickly and successfully adapt to a sudden diminution in the flow of resources currently going to the defence sector. Either of these developments would require demanding adjustments in the economy at a time when industry is struggling to make all the other adaptions which it is pressed into by wider world commercial and technological forces.

Views on how a British Government can best promote economic growth also affect consideration of the impact defence equipment spending has on the economy. On the general industrial front, the Government has adopted mainly what might be designated a market approach. This stresses the lack of governmental expertise in making commercial decisions and picking successful products. It further argues that the structure of industry is something best left to market forces, so that the efficient users of resources can prosper. This preference for minimal government intervention in industry has also meant that the government has been reluctant to have an explicit industrial policy for defence.

However, as has been noted on occasions through this study, reliance on market forces is of limited value in the defence sector. As *The Times* defence writer Rodney Cowton put it, 'The reality is that, where a government is a dominant customer, a hands-off policy is not possible.'[15] The Government is in a good position to pick successful defence products and companies since it is a major purchaser of defence equipment and foreign buyers rarely buy British military systems which have not been endorsed by purchase by the British Armed Forces. Moreover, even within NATO there is no free market in arms. All the major arms-producing states favour their national products, as they are legally entitled to do. Both GATT and EC regulations exclude defence equipment from commitments to free trade. Should Britain unilaterally cease to support its defence companies, those foreign companies which still enjoy their government's support will be well-placed to take advantage.

Moreover, the best-placed companies would very probably be American. Most explanations of American economic success, particularly in high technology, point to the value of American industry being able to service a large, unified market. In the defence sector, this market is much more unified than it is elsewhere since there are virtually only four customers — the Air Force, the Navy, the Army and the Marines — all coordinated to an extent by the Department of Defense. An order from the United States forces is usually large enough to act as a formidable base for further exports. There is no doubt that American protectionism in the defence area is less than it was, but it is still extensive. There is also little doubt that American readiness to collaborate with Europeans through such arrangements as the Nunn-Quayle proposals has been prompted by European determination to develop and produce indigenous weapons. United States defence industrial and market strength, coupled with American protectionism, logically means that European industries should be organised so that they can operate on a similar scale. Until this happens, the unilateral exposure of British companies to competition from the United States would risk their being severely damaged. On the other hand, the British assertion that trade on the 'Two-Way Street' should be roughly balanced seems to have been implicitly accepted by the United States.

Any market-based approach to the defence sector must take account of the longer-term. Over time, the implementation of unqualified competition policy would mean a trend towards monopoly and thus the absence of competition possibilities. Why is this so? First, because persistent losers in development competitions will be driven from sectors as they lose expertise. Second, if the rate of return on risk and effort in the defence sector falls below benefits in the civil sector, companies will leave defence of their own accord. Third, because the technological expertise and capital involved represent real barriers for companies wanting to enter many sectors of the defence market. Fourth because defence research, development and production in many cases involves substantial, commercially decisive economies of scale — the larger entity should almost always be able to defeat the smaller. In short, defence industries are natural monopolies and there will be a tendency towards monopoly unless governments take specific counter-action. It is thus a reasonable criticism of the present British Government's emphasis on competition that, while it may have short-term effects in improving the performance of British industry, its long-term effects on the structure of that industry will make competition impossible.

The non-interventionist strategy is clearly hard to apply in defence also because the sole customer specifies and finances expensive products. In the defence area, when finance is left to companies to raise, the consequences are usually products, such as some Vickers tanks and the Northrop F–20, which are meant to sell in the Third World but which have limited appeal to the British Forces.

The Government's overall non-interventionist, market-oriented industrial strategy has always been disputed and subject to the criticism — for instance, that it does not recognise the difficulty British companies face in the British financial system in raising money for long-term, risky projects. Also, British companies do not enjoy the services of an equivalent of Japan's MITI which oversees and provides guidance within a context of domestic competition protected from outside by overt and non-tariff barriers. That MITI does not itself spend much money is not seen as a Japanese commitment to non-intervention, but as a reflection of the fact that the closer informal, cultural ties between the Japanese Government, industry and the finance sector makes such expenditure unnecessary. Looking at Germany, the backing which the Land governments have given to industry has been central to industrial development. British industry itself is unhappy, as revealed by the Engineering Employers Federation July 1987 discussion document 'Towards an Industrial Strategy.' It included the observation that,

> We do not shirk the fact that building a strategy will mean making choices. Such choices will be difficult and may sometimes prove wrong — but not to have a strategy is feckless; it means other nations make the choices and we are left with the residue.[16]

The European electronics industry argued in 1987 that European integrated circuit manufacturers needed a degree of protection if European industry as a whole was not to suffer, in the face of unfair foreign competition. Specifically, it accused Japan of deliberately over-producing integrated circuits so as to create global surplus capacity and of dumping its products at below cost prices so as to destroy non-Japanese competition.[17] There are also signs that industry does not feel ACOST will be very effective in producing a more positive Government R&D policy.

As noted briefly in the previous chapter, in practice the government appeared to be moving away from its position that industry should be left largely alone and certainly, through ACOST, it tried to identify winning future technologies and even actual products. It established a Science & Technology Assessment office which 'will build up a picture of the relative contribution of the different R&D expenditures to the UK economy and will contribute advice on these matters to the new, strengthened central structure' (ACOST). By supporting the establishment of the Centre for Exploitation of Science & Technology, with some government financial backing but primarily funded by industry and the City, the government hoped to establish a process 'for identifying exploitable areas of science for the long-term economic health of the country. This body 'should have a major influence on R&D supported by the Government.'[18] In its stance on the French Eureka initiatives, Britain has encouraged the emergence of projects which are concerned with the commercial stage of development rather than early research.

Thus the Government has come to accept that it should have a greater supporting and coordinating role, helping industry and the financial sector to work together on technology issues. However, it only announced its intentions after a highly critical report from the House of Lords on national policy

TABLE 9.1
Military, Political and Economic Issues

---

1 Will deterrence require NATO to have a capacity for sustained conventional war?
RESPONSE: Yes, probably, given present trends.

2 What degree of autonomy will the United Kingdom need for its own armed forces?
RESPONSE: Some for out-of-area activity but with at least passive European support being likely.

3 Does Britain's foreign policy future lie primarily as a member of the Western European group of states, as a junior partner of the United States, or as a separate, independent entity?
RESPONSE: As part of a West European grouping.

4 Can defence policy be viewed as a discrete activity, isolated from other elements in government policy including those dealing with the economy?
RESPONSE: No.

5 Does the current defence effort damage British efforts to secure economic progress based on technological advance?
RESPONSE: No, the United Kingdom and other European economies face wider problems.

6 Can a non-interventionist, competition-based, market approach by government be applied towards the defence sector?
RESPONSE: Yes, but only in the short term. It is not a viable long-term strategy.

---

in relation to science and technology and, in 1988, it was too soon to see how the Government's policy would work out in practice.

To summarise this chapter so far, we argue that the approaches preferred to deal with the defence industrial base will depend in part on the responses given to the military, political and economic issues digested in Table 9.1 This table also includes a digest of the responses of the authors.

Using the responses offered to the questions discussed above, and building on arguments elsewhere in the book, some points can be offered which are particularly worthy of emphasis.

Overall, there is a need for DIB policy to avoid extremes. If the British DIB can no longer provide equipment which British forces need at prices which can be afforded, this must be recognised. Similarly a country's policy towards its DIB obviously must take account of the equipment needs of its armed forces. As the HCDC observed, 'there is little point in seeking to remain independent if it means relying on outdated equipment which will not be effective in countering a threat posed by an increasingly sophisticated enemy.'[19] For some years in the United Kingdom, indeed in Nato as a whole, rising equipment costs have posed major problems for the defence procurement budget and any policy towards the DIB cannot severely disrupt any efforts to hold down the rate of equipment cost increase.

However, it is difficult to accept that British suppliers across the board are less efficient than other producers operating on a similar scale. The Defence Minister vigorously defended the efficiency of British defence firms before an American audience in 1987.[20] In some cases, British industry has produced defence equipment which can compete effectively with equipment from firms operating on a much larger scale. While there have been substantial differences between projects and between companies, British defence companies overall would appear to be at least comparable if not superior to those in states of comparable size.

Balance also is necessary in relation to defence exports. On the one hand, it would be unwise to ensure the survival of a national DIB by concentrating efforts on the development and production of armaments for export, if necessary pressing such equipment on the national Armed Services. Defence policy's central aim is to ensure the deterrence of a perceived enemy and effective defence should deterrence fail. Such an effective defence capability in itself contributes to deterrence. It therefore makes little sense to define national equipment needs in terms of what is required by foreign forces. On the other hand, exports help to reduce unit costs by spreading fixed costs over more units and awareness of a need to export can sharpen company performance. DIB policy therefore needs to be coordinated with arms export policy, but in an explicit and coherent fashion.

It also seems unlikely that British security would be enhanced by relying on external suppliers which might prove unreliable in times of need or who could not be predicted to offer low prices once competition eased. In many fields, the United States could develop a monopoly position within a period of 10 to 15 years if other European states in a similar position to Britain also decided repeatedly to rely on America rather than using national and cooperative European action to maintain developmental and production capabilities.

Much assessment of the national security utility of the DIB depends on whether it is believed that the future market for military equipment will be dominated by the buyers. As more countries become arms manufacturers, a buyers' market will almost certainly continue for less sophisticated items. On the other hand, it is likely that the more sophisticated items will be developed by major powers and manufacturers which can afford the major investment costs. Given the size of the American defence market, and the protection and support which is afforded to American companies in it, it is such firms which would seem most likely to survive.

If the United Kingdom turns primarily to the United States as sources of arms imports, the relationship will inevitably become one of dependence since, as has been noted, the United States is a much larger market and the United States Government has a DIB policy of not relying on external sources of supply and of minimising dependence on outside states. The Anglo-American bilateral relationship is too asymmetrical to be a firm basis for broad British security and foreign policy, although individual deals with the United States, such as for Harriers, Rapier missiles, head-up displays, 81mm mortars and so on, are clearly significant for the particular companies concerned.

Political considerations must have a place in arms procurement. In crude terms, it would be considered unacceptable for the British Armed Forces to rely on Soviet or East European manufactured equipment, even if it was available. Politically, a central consideration is that, in a whole range of ways, Britain's long term future is tied up with the development of Western Europe. British foreign and defence ministers have repeatedly recognised the value of British participation in a coordinated and strong Western Europe. Clearly Western Europeans recognise and proclaim the value of American participation in their defence, but their aim is to establish a relationship in which Western Europe can deal with its partner across the Atlantic on a more equal basis.

Applying this thinking to the defence equipment field, Britain might support the maintenance of a comprehensive DIB within Western Europe as a whole. The DIBs of other Western European states are at best in a similar predicament to those of the United Kingdom and, if Western Europe's overall political weight in the world is to match its economic significance, its defence industries should be coordinated so that they have wide-ranging technological capabilities and opportunities for production on an efficient scale. A broad strategy for achieving such a European DIB could follow the lines indicated in the Vredeling Report to the IEPG. Initially, this would mean more open competition within Western Europe as a whole, mainly for goods already in production, and more collaboration for innovatory items.

Britain could also support an effort whereby Europeans would seek at least to monitor defence technological shortfalls in relation to the United States and to fill them by using a proposed European version of the United States Defence Advanced Research Projects Agency (DARPA).[21] According to the study commissioned by the Vredeling Report, existing gaps include areas of materials and electronics. To help strengthen the overall European defence industrial position, Britain could extend its existing tendency not to develop matching systems to those already in production in Europe but seek to buy the European model instead. In terms of purchases from the United States, licensed manufacture might be the norm as a means of achieving autonomy and acquiring technology. Collaborative projects with the United States should preferably have a number of European partners so that any reduction of United States commitment to a project would not threaten its survival.

Within the EC and NATO as a whole, the concept of a specifically British DIB is being slowly eroded by the growth of transnational interests by major defence companies. Companies such as GEC and BAe are looking for overseas acquisitions in Europe and the United States to strengthen their positions. Overseas acquisitions can provide access to both new technologies and markets.

Also over the longer term, it will be increasingly difficult to separate many of the defence aspects of such companies from the civil because of shared technologies. Britain has an interest here in seeing that the Europeanisation of British defence companies and the presence of European companies in Britain strengthens Europe's overall capacity to compete in defence markets against the United States and the Soviet Union. It also has an interest in ensuring that the British Government has similar authority over the subsidiaries of foreign firms operating in Britain as foreign governments have over the overseas subsidiaries of British companies. The Americans, as noted, while sometimes allowing foreign firms to own defence businesses in the United States, keeps control over their activities through government-approved boards of trustees.

More modestly, Britain could look to its companies to form collaborative networks in which the same companies become used to working with one another, developing trust and accepting common working practices, and learning to take advantage of their individual strengths. Such networks have begun to appear. British Aerospace, MBB and Aeritalia are moving from Tornado to EFA and Rolls-Royce has firm relationships with MTU and Fiat Aviazione in the same projects. Westland and Agusta are linked in two major helicopter projects, the EH101 and the Tonal. Such collaborative networks would be particularly valuable in the electronics sector where they are presently somewhat unusual. There are, however, signs that Europe's air-borne radar companies are recognising their need to work together in order to survive.

When the British DIB as a whole is considered, there will be problems of adjustment and contractions ahead. Britain has too many shipyards given the number of ships the Royal Navy will be able to order. Export prospects are not good, especially for hulls as opposed to equipment, and selling shipbuilding expertise overseas will not produce thousands of jobs. Ship-based missile and radar systems will be produced in fewer numbers and therefore it will become even more important to make them where possible as derivatives of more extensively produced air and ground-based systems. Britain's attitude towards its industry on the anti-air warfare system for the NFR–90 needs to be coordinated with the stance taken on the future medium SAM, Hawk replacement in Europe. In armour, even with Vickers as the only tank producer, it will be difficult to utilise British tank production capacity without substantial (and unlikely) exports. Such exports would probably require the production of more tanks designed specifically for Third World markets. Even West Germany, which is a much larger purchaser of tanks than the United Kingdom, has surplus capacity in Krauss-Maffei's tank plant. Since the Second World War aerospace has been a largely successful, expanding and exporting sector of British industry. However, this is less true of the electronics sector. With the increasing share of electronics and avionics in aircraft, the question is raised whether the British aerospace-electronics sector can be as successful in the future as it has been in the past. BAe's emerging response to this challenge is, understandably, to cut back its reliance on external electronics firms, to enhance its own electronics capability and to diversify its product range. Thus it can undertake itself important value added activities and rely on its in-house strengths for key technologies.

Britain's DIB needs continued scrutiny. The thrust of the Conservative Government's policy has seemingly been to stimulate British industry into greater efficiency by exposing it to external competition. This has served some function but it should not be overlooked that foreign firms competing in defence in the United Kingdom have normally done so from the base of a firmly protected, and in the case of the United States, huge market.

Until 1986, there was real governmental reluctance to have any clear industrial policy, beyond the national Alvey programme and participation in European collaborative exercises such as Brite, Eureka and Esprit. The training of more engineers and skilled industrial workers was encouraged but there seemed to be little government activity to highlight those industries where Britain had or should develop a lead, or to identify the key technologies which British industry needed to master. While companies were being encouraged to think about these issues for themselves, there remained a reliance on the pressures of the free market to generate competitive corporate behaviour.

Clearly government stances were changing somewhat, as indicated by the terms of reference given to ACOST and the Prime Minister's at least nominal association with it. Even in the Conservative Party's 1987 Manifesto there was commitment to governmental targeting of R&D resources for the good of the British economy. The Government seemed to be moving towards a policy of ensuring that, while industry had prime responsibility for identifying 'technological winners,' government could provide frameworks for discussion and consultation. In the defence field, however, companies have a case that government should take a much more prominent part in selecting technologies which will be of great future impact.

No DIB, technology or general industrial policy can be effective unless it is long-term. Although the differences between the British political parties on nuclear weapons make it difficult, as do their contrasting attitudes towards state intervention in industry, an effort could be made to establish a DIB policy which is supported in broad outline by all the major British political groupings. The House of Commons Defence Committee could play a role in such an effort. The 1986 Labour Party document on defence policy, which incorporated qualified but not unlimited support for British industry, means that such bipartisan policy is far from unimaginable.

Many of the possible directions in which the DIB could be steered have been discussed here. The central message of this study is that the British DIB needs explicit attention beyond a wringing of hands about over-capacity and the generation of favourable or unfavourable images through the occasional successful or unsuccessful project. The contributions now and in the past made to British security by the British, other European and American defence industrial bases cannot be ignored, nor can the rising costs of defence manufacture. Also it has been recognised that, not least for the sake of healthy cooperation with the United States, the United Kingdom DIB needs to be considered as one very significant element in the European defence industrial capability.

It would seem prudent to urge that the British Government (and not just the MoD) should think explicitly through the types of defence industrial capability which it wants to maintain and the grounds for so doing. Moreover the capacity for defence production should not be evaluated purely in economic terms; the security dimension should also be specifically addressed, preferably in terms of Western Europe as a whole. Western Europeans need a DIB policy of its own to complement that of the United States. In general, the DIB should be viewed in the light of wider forecasts about the future world in which Britain will have to operate. The British and wider West European DIB could prove to be a crucial element in the region's capacity to deal with an uncertain world.

Notes

Introduction

[1] House of Commons Defence Committee (HCDC), *Implementing the Lessons of the Falklands Campaign*, Fourth Report in Session 1986-87, London, HMSO, 6 May 1987, pp. 88-9.

[2] See, for example, the Rt Hon George Younger (UK Secretary of State for Defence), 'Defence: A Sense of Balance' *RUSI Journal*, December 1986, pp. 3-8.

[3] *The United Kingdom Defence Programme: The Way Forward*, Cmnd 8288, London, HMSO, 1981.

[4] HCDC *Statement on the Defence Estimates 1986*, Second Report in Session 1985-6, London, HMSO, 5 June 1986, p. 17.

[5] Using information provided in part by Greenwood, *The Independent* newspaper concluded before the 1987 British election that a defence review would be inevitable after the election, whichever party gained power (see issue of 22 February 1987). See also M. Chalmers, 'Trends in UK Defence Spending in the 1980s', Bradford, School of Peace Studies, University of Bradford, *Peace Research Report*, September 1986.

[6] See *UK Military R&D*, Report of a Working Party of the Council for Science and Society, Oxford, Oxford University Press, 1986, pp. 42 ff.

[7] Ibid. pp. 13 and 14.

[8] *Statement on the Defence Estimates 1987-8*, Volume 1, Cmnd 101-1, London, HMSO, p. 48; *Civil Research and Development*, Cmnd 185, London, HMSO, July 1987, pp. 7-8.

[9] HCDC *The Appointment and Objectives of the Chief of Defence Procurement*, Fifth Report in Session 1984-5, London, HMSO, 10 July 1985, pp. 12-13.

[10] These characteristics include the dominance of governments as customers for arms and as setters of requirements for defence equipment performance, the unwillingness of governments to allow free trade in weapons and the absence of perfect competition within the NATO arms market, an absence which is permitted both under European Community and GATT rules.

Chapter 1

[1] House of Commons Defence Committee (HCDC), 2nd Report, Session 1985-6, on *The Statement on the Defence Estimates 1986*, London, HMSO, 5 June 1986, p. 32.

[2] HCDC 3rd Report, Session 1985-6, on *The Defence Implications of Westland plc*, London, HMSO, 23 July 1986, p. 37.

[3] *Selling to the MoD*, 2nd edition, London, Ministry of Defence, 1986.

[4] HCDC 2nd Report, op. cit., p. 33.

[5] *Interavia*, August 1980.

Chapter 2

[1] *Jane's Defence Weekly,* 25 April 1987.

[2] For a brief description of what this entails, see the Ministry of Defence pamphlet, *"Selling to the MoD"*, 2nd edition, London, 1986.

[3] *Jane's Defence Weekly*, 23 May 1987.

[4] How many aircraft TNT eventually buy is dependent on the growth of its business.

[5] *Aviation Week & Space Technology (AWST)*, 15 June 1987, p. 150.

[6] *Jane's Defence Weekly*, 6 June 1987. BAe-sponsored VLSI research at Hatfield Polytechnic should also be noted, see *Janes's Defence Weekly*, 23 May 1987.

[7] *The Financial Times*, 22 July 1987.

[8] *The Economist*, 14 March 1987.

[9] Rolls-Royce Company *Prospectus*, 1987, p. 44.

[10] *Ibid*, pp. 23-4.

[11] For a review of Rolls' development and technology work in the military sector, see *Flight International (FI)*, 12 April 1986.

[12] Company *Prospectus*, op. cit., p. 24.

[13] See the House of Commons Defence Committee (HCDC), Third Report, 1985-6 Session, *The Defence Implications of the Future of Westland plc*, London, HMSO, 23 July 1986; HCDC, Fourth Report, 1985-6 Session, *Westland plc: The Government's Decision-Making*, London, HMSO, 23 July 1986; Lawrence Freedman, "The case of Westland and the bias to Europe", *International Affairs*, Vol. 63, No. 1, Winter 1986-7, pp. 1-20.

[14] *The Financial Times*, 12 June 1987.

[15] *The Sunday Times*, 2 November 1987.

[16] *The Guardian*, 1 September 1986.

[17] S. Faltas, *Warships and the World Market*, Helmond, 1985, p. 200.

[18] *Jane's Defence Weekly*, 29 August 1987.

[19] *The Guardian*, 17 April 1987 and 24 April 1987.

[20] *Jane's Defence Weekly*, 29 August 1987.

[21] *The Financial Times*, 19 January 1988 and *The Sunday Times*, 7 February 1988.

[22] *Jane's Defence Weekly*, 9 May 1987 and 22 August 1987.

23 *The Times*, 16 July 1986.
24 *The Guardian*, 19 December 1988 and *Jane's Defence Weekly*, 16 January 1988.
25 *The Sunday Times*, 9 August 1987.
26 *The Sunday Times*, 9 August 1987.
27 *The Times*, 16 July 1986 and *The Financial Times*, 15 December 1987.
28 *Statement on the Defence Estimates 1987*, Vol. II, Cmnd 101-11, London, HMSO, 1987, p. 21.
29 *The Guardian*, 21 August 1987.
30 A ship service life of up to 26 years including three major refits is now under consideration by MoD, see *The Times*, 23 June 1987.
31 *The Financial Times*, 7 July 1987 and *Management Today*, February 1988, p. 59.
32 *The Guardian*, 30 June 1987.
33 *The Times*, 9 January 1987 and 16 January 1987.
34 *The Times*, 22 and 23 February 1988 and *Management Today*, November 1987, pp. 50-56.
35 *Statement on the Defence Estimates 1985*, Vol. 1, Cmnd 9430-1, London, HMSO, p. 41.
36 *Jane's Defence Weekly*, 22 August 1987.
37 K. C. Macdonald, "Collaboration in Procurement versus National Interest", RUSI and Brassey's *Defence Yearbook 1986*, London, Brassey's, 1986, p. 174.
38 See data published annually by the US Arms Control & Disarmament Agency, Washington, in *World Military Expenditures and Arms Transfers*.
39 *Towards a Stronger Europe*, A Report by an Independent Study Team established by the Defence Ministers of the Independent European Programme Group, Vol. II, Brussels, December 1986, Vol. II, p. 22.
40 Ibid., p. 66.
41 *Defence Industry Digest*, June 1987.
42 Macdonald, op. cit., p. 168.
43 *The Financial Times*, 7 July 1987.
44 See the Minister's speech of 18 June 1987 to the American Chamber of Commerce in London, text available from UK MoD.
45 *Statement on the Defence Estimates 1987*, op. cit., Vol. I, p. 49; *The Times*, 13 July 1987.
46 *The Times*, 25 February 1987.
47 "Aerospace: A Strategy for the Future", digested in *The Financial Times*, 11 April 1987.
48 *The Financial Times*, 4 January 1988.
49 M. S. Levitt, *The Economics of Defence Spending*, NIESR Discussion Paper No. 92, May 1985, pp. 32-3.
50 Speech, op. cit., at Note 44.

Chapter 3

[1] R. Facer, 'The Alliance and Europe: Part iii, Weapons Procurement in Europe', *Adelphi Paper 108*, London 1975.

[2] The Independent European Programme Group (IEPG), *Towards a Stronger Europe*, Brussels, December 1986, Vol 2, p. 73.

[3] *Aviation Week*, 3 September 1987, p. 227.

[4] *Interavia*, January 1987, p. 46.

[5] *Jane's Defence Weekly*, 11 August 1987.

[6] IEPG December 1986, op. cit., pp. 73-5.

[7] I. Mackintosh, *Sunrise Europe*, London 1986, pp. 62-3.

[8] *The Times*, 17 February 1987.

[9] Software engineers in defence companies are now tending to move into senior management posts in the software industry. *The Times*, 6 October 1987.

[10] Professor Sir Ronald Mason, 'Political and Military Requirements and the Management of Technology', *RUSI Journal*, Vol. 132, No. 1, March 1987.

[11] The government's recent decision to write off £30 million spent on developing a computer controlled command centre for the Type 23 Frigate was triggered by the realisation that developments in hardware and software had rendered the original concept obsolete, and a new competition was ordered to provide an updated system. Significantly, the competitors for this contract are two consortia with both hard and software expertise. The first of the Type 23 Frigates will go to sea with a less than operationally satisfactory system.

[12] *The Times*, 2 July 1987; *Flight,* 27 June 1987, p. 56.

[13] *Aviation Week*, 8 June 1987, p. 81.

[14] E. Maddock, 'Civil Exploitation of Defence Technology', *Report to the Electronics EDC*, February 1983.

[15] G. Kennedy, *Royal Bank of Scotland Review*, June 1986.

[16] M. S. Levitt, 'The Economics of Defence Spending', *NIESR Discussion Paper*, No. 92, May 1985.

[17] *Interavia*, April 1986; *The Financial Times*, 5 August 1987.

[18] An interesting omission from the list of products in Table 3.3 is that of guided weapons. In the United States and France, electronics firms are also involved in guided weapons and missile systems integration. In the British, while electronics firms supply many components for missiles, the development and production of guided weapons are the sole responsibility of the two airframe constructors, BAe and Shorts. However, they in turn depend upon the electronics companies for key subsystems such as the homer. This was a direct result of past government policy to divide work on guided weapons between the airframe and electronic sectors. Marconi had to give up its interest in airframes, while in turn English Electric (now part of BAe) had to abandon its guided weapons electronics activities.

150   THE UK DEFENCE INDUSTRIAL BASE

Report of the Monopolies and Mergers Commission, The General Electric Company Plc and the Plessey Company Plc, Cmnd. 9867, London 1986, Para 10.48.

19 *The Financial Times*, 11 June 1986.
20 *Jane's Defence Weekly*, 11 July 1987, p. 57; *The Financial Times*, 2 July 1987.
21 *Electronics Weekly*, 12 November 1986.
22 See two articles on the EAP/EFA software-systems development in *Jane's Defence Weekly*, 21 March 1987 and 28 March 1987.
23 BAe's move was partly motivated by the need to protect access to outside software skills in the face of strong competition from other manufacturing firms as well as the City. *Sunday Times*, 1 March 1987.
24 *Financial Times*, 1 July 1985; *Jane's Defence Weekly*, 28 February 1987, pp. 340–341.
25 *Financial Times*, 10 August 1987.
26 Maddock, op. cit., p. 8.
27 EDC Report, *Policy for the UK Electronics Sector*, NEDO 1982, p. iv.
28 S. Willett, 'The Impact of Defence Procurement on the Electronics Sector in London', unpublished paper, Birkbeck College, October 1986, p. 4.
29 Levitt, op. cit., p. 13.
30 Maddock, op. cit., pp. 3–16.
31 Willett, op. cit., p. 14.
32 Maddock, op. cit., p. 13.
33 Ibid., pp. 13–20.
34 Ibid, Part 11.
35 K. Dickson, 'The Influence of MoD Spending on Semi-conductor R&D in the United Kingdom', *Research Policy*, 12, No. 2 (1973), p. 119.
36 Ibid, p. 117.
37 See also Europe's problems in this area, Mackintosh, op. cit., pp. 71–80.
38 E. Braun and S. MacDonald, *Revolution in Miniature*, Cambridge 1982.
39 F. Malerba, *The Semi-conductor Business*, London 1985, p. 196.
40 Ibid, pp. 196–7.
41 More recently, with the active urging of scientists from RSRE Malvern, ICI has invested £10 million in a gallium arsenide production process which should have specialised uses in both civil and defence fields. Ferranti, a pioneer in developing semi-custom integrated circuits could also claim some 30 per cent of the 1980 market for such components.
42 The troubled genesis of INMOS shows that the governmental sponsorship of British microelectronics over the last decade and a half has involved some highly complicated and politically charged issues, few of which can be directly related to defence and procurement policies. Indeed, while INMOS has maintained Britain's reputation for innovation, as Thorn-EMI, its owners since 1984, have discovered, making money from semiconductors is extremely problematic. INMOS has cost Thorn some £300

million, and only recently has it begun to show evidence of an upturn. However, although INMOS's main hope for the future, the transputer, has several commercial applications, its military applications may be more promising. See M. McLean & T. Rowland, *The INMOS Saga*, London 1985; *Financial Times*, 4 February 1987.

[43] M. Kaldor, M. Sharp and W. Walker, 'Industrial Competitiveness and Britain's Defence', *Lloyds Bank Review*, October 1986, p. 47.

[44] *The Financial Times*, 29 September 1986/11 March 1987.

[45] *The Financial Times*, 5 August 1987.

[46] We are grateful to Phil Gummett for this observation.

[47] *The Financial Times*, 24 June 1986; *The Guardian*, 20 December 1986.

[48] See in particular, the report on civil R&D policy from the House of Lords Committee on Science and Technology.

[49] *The Financial Times*, 27 January 1987/5 March 1987; *Aviation Week*, 2 March 1987, p. 94.

[50] IEPG, op. cit., vol. 2, p. 28.

Chapter 4

[1] K. C. Macdonald, 'Collaboration in Procurement versus National Interest', RUSI/Brassey's *Defence Yearbook 1986*, London, Brassey's, 1986, p. 174.

[2] T. Taylor, *Defence, Technology and International Integration*, London, Frances Pinter, 1982, p. 39.

[3] M. Levitt, 'The Economics of Defence Spending', *NIESR Discussion Paper No. 92*, May 1985, p. 36; Democratic Leadership Council, *Defending America*, Washington DC, September 1986, p. 8.

[4] Speech to the US Chamber of Commerce in the UK, 18 June 1987, text provided by UK Ministry of Defence.

[5] Certainly US Democrats believe that this is what happened during the first years of the Reagan Presidency: 'During the Reagan Administration's first four years, spending on procurement rose by 61 per cent (excluding inflation), yet the Pentagon bought only five per cent more tracked and combat vehicles and four per cent more combat ships than it purchased during the previous four years. The price of major weapons and military equipment shot up by 42 per cent (after inflation) during the first Reagan term'. See *Defending America*, Democratic Leadership Council, Washington DC, September 1986, p. 8.

Chapter 5

[1] The American journal *Aviation Week & Space Technology* noted in an editorial that 'one standard of American defense planning is that military spending must grow 3 per cent annually after inflation to maintain forces on constant size. The same holds true of buying new weapons and

maintaining combat readiness – although 3 per cent is not always enough',
7 March 1988, p. 9.

[2] In early 1988 the UK Public Accounts Committee was told by MoD of cost
overruns amounting to billions of pounds in British defence spending, see
The Times and *The Guardian*, 10 March 1988.

[3] *DoD's Defense Acquisition Program: a Status Report*, US General
Accounting Office, GAD/NSIA-86-148, Washington DC, July 1986.

[4] *Statement on the Defence Estimates 1981*, Vol. 1, London, HMSO, Cmnd
8212-1.

[5] Defence Committee, *Defence Commitments and Resources and the
Defence Estimates 1985–86*, Vol. 2, Minutes of Evidence, 3rd Report of
the 1984–85 Session, House of Commons, London HMSO, 23 May 1985,
p. 12A. This volume is referred to hereafter as HCDC-3 II.

[6] *Towards a Stronger Europe*, Report by the IEPG Special Study Team
(Chairman H. Vredeling) appointed by IEPG Defence Ministers, IEPG
Secretariat, UK Delegation, NATO, Brussels, Volumes 1 and 2, 1987.
This volume is referred to henceforth as Vredeling.

[7] D. Greenwood, in the *Three Banks Review*, June 1984.

[8] *The Independent*, 26 February 1987.

[9] M. Chalmers, 'Trends in UK Defence Spending in the 1980s', School of
Peace Studies University of Bradford, *Peace Research Report*, September
1986.

[10] Labour Policy Statement on Defence adopted by the Annual Conference
of the Labour Party, 3 October 1986.

[11] *The Independent*, 26 February 1987.

[12] Frank Kitson, *Warfare As A Whole*, London, Faber & Faber 1987.

[13] *Jane's Defence Weekly*, 12 July 1986; *The Times*, 14 July 1986.

[14] Defence Committee, 'Statement on the Defence Estimates', 2nd Report of
Session 1985–86, House of Commons, London, HMSO, Report, Proceedings and Minutes of Evidence, 5 June 1986, (p. xvi). This volume is
referred to hereafter as HCDC-2, 86.

[15] See *The Central Organisation for Defence*, London, HMSO, Cmnd 9315,
July 1984.

[16] Kitson, op. cit.

[17] See *Value for Money in Defence Equipment Procurement*, Defence Open
Government Document 83/01, October 1983; *The Procurement Executive*, booklet published by the Ministry of Defence, London, 1987;
testimony of Peter Levene and Sir David Perry, HCDC-2, 86; testimony
of Peter levene to Committee of Public Accounts, *Control and Management of the Development of Major Equipment*: Ministry of Defence, 6th
Report of the 1986–87 Session, House of Commons, London, HMSO, 18
February 1987, (hereafter referred to HCPAC-6, 87): and Peter Levene
speech to the Royal United Services Institute for Defence Studies, 25
February 1987 (lecture published in the *RUSI Journal*, June 1987).

[18] *Your Business*, January 1986, pp. 25–9; see also *The Guardian*, 26 January 1986 and *Jane's Defence Weekly*, 8 December 1986.

[19] HCPAC–6, 87, op. cit., p. 2.

[20] Rolls-Royce Company Prospectus, 1987, p. 32.

[21] *Statement on the Defence Estimates*, 1984, Vol. 1, London, HMSO, Cmnd 9227–I.

[22] HCDC–2, 86, op. cit., p. 33.

[23] *Defending America*, pamphlet from the Democratic Leadership Council, Washington DC, 1987, p. 10; and Sir Frank Cooper, "The Problem of Resources for Defence", Eurogroup Seminar, Copenhagen, December 1986, p. 9.

[24] *Statement on the Defence Estimates 1982*, Vol. 1, London, HMSO. Cmnd 8529–I, p. 18.

[25] HCDC, 4th Report, 1986–87 Session, *Implementing the Lessons of the Falklands Campaign*, London, HMSO, 1987.

[26] *The Guardian*, 15 March 1988.

[27] *The Guardian*, 1 March 1988; *The Independent*, 2 March 1988; and *The Guardian*, 15 March 1988.

[28] HCDC–2, 86, op. cit., p. xii.

[29] Ibid, p. 43.

[30] *Jane's Defence Weekly*, 9 May 1987; and SDE 87, op. cit., p. 44.

[31] PAC–6, 87, p. v.

[32] Committee of Public Accounts, *Production Costs of Defence Equipment: Ministry of Defence*, 23rd Report of the 1985–86 Session, House of Commons, London, HMSO, 28 April 1986. Hereafter referred to HCPAC–23, 86.

[33] See notes 2 and 26 above.

[34] See *Jane's Defence Weekly*, 14 February 1987; and *The Financial Times*, 27 February 1987.

[35] I. Mackintosh, *Sunrise Europe*, London, Blackwell, 1987, p. 233.

[36] *Air et Cosmos*, 4 October 1986 and 11 October 1986; *The Financial Times*, 9 November 1985. There is, however, some confusion about whether quoted French costs use current francs or estimates allowing for inflation.

[37] HCDC–2, 86, p. 59.

[38] *The Financial Times*, 5 March 1986 and 3 September 1987; *The Guardian*, 1 March 1988.

[39] SDE 1987 op. cit., pp. 48–9.

[40] See for instance, K. Hartley, F. Hussein & R. Smith, 'The UK Defence Industrial Base', *Political Quarterly*, Spring 1987; M. Kaldor, M. Sharp & W. Walker, 'Industrial Competitiveness and Britain's Defence', *Lloyds Bank Review*, October 1986.

[41] G. Kennedy, 'Managing The Defence Budget', *The Royal Bank of Scotland Review*, June 1986, p. 23.

[42] HCDC–2, 86, p. 134.

[43] HCDC–3, 85, p. 20.
[44] Op. cit., (note 17).
[45] *Value for Money in Defence Procurement*, Defence Open Government 83/01, Ministry of Defence, London, 1983.
[46] Alun Jones of Ferranti, in *Interavia*, February 1988, p. 148.
[47] HCDC–2, 86, p. 63.
[48] Ibid, p. xvii.
[49] *The Financial Times*, 12 April 1986.
[50] See, for instance, several industrial viewpoints expressed in *Aviation Week & Space Technology*, 14 March 1988.
[51] HCPAC—6, 87, op. cit., p. 10.
[52] HCDC–2, 86, op. cit., p. 49.
[53] Op. cit., at note 17.
[54] John Nott, address at the IISS, published as 'Economic Constraints and British Defence', *Survival*, Vol. 24, No. 2, March/April 1982, p. 90.
[55] Op. cit., (note 23), p. 9.
[56] Op. cit., (note 54).
[57] Vredeling, op. cit., at note 1.

Chapter 6

[1] *Financial Times*, 10 August 1987.
[2] *Aviation Week & Space Technology*, 25 May 1986.
[3] *Report of the Monopolies and Mergers Commission, The General Electric plc and the Plessey Company plc*, HMSO Cmnd 9876, London 1986, para. 9, 1 September 1966.
[4] Ibid, para. 10.52.
[5] Ibid, paras. 10.70, 76–7.
[6] Ibid, paras. 9.67–118.
[7] Ibid, paras. 10.82 & 10.55.
[8] Ibid, paras. 10.80–82.
[9] Ibid, paras. 10.73 & 10.113. In October 1987, GEC and Plessy merged their telecommunications interests. See also comments by Sir Ernest Harrison of Racal, *Electronics Weekly*, 5 February 1986. The MoD also helped Pilkington to fight off a take-over bid which might have threatened the firm's defence electronics interests.
[10] *The Financial Times*, 19 February 1987.
[11] *Electronics Weekly*, 16 April 1986.
[12] For the Royal Naval Dockyards' network computer system and the Defence Establishments' QAMIS system. *Jane's Defence Weekly*, 1 August 1987, p. 197 and 8 August 1987, p. 239.
[13] *Jane's Defence Weekly*, 24 January 1987, p. 122; *Financial Times*, 31 July 1987.
[14] The French evidently reacted with 'astonishment and ridicule' to the fact

that the British government intervened to halt the merger with Plessey. *Financial Times*, 9 July 1987.

[15] I. Mackintosh, *Sunrise Europe*, Oxford 1986.

[16] See *Management Today*, April 1987.

[17] *Value for Money in Defence Procurement*, MoD Open Government Document 83/01 London 1983.

[18] *Financial Times*, 27 July 1987; 1 August 1987 and 8 August 1987.

[19] See attempts by Dassault to compete against Thompson for the Rafale radar, *Air et Cosmos*, 27 June 1987, p. 76.

[20] *Jane's Defence Weekly*, 6 December 1987.

[21] *The Financial Times*, 18 May 1987.

[22] *Interavia*, April 1986, pp. 359–60.

[23] Ibid, *Flight*, 24 January 1987.

[24] *Financial Times*, 27 January 1987.

[25] Alan Jones, managing director, Plessey Electronic Systems, *The Financial Times*, 27 January 1987.

Chapter 7

[1] G. Snyder, *The Politics of British Defence, 1950–62*, Columbus, Ohio, Columbus University Press, 1964, p. 195 and pp. 210–224; M. Chalmers, *Paying for Defence: Military Spending and British Decline*, London, Pluto Press, 1985, pp. 50–53.

[2] See Sir Frank Cooper's contribution in A. Harrison and J. Gretton (eds), *Reshaping Central Government*, *Policy Journal*, 1987, report in *The Times*, 12 December 1987.

[3] *Statement on the Defence Estimates (SDE) 1984*, Vol. 1, London, HMSO, Cmnd 9227-1, p. 17.

[4] *SDE 1979*, Vol. 1, para. 339.

[5] *SDE 1981*, Vol. 1, London, HMSO, Cmnd 8212-1, p. 46.

[6] Ibid.

[7] *Report of the Committee of Inquiry into the Aircraft Industry*, London, HMSO, Cmnd 2853, 1985, p. 139.

[8] House of Commons Defence Committee (HCDC), 2nd Report, 1985–86 Session, on *The Statement on the Defence Estimates 1986*, London, HMSO, 5 June 1986, hereafter referred to as HCDC-2 1986, p. 34.

[9] See the testimony of Mr Michael Heseltine in HCDC, Session 1985–86, *The Defence Implications of the Future of Westland plc*, Minutes of Evidence, December 1985–June 1986, London, HMSO, 1986, p. 10; and quotation from the testimony of MoD official Mr W. D. Reeves, in HCDC, 3rd Report, 1985–86 Session on *Defence Commitments and Resources and the Defence Estimates 1985–86*, London, HMSO, Vol. III, May 1985, pp. 14–15.

[10] *The Falklands Campaign: The Lessons*, London, HMSO, Cmnd 8758, 1982, p. 26.

11 HCDC, 4th Report, 1986–87 Session, *Implementing the Lessons of the Falklands Campaign*, London, HMSO, May 1987, p. lxxxix.

12 *Jane's Defence Weekly, 25 October 1986, p. 984.*

13 J. Gansler, *"Needed: A US Defense Industrial Strategy"*, International Security, Fall 1987, p. 50 and pp. 61–2.

14 *SDE 1981*, op. cit., p. 47.

15 Snyder, op. cit., p. 92.

16 *UK Military R&D*, Report of a Working Party, Council for Science & Society, Oxford, Oxford University Press, Ch. 2.

17 *SDE 1976*, London, HMSO, Cmnd 6432, Essay on International Collaboration.

18 *SDE 1981*, op. cit., p. 46.

19 John Nott, "Economic Constraints and British Defence", *Survival*, Vol. 24, No. 2, March/April 1982, pp. 90–2.

20 See testimony of Michael Heseltine, op. cit., at Note 9.

21 Defence Open Government Document 83/01, *Value for Money in Defence Procurement*, London, Ministry of Defence, 1983, paras. 12 and 13.

22 K. Hartley & D. H. Hooper suggest, without offering evidence, that savings between 25 per cent and 40 per cent could be achieved by opening up the UK defence market to foreign bidders, see "Defence Procurement and the Defence Industrial Base", *Public Money*, September 1987, p. 24.

23 P. K. Levene, "Competition and Collaboration: UK Defence Procurement", *RUSI Journal*, June 1987, p. 6.

24 *Jane's Defence Weekly*, 9 January 1988 and 10 October 1987.

25 HCDC-2, 1985–86, op. cit., p. 34.

26 "Defence in the 1980s', *SDE 1980*, London, HMSO., Cmnd 7826–1, p. 79.

27 *The Guardian*, 5 February 1987.

28 *The Times*, 18 December 1986.

29 See for instance the offers to the MoD for the RAF's ASR 1238, *Jane's Defence Weekly*, 20 February 1988 and for the Magnetic Anamoly Detection equipment wanted for naval helicopters, *Jane's Defence Weekly*, 14 February 1987.

30 L. Freedman, 'The Case of Westland and the Bias to Europe', *International Affairs*, Vol. 63, No. 1, Winter 1986–87, p. 2 and p. 7.

31 *SDE 1981*, op. cit., p. 46.

32 The Government wrote down the book value of assets in the ROF in 1985 to take account of the fact that the TNT plant at Bridgwater had surplus capacity and had been built to give the UK a desired indigenous source of production, see *Ministry of Defence: Incorporation of the Royal Ordnance Factories*, Report by the Comptroller and Auditor General, London, National Audit Office, 23 April 1985, pp. 5–6.

33 HCDC, 3rd Report, 1985–86 Session, *The Defence Implications of the Future of Westland plc*, Report and Proceedings.

[34] Ibid., p. xxxvii–xxxviii.
[35] Ibid., pp. xxxvii–lxiii.
[36] HCDC, 4th Report, 1986–87 Session, *Implementing the Lessons of the Falklands Campaign*, 6 May 1987, p. lxxxix.

Chapter 8

[1] Keith Hartley, Farooq Hussain and Ron Smith, 'The UK Defence Industrial Base', *Political Quarterly*, Spring 1987.

[2] Keith Hartley, 'Value for Money in Defence: Strategic Choices and Efficiency Savings; *Public Money*, March 1986, p. 36.

[3] Vice Admiral Sir Jeremy Black, 'R&D Hard Choices', speech at Royal United Services Institute, 23 March 1988.

[4] Hartley, op. cit., p. 38.

[5] Policy statement adopted at the Annual Conference of the Labour Party, Blackpool, 29 September to 3 October 1986.

[6] See his speech of 18 June 1987 to the American Chamber of Commerce in London, text available from MoD.

[7] The 1981 Statement on the Defence Estimates Vol. 1 (Cmnd 8212-I, HMSO, London, April 1981) included an essay on defence procurement strategy which read, 'It may be false economy to opt for a cheaper foreign product if the result is to weaken or lose altogether British industry's own producing capacity in that line. We would then be dependent for future generations of equipment on foreign suppliers and on their ideas of what to produce and when, and how much to charge'. (p. 46).

[8] Speech on 'Hard Choices: Research, Development and Military Requirements' at RUSI on 23 March 1988.

[9] Op. cit., at note 3.

[10] Report in *The Times*, 2 March 1988.

[11] *Jane's Defence Weekly*, 29 August 1987.

[12] Black, op. cit.

[13] Hughes, op. cit.

[14] Ibid.

[15] *Interavia*, February 1988.

[16] Hughes, op. cit.

[17] *The Financial Times*, 12 January 1988.

[18] Jacques S. Gansler, 'Needed: A US Defense Industrial Strategy', *International Security*, Fall 1987, pp. 45–62.

[19] See for instance, The Further Education Unit and the Engineering Council, *The Key Technologies: Some Implications for Education and Training*, London, February 1988. This publication subdivided key technologies into material (with examples being magnetics, optical materials, biological materials, particulates and suspensions, ceramics, composites and structural materials, surface coatings, superconductors and semicon-

ductors, components (with examples being imaging devices, micro-electronics, optical components, hydraulics and micro-hydraulics, electro-optics and magneto-optics, microwave components, micro-mechanics and sensors) and manufacturing and process (with examples being condition monitoring, image processing, non-destructive testing, computer-integrated manufacture (CIM), expert or knowledge-based systems, software engineering and control systems).

20 Third Report from the Defence Committee, Session 1985-86, on *The Defence Implications of the Future of Westland plc*, London, HMSO, 23 July 1986, p. xliii. Such a Board had been recommended in the report which led to the establishment of the MoD Procurement Executive, the Raner Report ("Government Organisation for Defence Procurement and Civil Aerospace", London, HMSO, 1971, Cmnd 4641). However the recommendation was successfully resisted by officials who argued that Cabinet and Cabinet Committees would be able to resolve any conflicts of interests, see K. Hayward, *Government and British Civil Aerospace*, Manchester, Manchester UP, 1983, p. 188.

Chapter 9

1 US General Accounting Office Report, *The National Defense Stockpile*, Washington DC, GAO/NSIAD-87-146, May 1987, p. 21.
2 See, for instance, V. Suvorov, *Inside The Soviet Army*, Grafton Books, London, 1984, Part VI: R. L. Garthoff, *Soviet Military Policy: A Historical Analysis*, London, Faber, 1966, p. 103.
3 See Norman Clark, *The Political Economy of Science and Technology* (Blackwell, Oxford, 1985, p. 51) for a contrast between the civil service tradition of departmental autonomy and responsibility in the UK and the more collective spirit in Japan 'where departments of state tend to be more organic and functionalist'.
4 J. Gansler, 'Needed: A US Defense Industrial Strategy', *International Security*, Fall 1987, pp. 45-62.
5 Clark, op. cit., p. 9.
6 Ivan Yates speech to Royal Aeronautical Society of 10 December 1987 and report in *The Financial Times*, 1 March 1988.
7 *The Financial Times*, 8 January 1988 and *Jane's Defence Weekly*, 10 August 1987.
8 *The Times*, 29 February 1988.
9 *The Financial Times*, 9 June 1987.
10 H. Ergas, *Does Technology Policy Matter?* Centre for European Policy Studies (CEPS) Paper No. 29, Brussels, 1986.
11 See Sir Frances Tombs and A. Bain, in *The Guardian*, 17 December 1987.
12 See a report in *Jane's Defence Weekly*, 19 March 1988 digesting *Defence Finance Report No. 6* from Heriot Watt University on 'Defence R&D:

Perceptions & Realities'.

[13] Report in *Jane's Defence Weekly*, 29 August 1987.
[14] Economic and Social Committee, *Europe and the New Technologies*, European Community Economic and Social Consultative Assembly, Brussels, 1986, p. 1.
[15] *The Times*, 27 February 1986. See also Gansler op cit. for a similar argument regarding the US.
[16] Engineering Employers Federation, 'Towards an Industrial Strategy', London, July 1987.
[17] European Electronic Component Manufacturers' Association, 'An Integrated Future for Europe', Brussels, 1987.
[18] White Paper on *Civil Research and Development*, Presented to Parliament, July 1987, Cmnd 185, HMSO, London, 1987, p. 3. For Government views on technology policy, see also John Fairclough, Chief Scientific Adviser at the Cabinet Office, 'Setting priorities for science and technology', *Midland Bank Review*, Winter 1987, pp. 18–23.
[19] Fourth Report from the House of Commons Defence Committee, Session 1986–87, on *Implementing the Lessons of the Falklands Campaign*, HMSO, London, 6 May 1987, para. 335.
[20] Speech to the American Chamber of Commerce in London, 18 June 1987.
[21] See a piece by the former Conservative Minister, Sir Geoffrey Pattie, in *Jane's Defence Weekly*, 25 July 1987. He was impressed by the role in the US of DARPA, 'a small government agency whose job it is to foresee future trends and needs and make sure that the nation's technologists are geared up to meet them'. He felt that DARPA 'focuses on pure science and developmental technologies and has given the USA a capacity to respond rapidly to the most fundamental and enormous challenges'.

Appendix A

The Technology Threat – Summary Tables

Table 1 summarises the Technology Base position in terms of basic disciplines and their application to weapon systems.

TABLE 1
A Summary of the Comparative Defence Technology Base

Discipline	Typical weapons, weapon systems	Evaluation
Mechanical Engineering	Ship and submarine hulls and auxilliary systems Armoured fighting vehicles, land transport, engineering equipment Aircraft structures Propulsion systems for land vehicles, aircraft, ships, undersea weapons Large and small ordnance.	Europe has a strong technology base on most aspects of this discipline, in particular on naval ship construction, tanks/tank armour, guns. On military aircraft propulsion systems Europe is generally on a par with the US, though there are some (for the present) relatively minor US leads (but Europe ahead on VSTOL engines). US technology on closed cycle IC under water propulsion for torpedoes ahead of Europe. For the future, US work on advanced IC engines for land etc transport may produce a lead. Similarly, US research on advanced forms of propulsion for very high speed aircraft may become very significant. (This includes ramjets, scramjets, variable cycle engines). Japan has research on advanced IC engines which could result in an important lead over Europe (adiobatic engines, use of ceramics etc).
Materials	All weapon platforms Ordnance, guided missiles Munitions	In ferrous and lightweight metallic alloys Europe is on a par with the US (and possibly ahead in some new light alloy formulations). On composite materials Europe has lost its initial lead (CFRP etc) due to wider US applications experience. The US has also a technology base of greater depth in metal/composite constructional techniques and high

160

temperature engine materials.

In armour materials Europe is at least on a par with the US. Most Japanese advances in the field have been devoted to non defence, non aerospace applications, but Japan has a very good base in composites, ceramics, plastics that could read across to military applications.

For the future, though Europe is on a par or not seriously behind the US in this discipline, the massive US research effort, almost entirely in industry, coupled with applications experience, could significantly increase its lead over the next decade.

Aerodynamics	Fixed wing aircraft (including variable geometry) Helicopters Shells, bombs Guided missiles RPVs.	Europe is generally on a par with the US for sub-sonic and supersonic flight to Mach 3, but the US has a lead in aspects of computer fluid dynamics (CFD) technology, behaviour at high incidence (departure) and aerodynamics of novel* configurations. Though there is a deficiency in both Europe and US knowledge on hypersonic aerodynamics, the US is in the lead in this area, which could have significance for future very high speed aircraft and to a lesser extent for hypersonic missiles. *For "stealth", see under "Electronics".
Hydrodynamics	Ships, submarines, torpedoes	Europe is on a par with US on hull configurations, design of ships propellors, torpedo hydrodynamics (including those of sonar heads). Main problem now, in relation to ASW, is hydrodynamically generated noise. Here US and European technology base, test facilities etc comparable also.
Electronics	An all pervasive technology, applied to communications, detection, surveillance, guidance and control of missiles, night vision avionics, ships AIO, navigation, target marking, and weapon aiming robotics, electronics warfare. Includes "enabling" technologies like micro-electronics, opto-electronics, radio and radar, computing and data processing. Essential element of Information Technology, Artificial Intelligence, Expert Systems, C^3, "stealth technology".	A key, rapidly developing area. Overall the US has an overall lead in this technology base but in a number of areas the European base is adequate at present to enable the production of competitive products (in terms of technology) to be achieved eg in infrared surveillance and weapon systems, battlefield communications, some radar systems, sonar, low power laser based systems, intertial navigation for aircraft and missiles, jammers and other EW equipment, missile guidance systems and millimetre wave devices. The US prime lead is in high speed VLSI, applications of computers (inc. software) to systems, "stealth" and solid state radar applications. For the future the massive US efforts in this field could lead to the European lag becoming severely exacerbated with

further loss of autonomy, particularly in new generations of guided missiles. Japanese expertise in the electronics field, in some areas, superior to that of the US, could also be a serious threat in the longer term.

Chemical Explosives, Propellants, Pyrotechnics.	Warheads for torpedoes, guided missiles Shells, bombs, mines (land and sea) Propellants for ordnance, small arms, rockets GM and flares, smokes etc.	Europe is strong technologically in this broad field and fully competitive with the US. Some lag on insensitive explosives. US strong on theory underlying design of advanced warheads, but Europe building up comparable capability. For the future no serious competition from the US, provided technology base is continually updated.
Human Factors, Protection etc.	General area of human physiology, psychology and protection against environmental factors, chemical, nuclear attack, etc. Human factors as a basic technology in the design of all weapon systems with man/machine interface.	In human factors, man/machine interface in weapon systems, including display design, ergonomics, design of control inceptors, life support (excluding space aspects where US has a lead), general technology base generally on a par with that of US. In protection against NBC attack, Europe has a small lead but not an important area, industrially.

Table 2 summarises the comparative Development and Production status in terms of the chosen equipment sectors.

TABLE 2
A Summary of the Comparative Defence Development and Production Status

Sector	Subject	Evaluation
	Military Vehicles	
A	Armoured Vehicles	For conventional vehicles, no US threat is foreseen other than in power plant (particularly diesels) for tanks etc. Europe is at least on a par with (or may be better than) the US in tank armour, but this is a rapidly developing technology where European efforts must be maintained. There is a strong production base in Europe and no US threat is perceived.
B	Other Military Vehicles	
C	Engineering Equipment	
D	Conventional Weapons	Europe is on a par with or better than the US in this sector, with a few minor exceptions, having a good development capability and a strong production industry. The US technological threat is minimal.
E	Conventional Munitions	Europe is on a par with or better than the US in this sector, with a few minor exceptions, having a good development capability and a strong production industry. The US technological threat is minimal.

F	Guided Weapons and Torpedoes	Europe has considerable strength in the current generation of guided weapons and has achieved success in sales. However future missiles (smart to brilliant types) will be based on advanced sensors and computing technologies. This is an area of potential (retail?) weakness in Europe which must not be ignored, as the US will certainly try to achieve domination of the European market with such new missiles. This is a high threat area. European torpedo technology and production is adequate for its needs and no US threat is envisaged.
G	Powders, Explosives and Warheads	Europe is on a par with or better than the US in this sector, with a few minor exceptions, having a good development capability and a strong production industry. The US technological threat is minimal.
H	Aircraft and Helicopters	Europe has a strong development and production capability for all military aircraft except large transports but the European market is under constant threat from the US. This European capacity must be maintained, noting that it co-exists with (and because of) the development and production of civil aircraft. This is a high threat area but one where Europe should be able to maintain its capacity. There is also a strong helicopter industry which is again under threat from the US; this industry should be supported to ensure its survival.
I	Ships and Submarines	There is more than adequate development and production capacity in Europe — indeed over-capacity/shortage of orders is a greater threat to the industry than any menace from the US.
J	Electronics	This is a very rapidly advancing sector of industry with widespread applications in both civil and military equipment. Its importance has been recognised and Europe is making strenuous efforts to ensure that it has a development and production base at least as good as its main competitors (US and Japan) to achieve a reasonable share of the market. These efforts must be continued at all costs to ensure some degree of European autonomy and independence in this vitally important field. This is a high threat area from the US and to a lesser extent Japan.

| K | Protection Equipments | Europe is on a par with or better than the US in this sector, with a few minor exceptions, having a good development capability and a strong production industry and a limited production industry chiefly made up of small specialist firms. The US technological threat is minimal. |
| | Materials | Materials is a technology which permeates almost every sector of defence (and civil) industry. It is believed that the US is ahead of Europe in certain aspects of materials development and application. In this situation Europe should maintain and if necessary expand its technology base; at the same time it should consider, for each aspect of materials, whether it is preferable |

— to enter into a technology development programme or

— to 'buy' the technology from the US or

— to manufacture specific items using this technology under licence from the US or

— to buy US products

Source: 'The Vredeling Report' to IEPG.

Index